Executive's Guide to Personal Security

David S. Katz

Ilan Caspi

WILEY

John Wiley & Sons, Inc.

Library of Congress Cataloging-in-Publication Data:

Katz, David S., 1960–
    Executive's guide to personal security / David S. Katz, Ilan Caspi.
       p.   cm.
    Includes index.
    ISBN 0-471-44987-3
    1. Executives—Protection.   2. Executives—Crimes against—
Prevention.   3. Business travel—Safety measures.   4. Violence in
the workplace—Prevention.   5. Corporations—Security measures.
6. Office buildings—Security measures.   7. Emergency management.
8. Private security services.   I. Title: Guide to personal security.
II. Caspi, Ilan.   III. Title.
HV8290.K38   2003
658.4'73—dc21
                                                          2003000571

ABOUT THE WEBSITE

As the purchaser of this book, *Executive's Guide to Personal Security,* you have access to the supporting website:

www.wiley.com/go/personalsecurity

The website contains Word files for Appendix A, "Security and Awareness Checklists and Forms." These forms are easily downloadable and can be customized to suit your needs. Also available on the website is Appendix B, "Vendors," which provides a list of personal security vendors and their contact information.

The password to enter this site is: security

ABOUT THE AUTHORS

David S. Katz, a former senior Special Agent with the Drug Enforcement Administration, is an expert in conducting complex international criminal investigations, high risk arrests, undercover operations, physical and technical surveillance, and intelligence analysis. Former Special Agent Katz is a federally certified firearms and tactical instructor who also spent four years as a primary firearms instructor at the FBI Academy in Quantico, Virginia. During that posting, he taught firearms and tactics to several thousand federal agents, state and local law enforcement officers, SWAT team members, military personnel, and foreign counterparts. He is a recognized authority in the field of law enforcement arrest tactics and investigative techniques and has provided instruction to law enforcement officers around the world.

Mr. Katz also was the leading federal law enforcement expert in the design, testing, and use of body armor and related protective equipment. He developed the first comprehensive body armor testing program in the history of the DEA. Currently, he is collaborating with the Applied Physics Laboratory at Johns Hopkins University on a variety of body-armor-related projects.

During his assignment at Quantico, Special Agent Katz was the DEA liaison to the Israeli Secret Service, developing a cooperative relationship with its field agents and training staff. In August 2000, he provided advanced tactical firearms training to Israeli General Security Service (Shin Bet) instructors in Israel and provided firearms and tactical training to the Diplomatic Security Service Agents and U.S. Marines guarding the U.S. Embassy in Tel Aviv. He also provided tactical firearms training to many high profile police and military units, including the marine detail assigned to HMX-1, the president's official helicopter. Mr. Katz holds a degree of law from Hofstra University Law School.

Mr. Katz has written several articles about tactics and the selection and use of body armor. He is currently the president and chief operating officer for Global Security Group, LLC, a risk management and counterterrorism company. He can be contacted at *david.katz@globalsecuritygroup.com*.

Ilan Caspi is a security and counterterrorism expert with more than 10 years of experience in the military, intelligence, and security industry. A former member of the Israeli General Security Agency (*Shin Bet*), the Israeli Diplomatic Security Service, and El Al Israeli Airlines, he is an expert in security awareness training, conducting threat assessments, and developing comprehensive security protocols for international organizations.

Before joining the Israeli intelligence and security community, Mr. Caspi served in a combat unit in the Israeli Air Force and participated in many antiterrorist operations. During his service, he received the President of Israel's "Most Distinguished Soldier" award.

As a member of *Shin Bet,* Mr. Caspi served in the Office of the Prime Minister of Israel, where he specialized in the field of executive and dignitary protection.

With El Al Israel Airlines, Mr. Caspi acquired extensive operational practice in the field of airport security management and civil aviation. He conducted security surveys at various airports and served as an on-board security agent.

Mr. Caspi applied his knowledge and skills in the international arena as a member of the Israeli Diplomatic Security Service. He conducted vulnerability assessments of international facilities and updated security protocols. During his tenure at the Israeli embassy in Washington, D.C., he reviewed the embassy's existing security protocols, implemented improvements, and trained diplomats on personal security awareness while traveling and working abroad. As an expert in radical Islamic terrorist organizations, Mr. Caspi routinely analyzed intelligence data and formulated response plans to meet identified threats.

Mr. Caspi received his Bachelor of Arts degree (cum laude) in Political Science and International Affairs from Ptucha University in Tel Aviv, Israel. He can be reached at *ilan.caspi@globalsecuritygroup.com*.

*For my mother, Beatrice. Mom, everything I have been able
to achieve is because of you. My faults are my own.*

For my beautiful wife, Galina. Thank you for your love and support.

For my sons, Daniel and Michael. No father could be prouder.

For my in-laws, Nelli and Yefim, for all you have done.

*For my grandmother-in-law, Sofya, for making me
feel like a grandson again.*

To my dear friend and colleague, Ilan Caspi.

David S. Katz

To my colleague and friend, David Katz, for all his hard work.

To my parents, Etti and Yossi, for all you have done for me.

To my wife, Melanie, for her patience, love, and support.

*And most important, to my baby daughter, Ella, who gave new
meaning to my life and adds endless joy to each day.*

Ilan Caspi

CONTENTS

Appendix A: Security and Awareness Checklists and Forms and
Appendix B: List of Vendors are available on this book's companion
website, *www.wiley.com/go/personalsecurity* (password: *security*).

PREFACE

O N SEPTEMBER 11, 2001, thousands of people arrived for work at the World Trade Center in downtown New York City. They left their homes and families and began what they thought was another ordinary day. The majority were Americans but there were also citizens from nearly every nation on earth. It is likely that very few had ever heard the name Bin Laden or Al Qaeda. None of that mattered to 19 of their fellow human beings who set out that morning to kill as many of them as possible. Nearly 3,000 people died that day without knowing why.

In Pakistan, on November 12, 1997, four U.S. citizens, employees of an American oil company, traveled to Karachi, Pakistan, on a temporary assignment. They left their hotels early in the morning and were picked up by a local driver working for their company. Several minutes later, they were ambushed and shot to death by Islamic fundamentalists in revenge for the conviction of Aimal Kansi, a Pakistani citizen, for the 1993 slaying of two employees outside CIA headquarters in Langley, Virginia.

In Bali, Indonesia, on October 12, 2002, terrorist bombers killed more than 180 tourists. One month later, on November 28, 2002, bombers killed 11 tourists at a hotel near Mombassa, Kenya.

An American nurse assassinated in Lebanon. An American invalid thrown overboard from a cruise ship. A U.S. diplomat gunned down as he leaves his home. A German family in China stabbed to death by burglars. The list is endless. Ordinary people targeted by well-trained and well-financed terrorists. In addition, each day, in every part of the world, foreign travelers are victimized by local criminals. While we cannot control the criminal's or terrorist's desire to attack us, is there anything we can do to defend ourselves? Can we reduce our level of vulnerability? Can we lessen the chances that anyone who attacks us will succeed?

The way to lessen our chances of becoming a victim of terrorism or crime is by learning how to become less vulnerable. By becoming less vulnerable, we minimize the probability that anyone seeking to victimize us

will be successful. Often, this will cause cause criminals, and even terrorists, to move on to an easier target.

It is clear that the occupants of the Trade Center could have done nothing to prevent the attack. That task was the responsibility of the airlines
and federal law enforcement agencies. However, after the attack occurred,
there were many things that individuals and companies could have done
by way of emergency planning that could have minimized the number of
those killed and injured. There are many things that can be done to reduce
the chance of becoming a victim of terrorism. And the same methods are
also effective against the far more prevalent and mundane risks associated
with crime.

This book teaches executives, employees, students, and tourists how
to recognize and prepare for the real threats faced by ordinary individuals in today's world. It will provide you with the type of knowledge necessary to empower you to face these threats—information formerly reserved
for security professionals and government employees. You will learn about
situational awareness, risk analysis, and countersurveillance. You will learn
how to travel safely by selecting the right airline, the right hotels, and rental
cars appropriate to your security needs.

If you plan to live abroad, you will learn how to select a safe neighborhood, how to secure your home against intruders, and how to choose
the right road to drive on. If you are an executive responsible for the safety
of your employees and corporate assets, you will learn how to secure your
facility and information, how to formulate emergency protocols, and how
to handle a crisis. If you are a student abroad, or even just a tourist on
vacation, this book will arm you with the necessary knowledge to take the
actions that will enhance the physical safety and security of your property,
your family, and yourself.

INTRODUCTION

Effective security precautions require a continuous and conscious aware-
ness of one's environment as well as the need to exercise prudence, judg-
ment and common sense. This is especially true where the traveler must
adapt to new cultures, customs and laws. Personal security cannot be del-
egated to others; it is the responsibility of each one of us, as we promote
American and commercial interests around the globe.

—Former Secretary of State Warren Christopher,
"Personal Security Guidelines for the
American Business Traveler Overseas"

TENS OF MILLIONS OF AMERICANS travel outside of the United
States each year. The same is true for millions of citizens of Western European nations. Most are traveling for pleasure. However, there are
also millions of American and European citizens who live, study, work, and
raise their families overseas. While the exact number of these expatriates
is impossible to determine, a rough estimate can be made. As far as the
number of American expatriates, the 1990 census documented 925,845
Americans as residents of foreign countries. This number, however, tells
only a small part of the story, as the census figures do not reflect the total
number of Americans residing in other countries. The numbers only
account for U.S. military personnel and their dependents assigned to military bases on foreign soil. Also included are the crews of naval vessels
assigned to the 6th and 7th fleets, U.S. merchant marine crews, and the
federal civilian employees and their dependents serving at overseas posts.
Not included are the several hundred thousand Americans living abroad
while working for multinational companies or attending foreign universities. Also not reflected in the census figures are the hundreds of thousands
of Americans retiring abroad to countries where the cost of living is low

or those married to foreign nationals. The tens of thousands who return to their ancestral homeland or simply move overseas for other personal reasons are also not counted. How many Americans actually are residing abroad? While the exact number is unknown, the Association of Americans Resident Overseas (AARO) places the estimate at between 1 and 6 million. The lower estimate cannot be correct. The census numbers list nearly 1 million residents of foreign countries. Recent estimates indicate approximately 140,000 university-level students living abroad. Certainly an additional several hundred thousand Americans are living and working abroad for private corporations, not to mention the hundreds of thousands of hyphenated Americans returning to their native country. The actual number, therefore, is at least in the middle of the estimated range, which means that at least several million American citizens are currently residing outside of the continental United States at any given time.

A determination of the numbers of European citizens residing abroad is even more difficult to compile. Citizens of the United Kingdom (including Canadians and Australians) live and travel abroad in great numbers. The British Ministry of Tourism maintains statistics relative to the travel habits of British citizens. These statistics show that citizens of the United Kingdom made more than 58.3 million trips abroad between the years 1997 and 2001. Citizens of Germany, France, Italy, Spain, Greece, and other countries of Western Europe also make millions of trips abroad each year.

These Americans, Europeans, Australians, and Canadians, regardless of whom they work for or why they are living abroad, face many challenges in adjusting to life outside of their native lands. Often they are overwhelmed by the necessity of communicating in another language, adapting themselves to local customs, and living in a society devoid of many of the modern conveniences we take for granted. They also must face the prospect that, in many parts of the world, being an American or European citizen exposes them to a grave and very real danger of death or serious injury. Westerners abroad are increasingly at risk of being harmed or worse and have begun to focus on their physical safety more than at any time in our history. They have all begun to ask what they can and should do to prevent becoming another statistic.

Employees of the U.S. federal government and their dependents have an advantage; they receive at least some training regarding personal security matters. All government personnel, prior to being posted in a foreign country, must attend the Security Overseas Seminar given by the U.S.

Department of State in its training facility in Arlington, Virginia. This excellent and well-run two-day school is designed to provide the employee with some of the necessary knowledge about how to minimize threats to personal security. In addition, the State Department strongly encourages dependent family members to attend the training. The problem with even this excellent program is that two days is not enough time to properly prepare someone, especially a layperson with no background in security or law enforcement, for the real risks that Americans abroad will likely encounter. Furthermore, the course subject matter is the same regardless of which country employees may be posted to. An individual stationed at the U.S. Embassy in Ottawa gets the same training as someone posted to Peshawar in Pakistan, despite the very real and significant differences in the threats that may be encountered in those two countries. The important issues are all touched on and the instructors are all experienced professionals. However, as is common with most government training programs, they are forced to present too much information in too short a time period. This one-size-fits-all approach is, unfortunately, the rule rather than the exception in almost any type of program offered by the federal government. Although the State Department could spend more time providing country-specific training, local Regional Security Officers (RSOs) do provide more thorough training once employees arrive at their post, and the Congress has mandated that every U.S. Embassy receive a security briefing and evaluation by Diplomatic Security Service (DSS) agents every three years. In addition, employees of the State Department and the numerous other government agencies maintaining offices in embassies around the world have the advantage of being protected by the DSS as well as the embassy's marine guard detail. The RSO, a trained security professional, is always available to provide the embassy staff with the answers to their security questions and needs. This is not the case with private industry. No mandatory training program is provided to those Americans employed overseas by private companies. In fact, to our knowledge, no programs in private industry mandate that security training be given to personnel working abroad to familiarize them with the techniques that will increase their level of personal safety while living abroad. While many of the large multinationals do have security departments that offer some assistance in this regard, very little actual instruction is provided to enhance the safety of employees. Private security companies and security consultants can provide this type of training, but they are seldom contracted to teach corporate employees the fundamentals of personal security. Such training, when it does exist, is generally reserved for high-profile corporate officers. It is not made available to the rank and file.

The same is true for American and European students studying abroad. Many schools that participate in exchange programs with universities in foreign countries offer seminars designed to help students acclimate to their new environment. A basic language course may be offered as well as an overview of the culture of the host country. This training is designed to reduce the level of stress attendant to adapting to a new and perhaps very different culture. Typically, information relative to security issues is not presented or, if it is, is offered on a superficial level.

To partially remedy this situation, the U.S. State Department has created special divisions whose task it is to help Americans address their safety concerns while living in a foreign country. For the international business traveler, the State Department established the Overseas Security Advisory Council (OSAC) in 1985, in order to provide American companies that have overseas assets with a forum to share and disseminate information relative to security matters. OSAC has published several excellent publications that have provided guidance for the business traveler as well as Americans working abroad. In addition, to further improve the level of security awareness, the State Department sends DSS agents to large companies abroad to provide security briefings and related training. These DSS agents do a great deal of training for the employees of oil companies and other large American businesses overseas, such as Coca-Cola. However, the DSS responds only by invitation, and the availability of such courses depends largely on the personnel and resources available for teaching private concerns at any given time. The primary function of the DSS is to support the government mission overseas by providing protection for the local embassy and its staff. Assisting private companies, while it does further the goals and interests of the United States abroad, is secondary to that overriding protective function. DSS agents provide excellent instruction when availability of manpower allows. It is recommended that your company request DSS services. However, demand for such training far exceeds the ability of the DSS to accommodate it. If you happen to be an employee of a small company with offices abroad or are an American working for a foreign corporation, it is unlikely that the DSS will be able to accommodate your training request. The Service will, however, provide you with important and useful information and will direct you to other resources that may be of help. The gaps in providing instruction as well as other services related to security must be filled by private security consultants and other providers. It is, therefore, your personal responsibility to access these other options and take steps to enhance your own level of safety.

As an American citizen abroad, you have the opportunity to attend scheduled security briefings and training offered by the State Department in overseas embassies. Congress has mandated that every U.S. Embassy receive a complete security evaluation every three years. During these evaluations, the DSS provides a security seminar and briefing for embassy personnel and American citizens living in the host country even if they do not work at the embassy. If you are living abroad, contact the local embassy or consulate and ask when the next such seminar will be held. The security-related information presented during these seminars is invaluable. In addition, many embassies and consulates routinely provide in-house security workshops that are also open to Americans regardless of their employment status. These programs are in place and are available to American citizens living in the host country. Individuals must contact the embassy and find out when the next training date is scheduled. These workshops or courses teach the simple rules that must be followed to avoid becoming a victim of terrorism or violent crime abroad. Remember, the responsibility to learn about the availability of these courses is your own. The embassy is not going to contact all expatriate Americans and cajole them into attending the next security seminar. You need to seek out available training and learn to exercise prudence and caution while living abroad. If you are a citizen of another country, contact your own foreign affairs ministry before you travel. By all means register with your country's embassy or consulate when you arrive in a new country.

In the aftermath of the attacks of September 11, 2001, the potential for attacks against American and Western citizens and interests, both at home and overseas, has become increasingly likely. At the time of this writing, 189 organizations have been identified as terrorist entities. At the risk of sounding melodramatic, at this very moment there are terrorists and their sympathizers planning acts of violence against Americans all over the world. They do not distinguish between combatants and noncombatants, between civilians or government officials, or even among men, women, and children. Virtually every intelligence agency in the world has concluded that future attacks on Americans, their interests, and their possessions are a virtual certainty. It is not a matter of "if" but "when." However, even in this dangerous period in history, many people employed overseas ignore the vitally important personal security issues that affect not only themselves but their families as well. Even some of the largest corporations in the United States demonstrate extraordinary apathy in this regard. Shortly after the tragic kidnapping and murder of *Wall Street Journal* reporter Daniel Pearl, the authors had dinner with an acquaintance who is an executive with a major news corporation. This man travels abroad more than he is home and frequently travels to areas that are the subject of specific terrorist threat warnings posted by the State Department. We asked him what type of training he had been given relative to his personal security while traveling. We were more than a bit surprised when he answered that he had never received any training, despite frequent trips to the Middle East, Russia, India, the Philippines, and other countries where there are real and documented security risks to foreigners. We asked if he at least had access to intelligence information regarding security issues in the countries he was traveling to. Again the answer was negative. Nor did he even bother to access the State Department website and read the posted travel advisories. He said that his company had no program in place to gather information relative to country-specific dangers that its employees might face. He said that sometimes the company provided him with a bodyguard, but for the most part he was on his own. Furthermore, the only type of intelligence gathering he knew of in private industry was commercial intelligence. He explained that most large domestic and multinational corporations routinely spend hundreds of thousands of dollars to learn everything they can about individuals with whom they intend to do business—a prudent concern to be sure. Big companies hire investigators to compile complete dossiers on a prospective partner's personal habits, finances, bank accounts, romantic interests, and a variety of other confidential areas. They use excellent investigative firms, such as Kroll Worldwide, and try to obtain the same information on competitors as well. Millions of dollars are spent each year in this manner. Unfortunately, almost nothing is spent teaching employees how to be safe.

An important factor to consider is that terrorist activities are not the only source of danger Westerners must face overseas. In fact, you will have a far greater chance of becoming a victim of ordinary criminal activity than you will of becoming the target of terrorism. In many countries, there are criminal industries that thrive on victimizing foreign visitors to their country. A robbery or even a property crime against an American businessperson is almost guaranteed to provide a richer reward for their actions than crimes directed against their own fellow citizens. Fortunately, the security precautions that you should take to reduce your chance of being targeted by terrorists are also effective in deterring common street crime.

America's corporate interests can no longer afford to be negligent with respect to security matters. The same is true for companies from the European Union. Their employees and facilities are becoming increasingly attractive targets to terrorists and criminals. Furthermore, all Western citizens, even students or tourists, must understand that they are very desirable targets to those seeking to use terror to advance their political agenda or to vent their misguided rage at the United States, Europe, or Israel. And unfortunately for high-profile executives, government officials or employees, and celebrities, the level of this particular threat increases along with the level of the status or notoriety of the individual. However, even ordinary citizens are facing risks. They are also often the first choice to the local criminal element seeking an easy target for a robbery.

Each year hundreds of Americans and Europeans are injured or killed overseas. Traffic accidents, terrorism, street crime, and disease cause most of those incidents. The events of September 11 have only made matters worse. As we complete the final editing of this book, we have just heard word of the assassination in Amman, Jordan, of Lawrence Foley, a senior U.S. Diplomat working for USAID. Mr. Foley was shot to death outside his home. Thus far, no claims of responsibility have been made nor has any assailant been identified. It seems beyond question, however, that this senseless murder was an act of political terrorism by an Islamic terrorist group. It is also too early to have received an analysis of the act and whether any security precautions could have prevented his death. On this same date, we are reading a news account published by the Jewish press entitled "How to Kidnap American Citizens." The article describes how an extremist Islamic online forum recently posted a guide describing in detail the manner in which Americans can be kidnapped. The guide discusses how potential kidnappers can choose the best location to effect kidnapping, various methods to use, and how to gather intelligence about the intended victim. Inexplicably, although it can be found in other news sources on the Internet, this story has not been given any exposure in the mainstream media. In November 2001 nearly 200 people, mostly Australian nationals, were killed in a bombing of a night spot in Bali.

This year, hundreds more Western citizens will be robbed, assaulted, raped, kidnapped, or murdered. Most of these incidents could be prevented by adherence to basic rules of personal safety. Lives are lost needlessly because individuals do not know what to do during a fire or in a medical emergency. Money and other valuables are stolen because of simple inattention to a few commonsense security practices. Whether you are a highly placed executive managing your company's interests abroad or a student going overseas as part of an exchange program to promote diversity and understanding, this book will provide you with the necessary information to avoid becoming another statistic in a growing ledger book. This is your commonsense approach to personal security abroad.

CHAPTER 1

Target: Corporate America

I**N THE AFTERMATH OF THE ATTACKS** on the World Trade Center
and the Pentagon by the Al Qaeda organization, it has become clear
that Western economic interests, particularly American corporations, have
become the most desirable target of terror groups seeking to further their
own varied political agendas. In the past, the prime targets of terrorist
groups were military bases and personnel and official U.S. government
facilities. Striking at the American military was the foremost priority, especially for radical Islamic fundamentalist groups. Recall the murder of 242
Marines in Lebanon and the attacks on the Khobar Towers in Saudi Arabia
and the USS *Cole*. Governmental and diplomatic facilities were also primary targets of groups like Al Qaeda, which was responsible for the car
bomb attacks that destroyed the U.S. embassies in Tanzania and Kenya in
Africa. To be sure, there always were the occasional terror attacks that targeted civilians. Kidnappings were frequent occurrences in many parts of
the world, and hostages were taken to be used as bargaining chips or for
ransom. The spate of airline hijackings in the 1970s and 1980s, the attack
on the *Achille Lauro,* and the bombing of Pan Am Flight 103 over Lockerbie,
Scotland, are examples of incidents specifically targeting civilians. However,
in the not too distant past, the largest and most well-financed operations
seemed to be reserved for attacks on official targets. This is no longer
the case. Today most experts on international terror organizations agree
that terrorists have changed their targeting priorities. Unquestionably, the

1

current targets of choice are Western, or more specifically American, economic interests.

It may seem as if this shift in targeting priorities followed the attacks of September 11, 2001. This is actually not the case; the trend had already been well documented long before the Twin Towers fell. Remember, the first attack on the World Trade Center, on February 26, 1993, was undertaken with the goal of causing one of the towers to topple over and take its twin with it. Clearly, the intent in the first attack was to cause the deaths of many thousands of civilian noncombatants. The ugly truth is that terror groups the world over have made the murder of civilians the first priority. Exhibit 1.1 clearly documents the trend over the five-year period before the attacks on September 11, 2001. In fact, this exhibit shows that attacks against military targets, traditionally thought of as the prime target for these so-called freedom fighters, actually represent the smallest target category.

Exhibit 1.1   Facilities Targeted by Terrorists 1996–2001

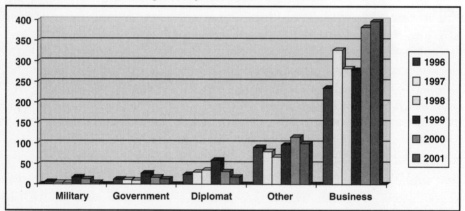

Source: U.S. Department of State, "Patterns of Global Terrorism 2001," Washington, DC: Office for Counterterrorism, May 21, 2001.

In the aftermath of September 11, 2001, this trend will certainly continue and is expected to do so at an accelerated rate. Why is this so? What makes civilian economic targets so important to terror groups?

If you ask the average person to describe his or her most vivid impression of the horrors perpetrated on September 11, virtually everyone will recall and describe the image of the collapsing World Trade Center towers, the terrible scene of ordinary people leaping out of the burning towers to their deaths and the thousands of office workers and rescuers killed. The attack on the Pentagon seems to have been largely ignored, almost forgotten. Why? Why do civilian deaths seem to shock us in a way that military casualties do not?

The very idea of terror attacks on civilian targets creates a visceral reaction in all of us. Those who died in the World Trade Center weren't soldiers or instruments of U.S. foreign policy. They were ordinary folks simply going to work to support their families. They kissed their spouses good-bye that morning never imagining that this was the last time they would ever come home to them. The media reported numerous stories of people trapped on floors above the impact of the planes phoning home on cell phones to the loved ones they knew they would not see again in this world. These images were enough to terrorize average citizens into changing jobs and moving away from crowded population centers. In the aftermath of the attacks, rentals of office space in the Empire State Building, once again the highest building in New York City, began to drop precipitously as people began to view the stately building not as prime commercial real estate but as the new prime target for the terrorists. As Vladimir Ilyich Lenin observed, "the purpose of terrorism is to terrify." Certainly attacks against innocent men, women, and children do just that.

However, other, more practical reasons better explain why economic targets are now so desirable to those seeking to destroy our way of life and diminish American influence throughout the world. One is the fact that the attacks on the World Trade Center resulted in consequences to the American and world economies that exceeded even the most optimistic expectations of Osama Bin Laden and his associates. They immediately recognized that economic targets were not only easier to hit but also that there was an unlimited supply of such targets that could be easily struck with more far-reaching effects than attacks against embassies and military bases.

Our system of government, with our constitutionally guaranteed freedom and liberty, is the enemy of radical fundamentalism. Fundamentalists loathe democracy because it is the antithesis of the repressive theocratic system they aspire to create. Radical Muslim extremists know all too well that the fanaticism they seek to promote cannot flourish within an open society where freedom of thought and expression is protected. They are also aware that the most effective way to combat the spread of Western-style democracies is to attack the foundations of economic prosperity that makes it so powerful. Damage the American economy and you damage American ability to spread its ideals throughout the world. Bin

Laden himself made this observation in a tape that surfaced shortly after the attacks.[1] World conditions and political realities guarantee that the United States and its interests, possessions, and citizens will continue to be targeted at home and abroad. Corporate targets have become more desirable as terrorists seek to use economic disruption to achieve political goals.

An examination of the practical advantages of attacking corporate targets will further illustrate the point and illustrate why civilian economic targets are so attractive. There is a distinction made between so-called hard targets, that is, well-defended military bases and well-prepared embassies, and "soft targets" with little or no security such as office building and industrial centers. Military targets:

- Are generally harder to strike because of enhanced security
- Result in military casualties
- Generally cause loss of government property
- Cause damage that is generally confined to the target itself

Attacks against civilian economic targets are more desirable to terror groups because economic targets:

- Are more vulnerable, easier to strike
- Result in loss of civilian life
- Cause loss of private and public property
- Create widespread damage to the fragile world economy

The September 11 attacks clearly illustrate the distinct differences between hard and soft targets as well as the effects of a successful attack on each. Two targets were selected and attacked: a hard target, the Pentagon, and a soft target, the World Trade Center. The disparity in the actual effects of those attacks is great. The destruction of the Twin Towers not only killed many more people than the attack on the Pentagon but also caused economic repercussions that were still being felt more than a year later.

Exhibit 1.2 shows some of the costs to private industry as well as the loss of tax revenue associated with these attacks. While the actual tally is still incomplete, even this partial accounting shows the enormity of the economic loss. Other data estimate in excess of $60 billion (some estimates put this closer to closer to $100 billion) in property damage and casualty losses alone. In addition, the attendant economic loss to the City of New York is estimated at more than $83 billion. These staggering amounts actually surpass the annual budgets of many of the world's governments.

Exhibit 1.2   Economic Impact of Terrorist Attack on the World Trade Center,
                  Dated May 29, 2002

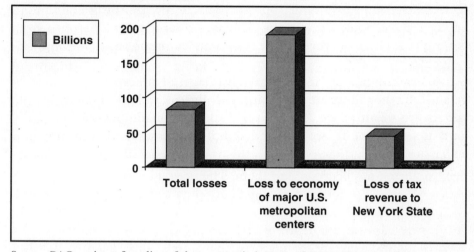

Source: GAO review of studies of the economic impact of September 11, 2001.

The insurance industry has been particularly hard hit. Recent estimates have placed the amount of insured loss at approximately $58 bil-
lion. The enormous financial loss to insurance companies will compel
underwriters to require that steps be taken to reduce the likelihood of
financial loss caused by terrorism. Corporations will likely find that their
insurers will exclude terror acts in their policies or require certification
that antiterrorist measures have been taken. Every facility, structure, or
organization that is deemed to be an attractive target for terrorist activity
is being charged more for insurance coverage. For example, small neighborhood synagogues in Brooklyn, New York, have had their liability pre-
miums raised by thousands of dollars per year simply because Jewish
interests and buildings are deemed as being at risk of attack.

The airline industry, which seems to be constantly facing economic
challenges even during relatively mild downturns in the national economy,
was also dealt a severe blow by the 2001 attacks. Many people viewed the
federally funded settlements given to the surviving family members of
the victims of the attacks as a bailout for the airline industry. To collect
the government benefit, the recipients were required to forgo their right
to any other legal action to recover damages, such as suing United or
American Airlines for negligence in not providing an adequate level of
security.

In addition, business was disrupted in New York City, the financial capital of the world, for months. The American stock market, already reeling under the collapse of the tech stocks, was further hard hit, as were global markets. Some estimates attribute more than 40 percent of the current economic downturn to the attack on the World Trade Center. No terror attack in history had ever created the same amount of widespread damage or generated such a powerful response.

Compare these far-reaching effects to the results of the attack on the Pentagon. Certainly the damage done was far more localized. While the pain and suffering of the families who lost loved ones in the Pentagon is no less than those who lost relatives at the Trade Center, comparatively little attention has been paid to them. The nationally televised interviews always seem to focus on the surviving family members from the Twin Towers. Civilian deaths and injuries always create a stronger reaction in the general public because the death of an ordinary citizen is far easier for the average person to relate to. Terrorists have, to be sure, grasped that fact and are focusing the bulk of their assets and abilities on planning additional attacks on U.S. civilian and economic targets. In October 2002, the Federal Bureau of Investigation (FBI) issued a warning that Al Qaeda might have been specifically planning attacks on U.S. economic interests. Al Qaeda leaders, the report stated, "aim to undermine what they see as the backbone of U.S. power, the economy." The FBI said that "an attack may have been approved" and that "Our adversary is trying to portray American influence as based on economic might and therefore seeks to strike an economic target prominent enough for economic aid and symbolic reasons that it would have immediate resonance around the world."[2] This analysis is actually quite correct. The economic might of the United States is what allows it to remain the most influential force in the world. Our system of democracy, with all its attendant personal freedoms, would not have captured the imagination of the oppressed people of the world were it not for the prosperity and economic success it has produced.

The State Department's Office of the Coordinator for Counterterrorism has documented this trend in its "Patterns of Global Terrorism" report dated May 21, 2002. Exhibit 1.3 shows a comparison of the number of anti-U.S. attacks for the year 2001.

More attacks targeted U.S. economic interests during the year 2001 than all other attacks combined. Furthermore, the trend exactly mirrors the statistics of terrorist incidents worldwide shown in Exhibit 1.1, which showed that the overwhelming numbers of terrorist attacks were directed

Exhibit 1.3 Anti-U.S. Attacks for the Year 2001

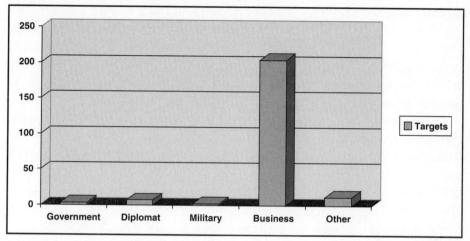

Source: U.S. Department of State, "Patterns of Global Terrorism 2001," Washington, DC: Office for Counterterrorism, May 21, 2001.

at business facilities. The same is true for the attacks specifically directed at American interests during the year 2001. In fact, the same is true for the past 10 years. Terrorists deliberately target business interests. This trend will certainly continue as the terrorists clearly understand the financial damage that the World Trade Center attack caused. They understand, correctly, that the government of the United States is subject to pressure from its citizens. That is the nature of our representative republic. The government also is subject to the influence of the leading U.S. corporations that have an arguably disproportionate power as a result of the enormous contributions they make to political candidates. If corporate profits are endangered, terrorists reason, corporations will use their influence to persuade the U.S. government from taking actions that may result in economic harm to big business. What the terrorists always fail to grasp is the level of resolve of the American people. Americans are refugees from the type of tyrannical regimes that many of the terror groups seek to impose. Americans have an understanding of right and wrong and will not be bullied or intimidated into doing anything that is not consistent with our core values. This is why we continue the fight against terror and why American business continues to thrive in virtually every market in the world.

This is the current political reality of our time. We continue to do business in the face of threats from those opposed to our way of life. We do this knowing that our mere presence makes us targets for the groups that seek our destruction. The only course of action open to us is to prepare ourselves to face this type of threat and counter the danger we face from well-trained and well-financed fanatical groups that are willing to kill themselves if it will cause harm to America. And, unfortunately, this is likely to be the reality for the foreseeable future. We must, therefore, appreciate this new reality and take the necessary actions to protect ourselves.

How should we begin to answer these new challenges? The first step is to understand that you are at risk and may very well be targeted for attack by terrorists or common criminals. Do not assume that you are not already in the cross-hairs of some radical organization. If you begin by honestly evaluating your risk, then you can take the precautions necessary to avoid becoming a target.

Common elements in criminal and terrorist attacks must be considered when determining a level of risk associated with a particular facility or individual. Focus needs to be paid to both the potential attacker and the potential target. Among these elements related to the potential assailants are:

- **Desire:** Individuals and organizations need to have a desire or motivation to justify their actions or receive some tangible benefit from their actions.
- **Ability:** Individuals and organizations need to recognize their ability (physical skill, knowledge, available assets) to conduct a strike.
- **Opportunity:** Individuals and organizations select their targets based on vulnerability.

Now the analysis must shift to the potential victim. Are you an attractive target? Criminals and terrorists manifest desire, acquire ability, and then look for opportunity. You may very well become a target if you meet these three elements:

1. **Suitability:** Would an attack on you further the goals of a criminal or terrorist?
2. **Vulnerability:** Are you vulnerable to attack?
3. **Probability of Success:** Is an attack on you likely to succeed?

A potential civilian target can do nothing to influence the desire and ability of terrorist groups. Concerted efforts by the military and law enforcement establishments of law-abiding nations certainly can have an impact on terrorists' ability to strike. Military action, arrest, and harrassment by directed law enforcement effort and stemming the flow of the money that finances these groups greatly interferes with their ability to operate. Even so, active and well-prepared terror cells still are ready to initiate strikes against U.S. interests. However, several factors in the equation are within the control of the potential target, and they all are tied to your particular level of vulnerability. Reduce vulnerability and you provide less of an opportunity to an attacker. Providing less opportunity dramatically reduces the probability of a terrorist group making a successful attack. Therefore, assessing and eliminating vulnerability is the most effective method of enhancing security.

What is the current situation as of today? At the time of this writing, the U.S. State Department had put out a general worldwide alert reminding all U.S. citizens abroad that they were targets and were likely to remain so. The caution stated:

> *This Public Announcement is being updated to alert Americans to an increased potential for anti-American violence, including terrorist actions against U.S. citizens, as a result of the military action in Iraq. The U.S. government remains deeply concerned about the security of Americans overseas. American citizens are reminded that it is more important than ever to maintain a high level of vigilance and to take appropriate steps to increase their security awareness. This Worldwide Caution supersedes that issued on February 6, 2003 and expires on July 20, 2003.*
>
> *As a result of military action in Iraq, there is a potential for retaliatory actions to be taken against U.S. citizens and interests throughout the world. Public demonstrations carry the potential for precipitating violence directed at American citizens, symbols associated with the United States or other U.S. and Western interests.*
>
> *The threat to U.S. citizens includes the risk of attacks by terrorist groups. Terrorist actions may include, but are not limited to, suicide operations, bombings or kidnappings. Possible threats include conventional weapons such as explosive devices or non-conventional weapons, including chemical or biological agents. Terrorists do not distinguish between official and civilian targets. These may include facilities where Americans and other foreigners congregate or visit, such as residential areas, clubs, restaurants, places of worship, schools, hotels, outdoor recreation events or resorts and beaches. U.S. citizens should increase their security awareness at such locations, avoid them, or switch to other locations where Americans in large numbers generally do not congregate.*
>
> *U.S. government facilities worldwide remain at a heightened state of alert and some have drawn down their dependents and/or personnel. These facilities may temporarily close or suspend public services from time to time for security*

*reasons. In those instances, U.S. embassies and consulates will make every effort
to provide emergency services to American citizens. Monitor the local news and
maintain contact with the nearest American embassy or consulate.*

*As the Department continues to develop information on any potential
security threats to Americans overseas, it shares credible threat information
through its Consular Information Program documents, available on the Internet at* http://travel.state.gov. *In addition to information on the Internet, U.S.
travelers can get up-to-date information on security conditions by calling 1-888-
407-4747 in the U.S. and outside the U.S. and Canada on a regular toll line
at 1-317-472-2328.*

Source: http://travel.state.gov/wwc1.html, March 24, 2003.

Clearly, the government of the United States anticipates further acts
of terror against American citizens. Virtually all of the governments of
Western European nations have issued similar warnings to their own citizens. It is only a matter of time before another such attack shocks the con-
science of the world. In the meantime, what can you do? As a company or
an individual you must immediately prepare to face the security challenges
of the post 9/11 world. You can effectively lower your risk of being attacked
by increasing security measures (physical, technical, and procedural). By
limiting access to your facility or home, you reduce your vulnerability to
any type of attack and therefore make an attacker realize that an action
against you is not likely to be successful. The less vulnerable we are, the
less attractive we are to any criminal or terrorist planning an attack. The
following chapters will teach readers how to be less vulnerable.

NOTES

1. According to a CNN report, Bin Laden stated that the September 11 attacks
    had "shaken the throne of America and hit hard the American economy
    at its heart and its core." Bin Laden said that if the U.S. economy suffers
    enough, Americans will withdraw from Islamic countries. Bin Laden observed
    that the attacks were easy to carry out and showed that America's economic
    strength has fragile underpinnings. "It collapsed very easily," he said. Source:
    CNN report on the Bin Laden video dated December 27, 2001.
2. This statement was released to state and local law enforcement by the FBI's
    National Press Office on October 9, 2002.

CHAPTER 2

Awareness

WE LIVE IN A DANGEROUS WORLD. You don't need anyone to tell you that. The goal of keeping yourself safe and free from harm seems to be almost impossible to achieve. Even the most cautious and security-conscious individuals sometimes get injured or killed. There are no guarantees. However, while safety cannot be guaranteed, it can be dramatically enhanced. All that is necessary for someone to improve his or her chances of avoiding danger is to learn a few basic rules of personal security. It is not as difficult as you might think. Learning to be aware of your surroundings, combined with prior planning and some common sense, is actually the biggest part of the job. Your familiarity of your own environs is your best defense against unforeseen danger. The first step is to teach yourself to become more observant of your surroundings and to appreciate the significance of the things you see. Doing this gives you a significant advantage over those who would do you harm.

Police officers and federal agents are taught observational skills, as are professional security officers. Virtually every law enforcement academy teaches its students how to be observant and what to look for. Law enforcement personnel scrutinize their environment. Their eyes are always moving and taking stock of what is going on around them. Law enforcement officers refer to this as having "cop's eyes," which merely means having the ability to observe the immediate environment and draw appropriate conclusions from those observations. An experienced police officer notices the unusual: things that look out of place, such as an unfamiliar car parked in a particular neighborhood or someone wearing an overcoat in warm weather. This skill is an absolute necessity for anyone in police work. It is also an indispensable skill for those seeking to reduce their chances of becoming victims. Fortunately, it is an easy skill to develop.

Awareness training is generally the first thing taught in the survival and security courses given to government agents, military personnel, and police officers. In the Office of Training of the Drug Enforcement Administration (DEA) in Quantico, Virginia, new DEA agents receive a special block of training entitled "Agent Survival" before graduating and embarking on their rewarding albeit dangerous careers. This particular course deals with how to survive the violent encounters that they will all face. Much of it is psychological preparation intended to train agents to be prepared to use all necessary means to stay alive by developing a combat mind-set. The course is very intense, and more than one individual has decided to resign after sitting through it. But before the psychological training begins, the first thing the agents are taught is the overwhelming importance of being aware of their environment. Because threats must be identified before they can be addressed, awareness is the first lesson in learning how to survive. You need to develop a little alarm bell inside your head that starts to jingle before a serious situation develops and to learn to trust that little bell and act before you become the latest story for CNN.

This level of awareness is common in some civilian populations that are, tragically, the targets of terrorism. Ilan, one of the coauthors, is an Israeli national. Apart from his extensive security training and experience, he learned to be observant at an early age. Israelis have, by necessity, learned these lessons from seeing their friends and neighbors murdered before their eyes. If someone leaves a bag unattended on an Israeli city street for even a second, citizens take the initiative by either calling for the owner to identify himself or herself or by alerting those around them. As a rule, Americans don't do that. For a brief period in post–September 11 New York City, people were cognizant of packages that were left unattended. However, people have short memories. The farther we are from an event like September 11, the more relaxed we become.

For a security officer, effective observational skills are critical. Prior to a terrorist assault, there is always a period of planning and surveillance. This is also frequently true of common criminal activities. The September 11 hijackers carefully planned their horrific attack over the course of several years. Imagine their patience. They spent years learning how to fly a commercial airliner and practicing knife fighting and unarmed combat. They took dozens of airplane trips to study airport security measures and develop ways to avoid being detected and arrested. They did their homework and were well prepared. But there is a flip side to this equation. Surveillance can be detected. If you are going to be the target of terrorism or common crime, it is very likely that the bad guys will be watching you for some time before they are ready to strike. It is during this period of pre-assault surveillance that the potential victim has the opportunity to identify the surveillance and take action to thwart their plans. This is true whether you are an agent protecting an ambassador or a civilian who may be in someone's cross-hairs.

COLOR CODE SYSTEM

How do you learn to become aware of your surroundings? DEA instructors teach a color code awareness system borrowed directly from Colonel Jeff Cooper's excellent book *Principles of Personal Defense*.[1] This system breaks down levels of awareness and readiness into four colors: white, yellow, orange, and red. It is a simple and effective system for teaching this most important lesson and is worth repeating here.

The white stage is the sleep state, the dream state, the state in which you are completely unaware of your surroundings. It is mentioned first because the most important point to take away from this chapter is that *you must never allow yourself to be out in public in condition white*. We can all relate to the experience of driving a car while lost in thought. When we arrive at our destination, we are somewhat surprised as we really have little or no conscious recollection of making the trip. Despite this fact, we were able to keep the car on the road, brake when necessary, and avoid other vehicles. While we were driving, we were on autopilot. Driving becomes an almost unconscious, reflexive ability. We become so used to driving that we allow our ordinary sense of awareness to slacken. This is common to many of the routine tasks that we perform each day. Routine actions tend to lull us into condition white.

The lowest level of awareness that you must ever allow yourself to reach in public is condition yellow. This condition will be your new state of preparedness each time you leave the house, whether at home in the United States or abroad. It is the state of relaxed alertness. You are aware of your surroundings and are not yet aware of anything warranting closer attention or an upgrade in your condition of readiness. Basically, you are just paying attention to the world around you. You are relaxed and you are able to notice the unusual. When in condition yellow and you leave the house, you naturally observe the street or parking area. You know what is usual for your neighborhood and what is not. You would immediately notice an unfamiliar vehicle parked in the area. Most likely it is nothing to concern you at all, but you notice it anyway. This is the appropriate condition to be in when you are out and about.

One frequently heard comment is that people don't want to live their lives in fear, waiting for something bad to happen. We agree completely. You won't live in fear. You will live with the understanding that this can be a dangerous world and that you are confident that you will be aware enough to see trouble coming if it happens to you or your family. It isn't all that difficult. Look around and pay attention. It is as simple as that.

PHYSICAL AND PSYCHOLOGICAL RESPONSES TO FEAR

Proper observational skills allow you to see a potential for danger or attack before it happens. While in condition yellow, you notice a small group of young men, unfamiliar to you, standing near your vehicle as you leave a local restaurant. Their appearance is suspicious, and they appear interested in you. Your attention is now focused on a particular potential threat, and you immediately move into condition orange. In this condition, you are focused on a particular potential threat and are evaluating it for danger. Perhaps this group is not a threat at all, but you still have that uncertain feeling in the pit of your stomach. As you size up the situation, you should be reviewing your options. What can you do? What should you do?

If your suspicions and instincts have proven correct and you are attacked, you now are in condition red. You may very well be fighting for your life. Fear and panic set in. There are only two alternatives: fight or flight. If you must fight, your counterattack must be swift and violent. If you flee, you must literally run for your life. In this situation, you will also likely experience the physical and psychological responses to fear.

Fear is generally a good thing. It is your body telling you that you are in danger. Unless fear becomes paralyzing, it can help you fight harder or run faster by causing the release of adrenaline into your bloodstream. However, the adrenaline rush also causes human beings to experience certain reactions that can be quite disconcerting to those who not prepared for them. These reactions include tachypsychia, auditory exclusion, tunnel vision, and cognitive dissonance.

Tachypsychia is the term that describes the perception of people under stress that time is moving in slow motion. During an attack, victims often perceive the attacker as if he is moving in slow motion. This is caused by the brain processing information more quickly to allow for a faster defensive response. Tachypsychia is a positive side effect that can enhance your defensive ability.

Auditory exclusion is another common effect. This is the brain's ability to block hearing while focused on an extreme threat. For example, many police officers involved in shooting incidents report that they never heard the sound of gunfire, either from the assailant's weapon or their own. The brain simply blocks auditory input to allow you to focus completely on the threat that you perceive. This effect has both positive and negative ramifications. The increased ability to focus is a positive. However, auditory exclusion can cause you not to hear things that you need to, such as the sound of another attacker coming at you from behind. We know of no way to moderate this effect. The only training technique that is successful is to train to "check six," or glance behind you each time the opportunity presents itself.

Tunnel vision refers to the narrowing of your field of view as you focus on a particular thing. The authors have experienced this effect many times and find it to be quite dangerous. With tunnel vision, you lose peripheral vision, which prevents you from identifying additional assailants or other dangers that may be approaching from the side. Training yourself to keep your eyes moving can mitigate the effect of tunnel vision. Combat shooters, for example, are taught to scan their immediate area after they engage a particular threat. They do this to avoid "tunneling" in on one threat and becoming oblivious to others.

A final effect that must be examined is known as cognitive dissonance. This refers to a disassociation with the actual events as they occur. Sometimes, during a crisis or attack, the victims feel they are watching the events unfold as if they were happening to someone else. Obviously, this reaction is perhaps the most dangerous of all. Disassociated minds are rejecting the idea that something so terrible could be happening to them. The disassociation is a way for the mind to cope with the sudden and unpleasant reality that is now confronting the person. The danger lies in the fact that a person in this state, by denying the event as it happens, is also negating his or her own ability to effectively fight back or run. Anyone can find him- or herself in a situation that is life threatening. Each of us must realize that it can happen to us. Every day we read of terrible events that have befallen others. There are only two reasons that it hasn't happened to you: providence or preparedness. If a life-threatening event happens to you, expect to be afraid. Simply stated, "Fear is the body's natural reaction to being put in an unnatural situation." There is no shame in being afraid. Everyone feels fear, even your assailant. Not being afraid is not what makes you brave. True bravery is doing something even when you are afraid to do it. By realizing that we may be the subject of a sudden and violent assault, we can mentally prepare ourselves for the reality if it ever comes.

MENTAL PREPAREDNESS

As a street agent, David had a practice of playing the "what-if" game with his partner. Often they would be sitting in their car on a lengthy surveillance in neighborhoods resembling Kosovo on a bad day. David would ask his partner: What would we do if a car pulled up behind us and two men got out with guns? How would we respond? What would the partner do? What would David do? Then they would change the scenario to something else. By talking about it, they were also preparing themselves for such emergencies. Each of us must ask ourselves what we would do in a particular situation. What would we do if we noticed a strange car following us? Or perhaps hear the sound of someone breaking into our home in the middle of the night? Or, while we are walking at night, we hear the sound of footsteps following us down a dark and deserted street? You need to consider these possibilities and ponder the what-ifs for yourself. There is a well-known axiom that best sums up this notion. It is known as the "6 P Principle": *Proper prior planning prevents poor performance.* We will discuss more about prior planning when we cover fire drills and evacuation plans. But for purposes of this discussion, it is sufficient to understand that even the practice of considering options in advance can allow you to act appropriately at the moment of crisis. When a person is under stress, the thought process becomes quite difficult. By planning in advance, you have, in effect, already done the thinking. Now all you need to do is act.

The worst thing that you can do is to freeze. Both of us have considerable expertise in the use of small arms and defensive tactics. While David was a firearms instructor at the FBI/DEA (Federal Bureau Investigation/ Drug Enforcement Administration) Academy in Quantico, one of his favorite pieces of advice he heard from an outstanding firearms instructor, DEA

Special Agent Allan Ponseigo, was "Don't freeze. Doing something, even the wrong thing, is preferable to freezing—if you make a mistake, make it going 100 miles an hour." Generally, this admonition was given to DEA Special Agent trainees as they stared numbly at a weapon that had just experienced a malfunction. Rather than executing the universal response to a failure to fire (tap, rack target, or bang), some trainees froze. That reaction is probably the only one that is guaranteed to get you killed. Taking action, even if it is not the best course of action, is better than doing nothing. Once you begin to move, your mind begins to work as well.

CONCLUSION

The bottom line for purposes of this discussion is for each of you right now as you read this book to make up your mind to pay attention to your surroundings and respect the little warning bell you have in your head. Everyone is observant under certain situations. Put an upper-middle-class guy in an inner-city neighborhood and he will become quite observant of his surroundings. The trick is to do it all the time. Don't get lulled into condition white under any circumstances. Remember, you are most vulnerable when you become comfortable and lulled by the false security of familiar surroundings. Generally, as you get closer to home, you tend to become more relaxed. That is the time you may be most at risk. Terrorists and bad guys know this and may very well decide to hit you in your comfort zone. Complacency on your part makes their job easier. Remember, becoming familiar with your surroundings gives you a huge advantage over a potential attacker. Becoming complacent shifts the advantage to them. You should use this advantage; your strengths are your attackers' weaknesses. Your biggest enemy is your daily routine. By becoming as familiar as possible with your surroundings and by changing your daily routine, you can easily prevent any attack while it's still in the preplanning stage. Ilan has had the occasion to interrogate terrorists subsequent to their capture. The ones who talk, and generally that is most of them, always mention how scared and uncomfortable they were while they collected intelligence information on the target before the attack. They all felt that someone was always watching them, and many times it caused them to choose a different target. Use this fact to your advantage. Stay alert and pay closer attention to your surroundings. Soon you will be able to pick out the unusual, including the presence of a terrorist or criminal who is targeting you. In addition, your alert demeanor will not be lost on anyone evaluating you as a potential target. Merely by becoming more conscious of your environment and alert to things out of the ordinary, it is likely that you will cause a potential assailant to move on to an easier target.

When David attended the security overseas seminar put on by the State Department, he heard an interesting story. A U.S. Army sergeant had been marked for kidnapping by terrorists while serving overseas. They knew that he had been selected because a raid on a terrorist safe house turned up a list of individuals targeted by this group. The sergeant's name had been scratched off the top of the list. Next to the name there was a notation indicating that he was a security-conscious individual who had a practice of looking up and down the street every morning before he left the house. Embassy security agents talked to the sergeant because they wanted to learn what extraordinary steps he was taking that actually dissuaded a dangerous group of terrorists from carrying out their plot. The sergeant was perplexed. He told the agents that he hadn't been doing anything unusual that he could recall. He did explain, however, that he had been having some problems with local kids throwing his early morning newspaper in unusual places. He said he checked outside every morning to see where those kids had hidden the paper. An amusing story. But think about it. The simple action taken by this man to look around outside every morning, despite the fact that it had nothing to do with antiterrorism, was enough to dissuade his potential attackers. They perceived him to be security conscious and alert and decided to move on to the next guy, who wasn't paying attention to security. Unfortunately, they did so with tragic results. The basic lesson that must not be overlooked is that even the mere appearance of taking security precautions often is enough to prevent an attack. Human nature is a funny thing. People, including bad guys and terrorists, often see what they expect to see. Terrorists planning an attack or abduction don't see a man looking for his newspaper. Instead, they see a soldier obviously well trained in counterterror techniques. Don't miss the point here. This story reminded David of some of his undercover deals as an agent. He would meet a bad guy and get his pager number to set up the deal. Later, when he paged the guy to complete the deal, he received no response. His first thought was that he blew it. Something he said or did made the dealer suspicious. David's senior partner told him to relax. Bad guys need to go to the bathroom, too. Point being, there were a thousand reasons why someone wouldn't call right back. David's perspective as a young and inexperienced agent made him choose the explanation suitable to his level of anxiety. The same will always be true for anyone watching you and sizing you up for an attack.

NOTE

1. Jeff Cooper, *Principles of Personal Defense* (Boulder, CO: Paladin, 1989).

CHAPTER 3

General Recommendations

FOR THOSE WHO LIVE IN NEW YORK CITY, it is always amazing how many millions of people come to visit New York as tourists each year. They come from all over the world. When you attend a Broadway show, more often than not you will hear the folks sitting next to you speaking a foreign language. (Come to think of it, in New York that really doesn't prove our point, as nearly 60 percent of New Yorkers were born somewhere else.) When you strike up a conversation with them, you find they are here visiting from Germany, France, England, Holland, Japan, and virtually every other country in the world. Sitting in a darkened theater, you really can't identify the tourists absent their conversation. When you walk down the street, however, you pick out the visitors immediately. They are the folks with the cameras around their necks looking up at all the tall buildings. Or their dress is a bit out of place. Sometimes you just know that a person is not a native New Yorker without even being able to say what it was that tipped you off. Average New Yorkers find it very easy to look down the street and immediately spot tourists. Unfortunately, the predatory criminals working the streets of New York can do it even better. When they see tourists, they also see dollar signs hanging on easy targets. Do you ever wonder if Americans and other Westerners look the same way to local criminals while they are walking down the street in Bangkok or Cancun or Cairo? The answer is: Yes, they do.

Why are tourists the frequent target of robbery and assault? The reason is obvious. Affluent Americans traveling abroad probably have a lot of cash and a minimal ability to fend off an attack. This phenomenon is not reserved only for American travelers visiting abroad. We have more than enough criminal predators in our own country. Only a few years ago in South Florida there was a horrific rash of robbery homicides in which several European tourists were murdered. Human predators deliberately targeted these unfortunate folks. They were picked because they were likely to have a great deal of cash. They were easy to spot because at that time, rental cars in Florida bore specific and readily identifiable plate numbers. Furthermore, Florida is a relatively liberal state as far as concealed weapons laws are concerned. A mugger targeting a native Floridian could never be sure if his intended victim was armed. It was, however, a sure bet that out-of-state or foreign tourists would not be. Nor would they be likely to know what to do in the case of an assault. The state of Florida ended up dealing quite harshly with persons convicted in such attacks and even mandated that rental cars no longer could be identified by specific tag numbers.

Certain countries have industries devoted to the victimization of foreigners. Sometimes it is through nonviolent means, as in the case of the simple theft of property without violent attack or credit card theft, as is common in Nigeria. When federal agents travel abroad, they pay for their accommodations and meals with their government credit cards. It was standard operating procedure for agents who had traveled to Nigeria to immediately cancel their cards upon returning to the United States. In virtually every case, unauthorized charges had already been made on the account even before it could be canceled. David's wife, who is originally from Russia, was well aware that groups of professional thieves and armed robbers stake out the airport in Moscow waiting for affluent foreign visitors. Once they spot people they believe to be worthwhile targets, they follow them to their hotel. Then they can follow the visitors at their leisure and wait for the opportune time to strike. Remember, as a nonresident, you will be unfamiliar with the places you visit. Locals know what areas to avoid. They know the dark alleys to steer clear of. Tourists or new foreign residents do not.

KEEP A LOW PROFILE

Victims of nonviolent theft can consider themselves lucky. Unfortunately, in many instances crime involves more direct forms of confrontation. The task that we as foreign visitors have is to make ourselves less conspicuous and thereby less attractive as potential targets.

This book is designed to teach you how to become a difficult and therefore less attractive target. This chapter in particular contains several general rules that you must learn to follow. You will learn how to keep a low profile and not stand out quite so obviously in a crowd. If you stand out in a crowd, you are also standing out to the criminal element. It is important to realize the importance of certain simple steps to avoid being the one selected for victimization.

Dress and behave conservatively. This is just simple common sense. If you are living in a country where $100 represents a month's salary, don't wear designer clothes while sporting a Rolex Presidential. Don't act in a boisterous manner; again, anything you do to make people take notice of you also applies to the local criminal element looking for a quick and easy score.

Social Encounters

If you are meeting with people who are unknown to you, meet only in familiar and very public places. One of the first lessons that David learned after becoming an agent is to always arrange undercover meetings in very public and well-lit places. Agents shun like the plague the common movie scenario of the narcotics agent meeting the bad guy in a dark alley. Narcotics agents felt safer, even while armed and supported by backup teams, meeting in a crowded restaurant. One veteran agent used to say "Make the bad guy kill you in public." The implication is that it is more unlikely that you will be assaulted in public, regardless of whom you are meeting. If armed agents choose public places to meet unfamiliar people, it is even more critical that tourists or resident aliens living abroad do the same. If you don't know someone well, stay out of the dark alleys. In fact, skip the alleys altogether.

When living abroad, try to have your phone number unlisted. If you live and work overseas, you may be even more vulnerable than tourists. This is merely a function of exposure to the local population. When you live abroad, you will come into contact with many more locals than the average tourist will. You travel to work; you shop in the local markets and explore your new surroundings much more than a tourist. Remember that you are still a foreigner even if you have lived overseas for several years.

Avoid Routine Patterns of Behavior

One of the most common points of attack comes while foreign nationals are on their way between home and work. This is particularly true relative to the crime of kidnapping. Most people settle into predictable routines. They leave the house for work at the same time every morning. They leave the office and return to their car at the same time each night. Anyone intent on assaulting you has a relatively easy time in setting up an ambush because of your unvarying routine. You will need to train yourself to change your route to work. Settling into a predictable routine makes it too easy for someone to make you a target. If you use company vehicles for transportation, it is a good idea to routinely and randomly exchange vehicles with your coworkers. Doing this will prevent someone who is targeting you from being certain that you will be driving a particular car at a particular time. You have to conduct yourself in a way that will make the bad guys move on to someone else. We discuss what you can do to protect yourself while driving in greater detail in the chapters about countersurveillance, vehicle safety procedures, and the principles of route selection.

Moderate Your Behavior

Several other points need to be addressed regarding the things that you, as a visitor to a foreign country, need to be cognizant of. Certain types of behavior can draw the wrong type of attention to you. Remember, you are living in a country where social mores and acceptable conduct may be quite different from what you are used to. Offense may be given where none is intended. Certain activities considered acceptable in the United States may actually be criminal in the country of your residence. Simple social contacts with politically active individuals may get you marked by a country's intelligence services. You need to be aware of what type of personal conduct is both acceptable and safe in the culture of your new country of residence. What types of activities should you avoid? There is a long list, but let's look at some of the more important ones.

In the United States, one of our most precious traditions is the right to be heard in the political process. Many people attend rallies, fundraisers, protests, or demonstrations. Even foreign visitors to the United States are afforded the privilege of making themselves heard in this manner. Unfortunately, many countries do not share our appreciation of political involvement. The Bill of Rights is not transferable to other countries. You are personally responsible for learning what activities normal to you as an American are off limits in your new country of residence.

PRECAUTIONS IN HIGH-RISK LOCATIONS

If you are traveling to a region designated as high risk by the State Department, there are additional measures that should be considered. If a terror attack is being planned against American civilians, the terrorists will seek to identify a location that will be certain to have a high concentration of Americans or other Westerners present at a specific and fixed time and location. For example, a horrific practice long used by terror groups is to target religious services at houses of worship frequented by Westerners. The reason is obvious; a Christian church serving the international community will provide them with a target that is guaranteed to be filled with a large group of individuals every Sunday morning at 9:00. This fact presents a tough choice for an individual to whom church service is an important part of life. Rather than be forced to make a choice between worship and personal safety, it may be necessary for the congregation to discuss enhancing security practices during worship. Whenever you or your family are planning to attend an event where large groups of Westerners assemble on a regular basis, you must always be aware of security issues. Many commercial districts, restaurants, or night clubs with a predominantly Western clientele also should be avoided whenever possible.

Maintain close contact with the local embassy or consulate. Often they will give very specific directives of certain areas or types of behavior to avoid. Pay attention to these directives. They are usually right.

For a more complete list of general and specific security recommendations and procedures, please download our own traveler's awareness form from this book's website. Instructions on accessing the website can be found on page iii.

CHAPTER 4

Know Where
You Are Going:
Pretravel Research

O UR WORLD IS EXTRAORDINARILY DIVERSE. A short plane ride can take you from the urbane, sophisticated culture of Paris to places where basic sanitation is not even a universally accepted standard. When going abroad, you need to realize that where you are going will dramatically change the level of attention you need to pay to security. Danger is common to all corners of the map. However, the nature and extent of those dangers change from country to country and even many times from locality to locality. You should take certain basic steps for security purposes no matter where you go. The extent to which you upgrade those steps depends on your exact destination. Most travelers know which countries have drinkable tap water and in which countries they must use bottled water and avoid salads, unpeeled fruit, and ice in drinks. You must perform the same basic research to familiarize yourself with country-specific security concerns.

There are many available databases to consult prior to travel. The U.S. State Department website at *www.state.gov* (*http://travel.state.gov*) is a good place to start. Consult its Consular Affairs home page. The State Department site offers many excellent suggestions and has published a guide through its Overseas Security Advisory Council. In addition to providing basic information about every country in the world, the State Department also posts advisories and alerts for those areas in which a developing situation could pose a danger to American citizens. If there is an alert for the area that you are going to, take it seriously. In the past, it took a bit of evidence and, unfortunately, the occasional tragedy before an alert was posted. The reason for this is political reality. It is important to remember that the State Department is a government (hence political) agency run by diplomats. The art of diplomacy is complicated. At the State Department, they are mindful of the fact that posting a travel advisory results in a large number of consequences. Many countries depend a great deal on tourist dollars. Alerts may have immediate and potentially dire consequences for many economies. They also put a chill on relationships between the United States and the country that is the subject of the alert. In the pre–September 11 world, political issues often delayed the posting of alerts. If circumstances required the maintenance of positive relationships with a particular country that ordinarily would have been the subject of an advisory, pressures within the State Department often delayed the issuance of an alert, or watered it down. This is not mere cynicism. Sometimes world political issues require delicate handling. However, in the post–September 11 world, alerts have been posted more rapidly and have been more explicit. For example, below is an excerpt of an alert posted on the State Department's Traveler Advisory website on November 20, 2002:

This Worldwide Caution supersedes the Worldwide Caution dated November 6. It is being issued to alert U.S. citizens to the need to remain vigilant and to remind them of the continuing threat of terrorist actions that may target civilians. This Worldwide Caution expires on May 20, 2003.

In light of the statement released by Osama Bin Laden on November 12, 2002, the Department of State reminds Americans that U.S. citizens and interests remain at increased risk of terrorist attacks, including by groups with links to Osama Bin Laden's Al Qaeda organization. Terrorist actions may include, but are not limited to, suicide operations or kidnappings. These individuals have proved that they do not distinguish between official and civilian targets. Because security and security awareness have been elevated within the United States, the terrorist may target U.S. interests overseas. Recent events include the terrorist attacks in Kuwait and Bali. We remind American citizens to remain vigilant with regard to their personal security and to exercise caution.

On November 14, 2002, the State of Virginia executed Mir Aimal Kansi, a Pakistani national, who was convicted in 1997 of the 1993 murders of two CIA employees. The potential exists for retaliatory acts against U.S. or other foreign interests in response to the execution.

Attacks on places of worship and schools, and the murders of private American citizens and other Westerners, demonstrate that as security is increased at official U.S. facilities, terrorists and their sympathizers will seek softer targets. These may include facilities where Americans or possibly other foreigners are generally known to congregate or visit, such as residential areas, clubs, restaurants, places of worship, schools, hotels, outdoor recreation events or resorts and beaches. Americans should increase their security awareness when they are at such locations, avoid them, or switch to other locations where Americans in large numbers generally do not congregate. There is a possibility that American citizens may be targeted for kidnapping or assassination.

U.S. government facilities worldwide remain at a heightened state of alert. These facilities may temporarily close or suspend public services from time to time to review their security posture and ensure their adequacy. In those instances, U.S. embassies and consulates will make every effort to provide emergency services to American citizens. Americans are urged to monitor the local news and maintain contact with the nearest American embassy or consulate.[1]

As you can see from the clear and unambiguous wording of this document, the State Department is greatly concerned about the safety of American citizens and possessions abroad and specifically recommends that citizens take responsibility for their own personal safety. Its website also offers country-specific warnings and contact numbers that should absolutely be consulted before traveling. While the State Department does a great deal to inform Americans of the risks attendant to travel to certain regions, even now in the aftermath of the worst terrorist attack in our history, political, business, and diplomatic considerations create bizarre reactions to the ways we protect ourselves. For example, as of the date of writing this book, new immigration regulations have been set in place as part of the new Homeland Security initiative. From now on, persons from countries on the terror watch list, such as Syria, Iran, Iraq, Sudan, and a few others, must be fingerprinted and photographed upon arrival into our country. They must provide information about where they will stay and check in with the Immigration and Naturalization Service (INS) at regular intervals. Although you may be wondering why anyone from these countries is allowed into the United States to begin with, there is an even more unbelievable twist. Citizens from Saudi Arabia and Pakistan were initially exempted from this requirement. Fifteen of the 19 terrorists involved in the September 11 attacks were Saudi citizens. Osama Bin Laden, arguably the world's most notorious terrorist, is also a Saudi citizen. What possible reason could there be for not subjecting Saudi citizens to the same

level of scrutiny as citizens of other nations with extremely active radical
fundamentalist movements? If, at this moment, you are racking your
brains trying to come up with a logical answer related somehow to legitimate security considerations, you can stop. There aren't any. In fact, log-
ically, Saudis should receive the highest degree of scrutiny. The reason
they don't is not complicated. American oil interests do billions of dollars'
worth of business with the Saudis. That is basically it. In a nutshell, it comes
down to dollars and cents. There may be other peripheral reasons, such
as the long friendship between the Bush family and the house of Saud.
President Bush values friendship and loyalty. There is also a need to maintain the goodwill of the Saudi government to obtain its support for any
military action against Iraq.

What about the exemption granted to Pakistan? Hundreds of Al Qaeda
fled Afghanistan and are now finding refuge in the mountains of Pakistan.
Seemingly every day, there are demonstrations in the streets of Islamabad
and Karachi calling for death to Americans. However, because the President of Pakistan, General Pervez Musharraf, courageously supported the
U.S. effort in Afghanistan, he is being rewarded with special status for his
citizens. This is understandable because our effort against the Taliban
would have been almost impossible to mount without Pakistani cooperation. However, from a security and law enforcement perspective, it is inde-
fensible. Several months after the initial decision to exclude Saudi and
Pakistani citizens from the more stringent immigration regulations, the
ruling was changed to include them as well.

Several private companies provide local intelligence updates to Americans abroad on the security conditions in virtually every foreign country,
and they are free to do so without the general constraints of diplomatic
niceties. Firms like International SOS offer overseas medical assistance,
emergency evacuations, and intelligence. Our own company, Global Security Group, LLC, and the Kroll subsidiary, IJET, both offer pretravel intelligence and travel monitoring. While it is true that the security briefings
are largely based on information disseminated by the State Department,
sometimes additional items are based on independent observations. These
companies maintain an intelligence database that deals with all manner
of dangers and includes information about local crime, terrorist activity,
medical dangers, and the medical infrastructure. The first stop you as a
tourist or future expatriate should make is to the intelligence division of
one of these companies. Each country is unique; there are a few basic
things that you must find out about the local criminal element, level of

terror cell activity, medical information, and political stability. Remember, there is no such thing as having too much information.

AVOID POLITICALLY UNSTABLE REGIONS

Political stability is something that Americans take for granted. In many parts of the world, however, this is not the case. In America, we transfer power via the electoral process. In many countries, governments change when the current leader dies or is overthrown. A government friendly to U.S. interests today may, literally overnight, become hostile to America and its citizens. The deposed Shah of Iran, Reza Pahvlavi, was a strongly pro-Western leader. His overthrow by the radical Islamic regime headed by the late Ayatollah Khomeini was as strongly anti-American, and its first action was to storm the U.S. embassy in Tehran and take American citizens hostage. Radical Iranian "students" held American citizens for 444 days.

While it is impossible to accurately predict an unexpected coup d'état, proper intelligence will provide you with an overall view of the government. What is the nature of the current regime? How is power transferred? Is there a tradition of democracy or dictatorship? Analysis should provide a historical overview of the nature of government as well as an in-depth history of how power was transferred over the last 50 years. The instability of the government in your country of residence is a critical element in formulating security plans for yourself, your family, and your company. Unstable political situations, especially in countries with a history of the violent overthrow of past regimes, require that you have an emergency evacuation plan in place during your stay.

At the time of this writing, there is currently an emergency situation in the Ivory Coast (Côte d'Ivoire). A brief overview of the history and development of the situation in this volatile African nation should serve as a practical example of what we are talking about. If American citizens, contemplating travel to the Ivory Coast, had consulted the State Department website, they would have learned that the political situation in that nation is anything but stable. The official security warning reads, in part, as follows:

> *U.S. citizens traveling to and residing in Côte d'Ivoire are urged to exercise caution and maintain security awareness at all times. Côte d'Ivoire is undergoing a period of extended political, social, and economic change. There have been several instances of brief, but extensive violence since December 1999, when a*

military coup d'état overthrew the civilian government. Although Côte d'Ivoire returned to civilian rule following presidential elections in October 2000, there have been several violent encounters since that time, with the most recent occurring during a failed coup d'état in January 2001. At the same time, the country experienced a period of economic decline after years of growth, creating the potential for labor unrest. However, in recent months, there have been signs of growing political and economic stability. Nevertheless, U.S. citizens should bear in mind that violent demonstrations have occurred in Côte d'Ivoire in the past and that further unrest or military action could recur with little or no warning *[emphasis added].*

> *The Liberia/Côte d'Ivoire border region is unsettled and potentially dangerous. Travelers to this region and other areas of the country may encounter roadblocks, armed military personnel, vehicle searches, and police shakedowns. . . . All U.S. citizens who travel to Côte d'Ivoire should be aware of their surroundings and use common sense to avoid situations and locations that could be inherently dangerous. Travel at night is strongly discouraged.*

This report, dated July 18, 2002, well before the state of emergency, which began in September of 2002, is a well-prepared document that calls for prospective travelers to pay close attention. Not only is it well written and concise, but it also turned out to be quite prophetic. Now that you have read it, ask yourself if you would follow through with plans to travel to the Ivory Coast under these conditions. Let's track the progression of warnings as the situation deteriorated. On September 19, 2002, a warden system[2] warning was posted to Americans resident in country:

> *There are reports of shooting in Abidjan, Bouaké and Korhogo, Côte d'Ivoire. American citizens in Côte d'Ivoire are urged to stay home. The U.S. embassy will continue to provide updates to American citizens in Côte d'Ivoire via the warden system. For emergency situations involving an American citizen, please contact the U.S. embassy at 20-21-09-79, ext. 6000.*

The following warden message on September 20, 2002, seemed somewhat more reassuring:

> *The situation in Abidjan is stable and life is returning to normal. The situation in Bouaké and Korhogo remains fluid. All Americans are advised to stay at home and indoors. In the event the situation changes, this will help ensure your safety. The Embassy will continue to provide updates throughout the day. If you need to contact the consular section, please call 20.21.09.79, extension 6684 or 6602.*

However, the situation worsened the following day, prompting this message on September 21:

> *In the pre-dawn hours of Sept. 19, 2002, widely dispersed gunfire erupted in Abidjan, Côte d'Ivoire and in Bouaké and Korhogo, the country's second and third largest cities. An unknown number of armed men attacked national Gendarme and Army installations. They attacked the home of Interior Minister Emile Boga Doudou in a residential neighborhood and the home of the Defense Minister in Cocody near President Gbagbo's residence. Before mid-day, government forces put the attackers to flight and re-established control in Abidjan.*
>
> ***The current situation:*** *Government forces re-established control in Abidjan by mid-day September 19. Patrols throughout the afternoon continued to mop up pockets of resistance. On the morning of September 20, anti-government forces were still in control in Bouaké and Korhogo. The Minister of Defense assured the nation on government television the previous evening that loyal forces would move to regain control of those two cities. In a televised interview at 11:30 a.m. September 20, the Defense Minister said government forces would retake Bouaké by late afternoon that same day.*

The message goes on to address some of the developments of the ongoing fighting and then provides additional information for resident Americans, including the status of outbound commercial airline service.

> ***Airport:*** *Ivorian civil aviation authorities are keeping Abidjan's Houphoet Bougny International Airport open and the control tower manned. KLM and Air France, the only lines offering direct service from Europe, canceled their flights September 19, but Air France announced early in the day that on September 20 it would return to its regularly scheduled afternoon departure from Paris. KLM's next scheduled flight from Amsterdam to Abidjan is September 21.*
>
> ***American citizens:*** *From early on, the Embassy announced via radio and via telephone calls throughout the country that Americans should stay in their homes and under cover. The announcement was repeated the morning of September 20.*
>
> *The Embassy: Embassy Abidjan was closed September 19 and is closed again September 20. There is a small core group manning the Embassy.*

The next situation update was dated September 23:

> ***Abidjan:*** *The situation in Abidjan remains calm. Some shops have reopened for business. The hours of curfew were reduced to run from 20:00 to 6:00 for the entire country except for Bouaké and Korhogo, and the curfew has been extended*

until Sunday, September 29. The curfew in Bouaké and Korhogo remains from 18:00 to 8:00. Some poorer neighborhoods of Abidjan, many inhabited by foreigners resident in Côte d'Ivoire, have been burned during the government's searches for pockets of rebellious soldiers.

International flights: *The international airport in Abidjan is open and operational during non-curfew hours. Air France and KLM, the two airlines that service Europe from Abidjan, flew into Abidjan over the weekend, rescheduling their flights to conform to the curfew. South African Airways has also serviced Abidjan over the weekend.*

Bouaké and Korhogo: *The rebels are still in control of Bouaké and Korhogo. The Minister of Sports remains held hostage by the rebels in Bouaké. The rebels have appealed to the government for negotiations and the government has demanded that the rebels lay down their arms prior to any negotiations.*

French troops arrived in Abidjan on Saturday to help ensure the safety of French and third-country nationals in rebel-held Korhogo and Bouaké. The U.S. is coordinating with French authorities.

Americans in Côte d'Ivoire: *All official Americans, including all Peace Corps volunteers, in Côte d'Ivoire are safe and accounted for. There have been no reports of attacks against Europeans or Americans or their property. There are no plans to evacuate official or non-official Americans from Abidjan. The U.S. consul has been in frequent contact with American citizens in Bouaké and Korhogo to advise them of any instructions through the official warden system.*

The September 22, 2002 Public Announcement for Côte d'Ivoire urges U.S. citizens to postpone travel to Côte d'Ivoire at this time. American citizens in the cities of Abidjan, Bouaké, and Korhogo are advised to stay home.

International Christian Academy: *The International Christian Academy, a school primarily serving the children of missionaries posted throughout West Africa, has approximately 160 U.S. citizens on the campus located in Bouaké. The school has adequate supplies and the students are reported safe, despite reports of gunfire close to the school. The Embassy remains in regular contact with the school.*

The Embassy: *The U.S. embassy in Abidjan will be closed to the public on Monday, September 23. A small core group of employees will report to work. The International Community School of Abidjan will also be closed on September 23. As a result of security concerns, U.S. Embassy Abidjan may close for general business periodically to review its security posture in the future.*

By the following day, the situation worsened to the point where U.S. troops were dispatched to provide for the safety of American citizens endangered by the fighting. On September 25, American troops arrived in the city of Yamoussoukro, the central capital of the Ivory Coast to help evacuate the more than 300 American citizens trapped by the fighting in the city of Bouaké. More than 100 French soldiers had reached the International Christian Academy, where 200 Westerners, including 100 Americans, had been trapped. Fortunately, the presence of the French and American soldiers prevented the deaths of foreign nationals in the country. However, we must ask why those trapped Americans chose to disregard the frequent and clear warnings that a situation of this sort was not only possible but actually probable. Warnings, updates, and warden messages are useful only when they are heeded. All the people who sought refuge in the school could very well have been killed. The fault would not have been with the State Department but with the victims themselves who had chosen to ignore the advice of trained security professionals and diplomats.

It is inexplicable to us as to why situations like this happen. Some people listen, act, and avoid the worst. Others prefer simply to hope for the best or trust their own luck. It is somewhat analogous to the reaction that people have to posted hurricane warnings. Again, at the time of this writing, people along the coast of Louisiana are bracing for Hurricane Isadore, which is expected to make landfall within hours. There are, of course, many reports of heavy traffic on roads leading away from shore as most people evacuate. However, there are also reports of folks who refuse to pay heed and are staying despite the issuance of an evacuation order. Hurricanes kill people, most often by drowning. It simply does not make sense for anyone to stay put during a hurricane, just as it is irrational for people to remain in a war-torn region where there is a high probability that the violence will lead to their own deaths.

If you think this situation in the Ivory Coast was an isolated occurrence, you are mistaken. On October 12, 2002, at approximately 11:00 P.M. local time in the Indonesian city of Bali, a car bomb exploded outside of the Sari Club at the Kuta Beach Resort. Approximately 200 people, mostly foreign tourists, were killed. That it was an act of terrorism was immediately apparent. Currently, no group has claimed responsibility for the attack, but it has been linked to Al Qaeda by many law enforcement authorities. Could anything have prevented this attack or, at the very least, enabled people to have acted in a manner as to avoid becoming one of the victims?

COUNTRY-SPECIFIC TRAVEL WARNINGS

One of the most important factors that must always be considered while traveling abroad is whether a specific travel alert has been posted for the country in question. Let us examine the alert status for Indonesia prior to this attack. Almost a year earlier, on November 23, 2001, the U.S. State Department posted the following alert:

> *The Department of State warns U.S. citizens to defer non-essential travel to Indonesia. Although the Department of State has authorized the return of all Embassy and Consulate personnel and family members effective November 25, the security situation in many parts of Indonesia puts Americans at potential risk . . . There are indications that the bombings that have recently and regularly struck religious, political and business targets throughout Indonesia—such as the attacks on several dozen churches on December 24, 2000, leaving 16 dead and over one hundred injured—will likely recur. . . . . Additionally, there is information that extremist elements may be planning to target U.S. interests in Indonesia, particularly U.S. government facilities, but also possibly including commercial and other private targets.*
>
> *American citizens who travel to or reside in Indonesia should exercise maximum caution and take prudent measures such as avoiding crowds and demonstrations, keeping a low profile, varying times and routes for all required travel, remaining acutely aware of their immediate environment, and notifying the U.S. embassy or Consulate in case of any change in the local security situation. American citizens are also urged to treat mail and packages from unfamiliar sources with suspicion.*

The State Department does not issue travel alerts without considerable cause. This alert should immediately give pause to anyone considering going to Indonesia simply for pleasure. State is quite clear in identifying the threat. Bombings have occurred, are likely to recur, and the likely targets are named. If you learn nothing from this book other than this—heed travel warnings! If you must go to a country deemed unsafe for work or some other compelling reason, follow the recommended precautions.

You can read the reactions to the travel advisory in comments posted on the Internet by a few expatriate British citizens and one American residing in Indonesia. The Brits were somewhat smug in their assessment. Why, one of them wondered, didn't the U.S. State Department issue an advisory against travel to New York City and Washington, D.C., after the attacks on September 11? The odds of being in a car crash, he continued, were far greater than becoming the victim of a terror attack. While statistically this argument could be made, it is the height of foolishness to draw the parallel in the first place. When assessing the safety of a country for foreigners, the history of the country must be taken into account and the recent trends must be analyzed. Has anyone taken the time to research some of the recent happenings in Indonesia, particularly in the region of Borneo, where Muslim Dayaks and Malays have been slaughtering a group of immigrants known as the Madurese? The Madurese tend to be mostly Christian and Animist, and hundreds of Madurese have been hacked to death with machetes wielded by their Muslim neighbors. There have been numerous and well-documented cases where such slaughter occurred before the eyes of the local police, who did nothing, fearing for their own safety. Dayaks have routinely displayed the dismembered bodies of their Madurese victims in public. There have even been reports of isolated recurrences of the practice of cannibalism, once common to the island of Borneo. We would say to our British friends that if wanton butchery and cannibalism reared its head in the United States, we would certainly understand their reluctance to come for a holiday. However, despite the recent warnings by numerous Western countries not to travel to Indonesia, Western tourists continue to flock there. We wonder if any of the victims of the latest attack shared the attitude displayed in the various chat rooms. There are many places to visit and vacation in the world. Select places with stable governments and a history of racial and religious tolerance and tranquility.

Additional concerns also must be addressed. Even if the ruling government seems likely to remain in power, it is important to consider the nature of opposition parties. Have they engaged in acts of violence before to further their political objectives? Are there terrorist groups active in the country you are traveling to? Do they have popular support, or do they work clandestinely? In addition, other considerations, such as the potential for the nationalization of private property or the destruction of your corporate assets, must also be weighed. The major oil industries of the United States and Great Britain are all too familiar with the billions of dollars lost to nationalization.

EMERGENCY MEDICAL CARE

What is the state of the medical infrastructure of the country? Where are the country's doctors trained? How well staffed and supplied are their hospitals? The State Department has all of this information and has designated regional areas as evacuation points in the event of medical emergency. For example, if you are traveling in Southeast Asia, the medical evacuation point is located in Bangkok, Thailand. Among the countries in that region, Thailand has an exceptionally good medical system with well-trained doctors. If you are visiting ancient Khmer ruins in Cambodia and you need surgery of any level of complexity, your chances of survival may be greater if you wait for transportation to Bangkok rather than trust local hospitals. However, even in Thailand, if you are in a remote village area and are sick or injured, you may be the better part of a day away from an emergency room. Learn about the locations of hospitals and the level of medical care. By the way, this is done routinely in law enforcement, even in the United States. Agents and police officers also know which hospitals are trauma centers and which are not. That information is listed in the operational plan prepared before undertaking an anticipated enforcement action. Street cops and firefighters always know where to take their own in an emergency. There are definitely some hospitals that you want to avoid at home. This is doubly true overseas.

Research the availability of medications, both over the counter and prescribed. Many countries have no pharmacies except in the major cities. Prior knowledge of the availability of a local drugstore will allow you to prepare an emergency kit with appropriate medications taken from home. In this same regard, the prevalence of local diseases must be researched. In many countries, malaria, hepatitis, cholera, and rabies are at epidemic levels. Know the country and you will know how to protect yourself with appropriate vaccinations before you land in it. Both the State Department and the Centers for Disease Control can provide you with this information.

LOCAL CRIMINAL ACTIVITY

An often-overlooked fact is that most Americans overseas have a greater risk of being the victim of a criminal rather than terrorist act. Many countries have criminal industries devoted entirely to victimizing Western tourists. In poor countries, people traveling from abroad are almost guaranteed to have more cash and valuables that the local populace. The same is true for expatriate Americans. You are simply a very desirable target. In addition, locals know the places to avoid and the places that are safe. Not being familiar with the neighborhood or district you are wandering around in is one sure way of becoming victimized. The contents of your wallet may very well represent several months of salary to persons living in undeveloped countries. The same is true for an expensive watch or fine jewelry. Chapter 21 discusses the issue of avoiding becoming the victim of crime.

While David was attending law school, he knew a young woman who worked out in the gym he went to. Although he didn't know her very well, he liked her. One winter she accompanied her parents on a vacation to the Dominican Republic. She stayed with her family for a week and then needed to return to the States earlier than her folks, as her school break was over. Her father and mother rented a car and drove her to the airport. While driving through a small town, their car was deliberately rammed broadside by an old truck. The small rental car they were in was crushed. The young woman and her mother were killed. The father survived. As he lay bleeding and unable to move, he watched the locals pull the jewelry off the bodies of his dying wife and daughter. No one even bothered to call for help. To our knowledge, the perpetrators were never caught.

Crimes like the incident just described happen every day. This was undoubtedly not the first time these criminals had used this tactic. Did the local consulate know about this type of criminal activity? If it did, why didn't it post a travel advisory to Americans visiting the Dominican Republic? And even if one had been posted, would anyone have checked to see whether there were any such alerts? Might they have been dissuaded by the alert if they had checked? Could a little prior research into the nature of the criminal situation have prevented a warm and lovely young woman of twenty from dying such a senseless death? People who have never been victimized always tend to view crime as something that happens to other people. It can happen to you. Read the alerts, pay attention, and your chances of becoming a victim will be drastically lowered.

LOCAL LAWS AND CUSTOMS

Give special attention to learning the local laws and customs of the country to which you will be traveling. Many seemingly innocuous actions here in the United States will give extreme offense in some countries or might even result in your arrest. In Thailand, for example, the feet are considered the lowest and dirtiest part of the body. The head is the most sacred. To sit with your feet up pointing toward someone, especially someone's face or head, is considered unspeakably rude. Therefore, if you are riding in a train in Thailand and put your feet up to get more comfortable, you are not only running the risk of being considered an uncultured slob but may actually find yourself in a physical confrontation with a Thai national who thinks you just mortally insulted him. This type of behavior certainly won't make you friends and might even provoke someone to assault you. A dear friend of ours, a wonderful Thai woman named Wongchan Wongching-chai, lives in the suburbs of Washington, D.C. One day, while on the Washington Metro system, she sat across from a young man who was leaning back in his seat and had his feet propped up against the pole used by standing commuters to keep upright while the train is in motion and no seats are available. She was very distressed by the actions of this man, who probably had no idea that someone was viewing his behavior as being so offensive. If he had put his feet up on a train in Bangkok, he may very well have been assaulted. Know where you are going and get at least a passing familiarity with local manners and etiquette.

The Thai people are overwhelmingly Buddhist. Some of the most exquisite artwork in the world can be found in the religious structures and statues of Thailand. However, if you are visiting some of the beautiful Wat Thai or Thai Buddhist temples and you decide to have a picture taken as you sit atop a statue of Buddha, it is very likely that you will be arrested. The police don't want to hear any excuses about not knowing the local laws. You sit on the wrong statue, you are going to jail. It is only common sense to learn as much as you can about the local laws and customs before you go. Along the same lines, learn a bit about the social mores and customs of the country you are traveling to.

NOTES

1. U.S. Department of State, Office of the Spokesman, Worldwide Caution, November 20, 2002.
2. A consular warden system is an embassy's method of maintaining communications with the local American community. A consular warden notice contains information about safety risks as well as more benign subject matter. Information may be circulated by local wardens via phone, fax, or e-mail.

CHAPTER 5

Preparing to Travel

AFTER YOU HAVE COMPLETED YOUR INITIAL RESEARCH, you are now able to begin actual preparations for your journey. The research time you have spent has given you a much better idea of the steps you must take and the items you must bring. Where should you start? The U.S. Department of State offers a wealth of information for the traveler about which items to bring, which to leave home, and a whole host of other helpful things. Go to the website and download its travel checklists. Doing so will help you immeasurably in packing the right way. Also consult some of the many commercially available travel books about the types of items you should bring to the country you're traveling to. The excellent Frommer's travel series is a treasury of important travel knowledge. However, for our purposes, we will deal only with issues of safety and health in our preparatory travel section. State Department personnel travel more than anyone in the world, except for pilots and flight attendants. The State Department's website contains a tremendous amount of valuable information from the most experienced foreign travelers around. It will be more than adequate to help you identify the dozens of other items to take care of before your trip.

NECESSARY DOCUMENTS

Check your passport. Has it expired? Will it expire while you are abroad? Some folks like to live a bit dangerously in this regard. For example, if your trip will last two weeks and your passport has three weeks until the expiration date, you may be tempted to put off getting a renewal. Don't do this. Unforeseen events, illness, or just a change of mind can easily have you abroad with an expired passport. Passports become useless the day they expire. New passports can be reissued at the nearest embassy or consulate, but securing one can be time consuming and just another unnecessary headache. Always make several copies of the passport and place them in separate pieces of luggage. In addition, make sure you have obtained the necessary visas if the country of your destination requires them.

As soon as you have finalized your itinerary, give a copy of it to someone at home. Include all the phone numbers and e-mail addresses that you can and arrange to check in with a friend or relative at regular intervals. Checking in is particularly important. If you are missing for some reason, no one will come to look for you unless someone knows there is a problem. You also must use a bit of common sense while selecting your own personal "lifeline" back home. Besides being a responsible individual, he or she should also be the type of person who can handle an unexpected crisis.

MEDICATION AND MEDICAL INSURANCE

What happens if you need medical attention while you are overseas? Several years ago David took his wife on a trip to Malta, where he was to provide training for the Maltese police. It never occurred to them to check to see whether their policy covered care while traveling abroad. (It did not.) While government employees are traveling on orders, the local embassy will provide medical care and access to the in-house medical services. Dependents, however, unless they are traveling on orders as well, do not qualify. On the return trip between Malta and London, his wife experienced excruciating pain from a sinus infection. They decided to stop over in London and find a doctor. The hotel offered to arrange a house call from a local doctor for the "reasonable" fee of £100. Or, they were told, they could just walk down the street to the hospital. They decided to go to the hospital. Although they had to wait a few hours, they were seen by an excellent physician who treated David's wife and provided enough medication to see them home. When David asked about insurance forms for the payment, he was pleasantly surprised to learn about British socialized medicine. Treatment was provided courtesy of the British taxpayer. However, had they been somewhere else, they would have had to pay out of pocket. Many domestic health insurance companies don't cover out-of-network expenses even within the United States. It is a sure bet that they won't cover you out of the country. Other health plans do provide such coverage. Call your insurance provider before you travel and find out.

If you do not have coverage (seniors take note: Medicare and Medicaid do not cover you overseas), several companies provide inexpensive overseas coverage to travelers. This issue is even more important if you are going to be residing abroad for extended periods of time. International SOS is a good company to contact with these types of questions. It specializes in providing worldwide medical assistance to individuals living or traveling abroad. International SOS is the premier company of this sort and is able to provide for your health needs even in the most remote areas of the world. The company also specializes in dealing with medical emergencies, which require rapid evacuation to a quality healthcare facility. In addition, International SOS can provide evacuation assistance in cases where political unrest or civil disturbances abroad require immediate evacuation to an area of safety. Its complete worldwide contact list can be found in Appendix B.

If you are currently taking prescription medication, make sure you take enough with you. Splitting the contents up and placing some in carry-on luggage and some with checked baggage is a good idea. Try to do the same for glasses or contact lenses, and make sure you have a copy of your prescription. Leave prescription medicines in their own properly labeled bottles to avoid any questions with foreign customs agents or police officers. When you split your prescriptions as recommended above, have the pharmacy provide you with a second labeled bottle. It isn't a bad idea to have a doctor's letter explaining your need for certain medications if they might be unlawful to possess in the country you are traveling to. Make sure you consult the State Department for country-specific recommended inoculations and health alerts as well.

CHOOSE THE RIGHT AIRLINE

When booking your flight, check the safety record of your intended carrier. The extra few bucks you may save flying a bargain airline is not the place to look for savings. Both of us and our wives always fly wide-bodied jets like the 747. David and his wife initially started doing so for nonsecurity reasons. His wife doesn't like the steep takeoff trajectories that you get flying a 727. A bigger plane tends to treat you more gently in this regard. David, his wife, and Ilan's wife are not big fans of flying. They do it because it is necessary to travel. It is somewhat comforting, however, to be flying on a plane with four engines instead of two. These days, flying on a wide-bodied jet has an added benefit that might come as a surprise. Hijackers tend to avoid targeting wide-bodied planes because of the tactical problem of covering that many passengers and three rows of seating instead of two. Ilan, who has experience as a security officer on board El Al planes, certainly agrees with that assessment. Flying a wider plane gives you a smaller chance of getting caught in a hijacking. We'll discuss the risk of becoming a victim of hijacking or being taken hostage in greater detail later on.

The authors try to fly El Al whenever possible because it is one airline that you can be sure takes security seriously. Other carriers have not yet caught up to the impressive security considerations of the Israeli national airline, but some are trying to. At the current time, no other airlines equip their passenger planes with the type of protective equipment that El Al does. Its planes have had a virtually impregnable access system to the cockpit for many years. Another little-known fact is that El Al planes also are equipped with countermeasures to protect against a missile attack. While other airlines are upgrading their planes to copy the Israeli cockpit access system, to date no one is equipping planes with missile defense systems.

AIRLINE SAFETY TIPS

Try to schedule direct flights if possible. Besides the fact that direct flights are more convenient, there are two security-related reasons for this practice. The first is the fact that most airline accidents occur during takeoff and landing. It therefore stands to reason that if your flight is not making many of these takeoffs and landings, you have a statistically lower chance of being in an accident. The second is to minimize the risk of being involved in a hijacking. Despite the success that the September 11 hijackers enjoyed while commandeering American planes flying out of domestic airports, the usual points of infiltration by hijackers are the less secure airports at which many connecting flights must stop. Terrorist hijackers are well aware of which airports they can operate in and which they cannot. If you must take a connecting flight, make sure you are not transferring in an airport that has a history of poor safety practices or is in a high-risk area. Even in the continental United States there is a wide disparity between the levels of security from airport to airport. The recent legislation federalizing the position of airport security screeners may address and correct some of these disparities, but this remains to be seen.

Moreover, there are still many problems even in some of the larger airports in the United States. Most former El Al security specialists are stunned when they pass through metal detectors in U.S. airports. The sensitivity settings here are far lower than is generally used in Israel or in any El Al terminal. In many airports the settings are geared more toward keeping the flow of passenger traffic moving and less on keeping potentially dangerous weapons off planes.

In most countries, with the notable exception of Israel, most airport lobbies are open to the public and are not secure. The secure area is beyond the screening booths; theoretically, no one should be in that area unless he or she has a ticket and has passed through the metal detector. Once you check in, move directly to this part of the airport. Virtually all of the terror attacks at airports have occurred in the unsecured common ticketing area. The recent attack at the El Al counter in Los Angeles also fits this pattern.

THE FLIGHT

Finally, you are ready to get on board the plane and fly off to begin your new life. You feel excited as well as apprehensive. While you are traveling, there are several things to consider to ensure that your trip is not only safer but more convenient as well. We are assuming that you have packed correctly and have utilized some of the travel checklists provided in this book's website to do so.

Check-In

At the airport, expect to experience the usual long delays that have become associated with international air travel since the attacks of September 11. Plan to arrive at the airport at least three hours before your flight. Watch your luggage and carry-on bags at all times. You will have to put your bag through the X-ray machine before you get to the boarding area. Pay particularly careful attention to your bag now. Teams of practiced criminal groups stalk major airports and specialize in grabbing bags off the X-ray machine's conveyor belt while their owners walk through the metal detector. If you are traveling with someone, have one person go through the detector and wait while you place your bags onto the conveyor for the X-ray machine. The person on the outside should watch the bags as they pass into the machine. The person who has already cleared the checkpoint watches the bags as they pass through and collects them. In this way the bags are never unattended except for the few moments when they are physically passing through the machine.

Make sure that you are not carrying anything that could even remotely be considered a weapon. Nothing sharp or pointed and, unless you don't mind spending time in a federal holding cell, don't forget to check any firearms you may have. Never, under any circumstances, agree to take anything on board for someone else. This, of course, does not apply to bringing a box of Grandma's cookies overseas to your relatives. But it does apply to just about everyone else. Do you remember the preflight question that used to be asked of travelers on airplanes? Passengers used to be asked: "Has anyone unknown to you asked you to carry an item on this flight?" This is no longer the case, as bombs have been unwittingly carried by persons taking a package for someone they knew, or thought they knew, very well. Consider the case of Anne Murphy, five months' pregnant by her Jordanian boyfriend, Nezar Hindawi. Hindawi gave her a package containing three pounds of plastic explosives, more than enough to bring down the plane, to carry onto an El Al flight between London and Tel Aviv. Murphy and the package were intercepted before she boarded, and no one was harmed. But consider the absolute abrogation of every instinct of humanity in this act. Hindawi was indifferent not only to the murder of his girlfriend in furtherance of his attack but of his unborn child as well.

In-Flight Briefing

While flying, pay attention to the security briefing given by the flight attendant. Almost everyone tunes out this presentation instead of paying attention to it. Locate the emergency exits and decide which one will be easier to access in an emergency. Know where the next closest one is as well in case you are unable to get to your choice. In the event of an evacuation during smoke-filled conditions, it is a good idea to carry disposable emergency escape hoods with you for each member of your party. We will discuss these types of devices later on.

Once you arrive at your destination, you will need transportation to your hotel or new place of residence. Whenever possible, try to arrange transportation before you go. Many hotels have their own transportation vans, which make regular runs between the hotel and the airport. If you cannot make prior arrangements, use only properly marked and identifiable livery vehicles. Do not accept the services of local residents using personal vehicles to take fares from the airport.

BEHAVIOR ON ARRIVAL

While you are out and about in a foreign country, or anywhere for that matter, the way you walk will allow a potential assailant to classify you as a victim or someone to pass by. We all present a certain body language while we walk. If we have a strong, purposeful stride, we present the image of being a direct person with a place to go. Such people walk with confidence, with a stride that tells the world that they know what they're about. Not exactly the type of person to invite an attempt at mugging or other street crime. However, those of us who may walk with a bit of uncertainty or trepidation send a different message: Take me! I would be an easy mark! C'mon, do it, you know I won't resist.

If you think we are exaggerating, consider a study undertaken several years ago to research how rapists select their targets. Several convicted rapists were asked to watch a series of videos showing women walking about town and evaluate them as to whether they would have selected them for rape. Some of the women depicted in the videos had, in fact, been rape victims. Others had not. The group that had no prior experience as the victims of sexual assault was split between those women that were selected as potential targets of sexual abuse and those that were not. The felons were then asked to explain why they would have targeted one woman over the next. Their responses largely concerned the way the women walked. Rapists were likely to ignore women with a strong confident stride while focusing on victims with a less assertive manner of walking.

The most interesting result of this study related to the group of women who had been prior victims of sexual assault. All of these women were chosen as targets by the convicted rapists. The incarcerated rapists were able to see something in the way each former victim walked that made her more attractive as victims to them as well. Do not walk like a victim. Walk with purpose and confidence, and look as if you have somewhere very important to go. Also, do not ask directions from people on the street. Try to find a police officer or someone in a position of authority. Not only will asking for directions tell a potential criminal that you have no idea where you are, but you will have told a complete stranger where you will be going. Don't do that. Buy a map or a global positioning system, or find a cop, cabbie, or someone else more likely to assist you.

Exhibit 5.1 provides a sample checklist that you can use to assist you in making safe travel decisions. Some of the recommendations have already been discussed; others are explained in greater detail later in this book. Use this form as a guide to help you make the right decisions and take the appropriate precautions. Our checklist is mainly concerned with safety, security, and health. Remember, for additional tips to make your trip more enjoyable, consult the State Department website or one of the travel companies' websites. Use the checklist below along with the traveler's awareness form discussed on page 24.

Exhibit 5.1 Security Pretravel Checklist

Documents

☐ Check *passport validation* (at least 6 months remaining validity).

☐ Arrange *visas* for entry into countries to be visited, including those that you will transit.

☐ Pack an extra set of *passport photos* along with a photocopy of your passport information page to make replacement of your passport easier in the event it is lost or stolen.

☐ Carry a current U.S. *driver's license* with your photo on it. Make sure it will not expire during your trip.

☐ Leave a *copy of your itinerary* with family or friends at home in case they need to contact you in an emergency. Arrange to check in with them at regular intervals.

☐ Make two *photocopies* of your passport *identification page, airline tickets, and driver's license* that you plan to bring with you. Leave one photocopy of these data with family or friends at home; pack the other in a place separate from where you carry your valuables.

☐ Make a list of addresses and emergency telephone numbers for U.S. embassies and local consulates.

☐ Make a list with your blood type, allergies, medical conditions, medications you are taking, and other special medical requirements.

☐ Check with the airline and your personal insurance company regarding coverage for lost luggage. Hard-shell type suitcases with locks are preferable.

Health

☐ Take a copy of your prescriptions and the generic names for the drugs.
☐ Take an extra set of eyeglasses or contact lenses.
☐ Take a health book (record of immunizations).
☐ Carry a small first aid kit.
☐ Take any medicines you need in your carry-on luggage.

Money, Cards, and Phone

☐ Obtain a modest amount of *foreign currency* before you leave your home country.
☐ Take only the *credit cards* you need.
☐ Bring *travelers' checks* and one or two major credit cards instead of cash.
☐ Carry the minimum amount of *valuables* necessary for your trip and plan a place or places to conceal them.
☐ Make two copies of the numbers of credit cards and travelers' checks, along with telephone numbers to report their loss, and air ticket numbers and store them in your wallet or briefcase.
☐ Ask your credit card company *how to report the loss* of your card from abroad. 800 numbers do not work from abroad, but your company should have a number that you can call while you are overseas.
☐ Consider getting a *telephone calling card.*
☐ Consider worldwide paging or satellite cellular service.
☐ Access numbers to U.S. operators are published in many international newspapers. Find out your access number before you go.

Luggage

☐ Put your *name, address, and telephone numbers* inside and outside of each piece of luggage. Use covered luggage tags to avoid casual observation of your identity or nationality.
☐ Buy *locks* for your luggage.

Insurance

☐ Check on whether your *health insurance* covers you abroad. Medicare and Medicaid do not provide payment for medical care outside the United

(continues)

Exhibit 5.1   Security Pretravel Checklist *(Continued)*

States. Even if your health insurance will reimburse you for medical care that you pay for abroad, normal health insurance does not pay for medical evacuation from a remote area or from a country where medical facilities are inadequate.

☐ Consider purchasing one of the *short-term health and emergency assistance policies* designed for travelers, such as a policy from International SOS. Also, make sure that the plan you purchase includes medical evacuation in the event of an accident or serious illness.

☐ If you do not have comprehensive medical coverage, consider enrolling in an *international health program.* (Hospitals in foreign countries do not take credit cards and most will not honor U.S.-based medical insurance plans.)

☐ Find out if your *personal property insurance covers* you for loss or theft abroad.

☐ Check what exclusions are written into your life insurance policy.

Education

☐ Learn as much as you can about the *local laws and customs* of the places you plan to visit. Good resources are your library, your travel agent, and the embassies, consulates, or tourist bureaus of the countries you will visit.

☐ Learn a few *important words* of your country destination.

☐ Get a large regional *map.*

☐ Get a foreign language/English pocket *dictionary or electronic translator.*

CHAPTER 6

Residing Abroad

A T ANY GIVEN TIME, there are more than 1 million American citizens living in foreign countries. Many in the expatriate community are working for American companies with interests in countries all over the world. They live on the local economy and reside in local neighborhoods. Many are retired Americans who have moved back to their family's country of origin or have decided to live in a country that will allow them to enjoy a more comfortable lifestyle on their limited resources. Hundreds of thousands of other Americans live abroad while working for the federal government.

Those Americans living abroad while working for the U.S. government have the luxury of having security guidelines for government-provided housing. Security officers at the local embassy do their best to make sure that residential housing complies with those security guidelines. Private citizens, however, do not have that luxury. Often they are left to deal with these issues on their own. This chapter provides a checklist for those living abroad of minimum standards that all housing should meet.

CHOOSING A PLACE TO LIVE

Long before your actual move, you will need to make many plans concerning your new life abroad. Where will you live? Will you buy a private home or condominium, or will you be a renter? How about your furniture? Take it with you or buy locally? Do you intend to bring a vehicle with you from home or buy one locally? Where will you educate your children, or where will you attend a house of worship? Many of these decisions can be left to personal preference. Others should be made only after consideration is given to what impact any of these choices may have on your safety and that of your family.

Every country in the world has neighborhoods that are considered to be safer than others. How do you know which neighborhood is the best and safest choice? You can take several steps in this regard, beginning with asking the local embassy or consulate in the country you are moving to. Ask the consular staff for recommendations. Where do most embassy employees live? In some countries, embassy personnel live in a compound and not in the local community. Even so, they will be able to provide you with all the information you need to get started. If at all possible, go on a house-hunting trip prior to your move. It is a good idea to spend some time exploring the neighborhoods in the city you will be living in. After receiving some thoughts from the embassy as well as friends and coworkers already resident in the country, consult a map and judge the area on more than merely whether you like the neighborhood or not. One of the most important things to consider is the accessibility of your intended home while driving. If there is only one way in and out of the neighborhood, look elsewhere. The more desirable situation is to be able to use several different routes to travel between home and work. Selecting a residence along a multilane road with traffic flow in both directions is preferable. We go into this subject in greater detail in Chapter 8.

Drive the route between your place of employment and the various neighborhoods you are considering moving to. Locate the schools that you are considering and determine the length of time it will take to get there from both home and work. Do the same for local hospitals. By the way, as we all know, not all hospitals are alike. Even here in the United States, the police officers and firefighters, not to mention doctors and nurses, all know which hospitals to go to in the event of an emergency. Overseas, this decision is even more critical. Often there is a big difference between local hospital care and the facilities that cater to the international community. Call the embassy and find out which hospitals their personnel use.

Evaluate each neighborhood for its proximity to shopping areas. Living in a secure neighborhood is certainly important, but if you must shop for groceries in an unsafe area, consider changing your living plans.

Determine the location of local police stations. In general, even in countries where there is considerable anti-American sentiment, police stations are likely to be a place of relative safety in an emergency. In Western countries or regions with good relations with the United States, they should be considered safe havens in the event you are in danger of assault or are being followed.

SECURING YOUR RESIDENCE

What type of dwelling are you considering? A private home offers somewhat more privacy than an apartment building but, depending on the surrounding area, may offer less security. Often foreign nationals reside in apartment complexes with private security guards and limited access. This may be a more desirable option. A private home may be made secure by the use of fences and other devices to establish a secure perimeter.

It is extremely important to remember that physical security comes first. Alarms and monitors are excellent tools that can greatly enhance security. (See Chapter 13 for a discussion of technical security.) But the fact remains that these measures are a second consideration after you have made sure that your residence is physically secure. This does not mean that you live in a fortress. A determined method of attack can breach any fortifications. Your goal is to make it as difficult as possible for a criminal or terrorist to gain entry. For example, an open window is one of the most inviting signs for a would-be intruder. The best security designs and alarm systems are rendered completely useless if you leave a window open or if the system is not activated. The late former Beatle George Harrison was stabbed by an intruder in his home several years before his death. It was widely reported that although Harrison's home was equipped with an extremely sophisticated alarm system, it was not turned on at the time of the attack. Limit access. If someone is intent on breaking in, he or she probably will be able to do so. The task is to make it difficult for intruders. Force them to make a lot of noise and spend a great deal of time, and you have drastically reduced the likelihood that you will be selected as a target.

ENTRY POINTS

When looking for a residence or while assessing the current level of security at the home you live in, assess the physical entry points first. Check the windows. Always keep in mind that windows are an intruder's favorite source of entry. Look for solid windows and frames. Avoid windows that are sectioned into numerous panes; they allow intruders to remove an individual pane easily and quietly. Once that is accomplished, the intruder can reach in and disengage the lock on the window. Someone you definitely don't want in your home has just gotten instant access to you and your family. Solid-pane windows set in sturdy frames require greater force to open. Of course, they can always be shattered, and generally they can be pried open as well. The trick here is to make would-be intruders use a great deal of force to gain entry. If someone tries to force your window at night in this manner, the attendant noise will be sufficient to wake you up. Remember, most thieves and terrorists will spend time watching a target before making an attempt. Make sure that when they look your house over, they instantly realize that they will need to expend some effort to get in. The preferred approach is to secure windows with protective grilles. Again, criminals can defeat grilles with tools and time, but the idea is to cause potential intruders to consider how long they will need to be exposed while attempted to get through the grilles. If grilles are used, emergency releases must be installed to allow for evacuation in the event of a fire.

Sliding doors are common all over the world. Depending on their design, they can either offer easy access to a criminal or present great difficulty. The first thing to remember is that a glass sliding door can always be shattered. This is not always as easy as it sounds. During a joint Drug Enforcement Administration (DEA)/New York State Police investigation in Long Island, New York, an entry was being made into the home of a suspected cocaine dealer. Once inside, the team encountered a sliding glass door in the *interior of the house*. The home's owner had added on several rooms to the back of the house. The sliding door, which had originally provided access to the backyard, was now in the middle of the new, larger structure. This unexpected impediment stopped the New York State Police Mobile Response Team (MRT), the lead element in the raid, cold. They had breached the entry door and had left their heavy tools outside. One intrepid team member picked up a large television and hurled it against the glass. Although this big, athletic guy threw the TV with great force, the agents and officers watched it bounce harmlessly off the glass door. The team then had to hold position in the middle of the entry while someone went out to the truck and brought in a large pry bar called a hallagan tool, which was used to smash through the glass. However, the delay gave the drug dealer time to flush several kilos of cocaine down the toilet. The point of retelling this account is to illustrate that the right design can provide relatively good security, but it does not make the residence a fortress. Just remember that glass is still just glass. It may deter but it cannot stop, as the right type of tool will easily smash through the door and allow entry.

DOORS AND LOCKS

Check the locks on the sliding doors. Make sure they are functioning properly. Many sliding doors have a tiny latch lever that provides the only lock. A quick twist with a crowbar or heavy screwdriver is all that it takes to force entry. A straight bar placed behind the closed door can improve security dramatically. Don't forget that while the locking mechanism itself can be made effective, all it takes to get through a glass door is a hard strike with a brick.

Solid doors must also be scrutinized. You would be amazed at the enormous number of people who have spent a lot of money on steel doors and dead bolts on doors that they have set into wood frames. During his career with the DEA, David smashed through hundreds of such doors. Remember, the strength of the door depends on the strength and construction of the door *frame*. Look at the doors in your home right now. The hinges are screwed into the frame, aren't they? If the frame is wooden, the hinges can be easily forced off the frame. That strong and expensive steel door will simply be torn right off the frame. Select a sturdy steel door with dead-bolt locks set in a metal frame. Standard dead bolts must have a throw of at least one inch. A better choice is a multipoint lock design. This type of lock secures the door to the frame in several places, making it more resistant to prying or battering attacks. The lock companies Rav-Bariah and S.E. Yardeni, as well as the German firm Winkhaus, offer very strong designs. Another suggestion is to use cross bars on the inside of the door that bolt into the top, bottom, and sides of the frame. This type of locking system is also a good idea on the door to your residential safe haven, which we will discuss below. In addition, antiram bars are a good idea on any door that is not used frequently, like the door to the basement.

The door must then be securely fastened to the frame. Make sure that the hasps are screwed into the frame and door with long, heavy-duty screws.

Good dead-bolt locks are worthless if the door can be forced off its hinges. The next critical point is to make sure that the frame is properly mounted into the structure itself. The door frame should be steel. Strong steel doors mounted into wooden frames won't do the trick. A steel frame, however, can be easily mounted into the wooden structure of the dwelling with long, heavy-duty screws. Once the steel frame is securely mounted, the steel door won't be too easy to force open. One note of caution: Many police officers have attempted to serve search or arrest warrants to people living in tenements with steel doors mounted into steel frames. Frequently, upon application of a battering ram, the entire wall starts to buckle in. Overall sturdy construction cannot be overlooked.

Doors also should have a peephole or eyepiece large enough to see a significant area in front of the door. Many excellent designs have a lens providing a 180-degree panoramic view. They are definitely worth the few dollars that they cost. Every family member, including children and domestics, needs to look through the peephole prior to opening the door. Even when someone is expected or if a known visitor acknowledges his or her presence verbally, look through the peephole. It is very common for intruders to wait for someone to arrive home before attempting entry. They may either attempt to rush the door as it is opened or may try to gain entrance by forcing a familiar person to announce him- or herself. The simple step of looking before opening the door can provide an added level of protection against this tactic.

Outside doors must have sturdy dead bolts. Once again, the construction of the frame is critically important. A steel door and heavy dead bolt is rendered worthless if the bolt is secured into a flimsy frame. This must be given a great deal of attention. A variety of after-market products are available to reinforce door locks. Most are excellent, effective, inexpensive, and easy to install. Some, such as three- or four-point lateral sliding bolts, which are common in countries like Israel, are more expensive but are worth the cost. It is worth repeating again that all of these measures are worthless if the frame is substandard.

Several companies manufacture excellent security doors, which are also quite attractive and are available in numerous designs and styles. The Israeli firm Rav-Bariah is one of several. Its security products are among the best in the industry. Exhibit 6.1 shows examples of residential doors offered by Rav-Bariah.

All Rav-Bariah doors are available with many desirable accessories, such as a four-way lock, high-security cylinder, double cylinder protector,

180-degree panoramic door viewer, floor door stopper, and several other security options. Rav-Bariah manufactures double doors, French doors, and numerous designer models that were formerly marketed under the Mul-T-Lock name. Many are certified for use by the Israeli government, particularly the Israeli Foreign Service, for securing the residences of Israeli diplomats and governmental representatives abroad.

Exhibit 6.1   Examples of High-Security Doors: Rav-Bariah Model 790 Residential High-Security Door (left), Rav-Bariah Model 790 Satin Nickel Door (center), and Rav-Bariah Forced Entry Model 9315 High-Security Door (right)

Photos courtesy of Rav-Bariah.

If you choose not to install a high-security door, there are several security measures that you absolutely must take. For example, every lock to the outside must be changed or rekeyed. You have no way of knowing how many copies the last tenant or owner made. In addition, think how easy it is to have copies made of keys. If you consider all the people who have had access to your keys—for example, in parking garages or domestic help—you will appreciate how easy it would be for someone to have unauthorized copies made. Many locks have keys that cannot be duplicated at the local hardware store; the keys can be made only by an authorized professional locksmith. The locking systems should be dead bolts at a minimum. Even better choices are the multiple-point locks available from Mul-T-Lock or Winkhaus. The Winkhaus locks have multiple, very strong dead bolts. Other models have hook-type locks that engage the door frame in an additional location. More locking points make forced entry difficult unless the intruders are equipped with heavy entry tools. Properly installed, they will prevent the door from being kicked in.

ADDITIONAL POINTS OF ENTRY

The roof is another potentially vulnerable access point. Most houses have ducts for the cooling system, vents, and fireplace. Make sure they are secure. Often adjacent buildings provide easy access to the roof. Don't overlook this point. A German family living in mainland China several years ago was murdered by intruders who gained access in just this manner. Get a competent contractor to seal off these points if you can't do it yourself. In addition, if tree limbs in your yard or adjacent to your home could provide access to the roof or to upper-level windows, they must be cut down. If the landlord refuses, go live somewhere else.

LIGHTING

Indoor and outdoor lighting are valuable means of enhancing security. Thieves hate bright lights. So do terrorists and, for that matter, anyone attempting to surreptitiously gain entry to your home. Motion-sensitive lights are cheap and easy to install and are quite effective in discouraging potential intruders. They make a great difference. Make sure you position the lights where they are of most use. Often lights are placed in the front and back of the homes by doorways. This may be acceptable if those doorways are the only ways in and out. However, if you have side windows located in a poorly lit area, you will only be directing a potential intruder to move his or her attempted point of entry to those windows. Lighting should cover all exterior walls of the residence. The external perimeter, along the fence or property line, should ideally be illuminated as well.

While we are talking about lower windows, it is a good time to mention that often homes have decorative bushes or trees near or under windows. Look at these areas and use a bit of common sense. If an intruder could use them for concealment, have them removed or cut back. The key to remember is to make assailants feel exposed and vulnerable to discovery no matter where they attempt to get in. There is nothing more to it. Make them uncomfortable with the prospect of trying to get into your house, and they will most likely move on to an easier target.

RESIDENTIAL SAFE HAVEN

Another consideration may be the installation of a secure area within the home in case of a determined attempt at forced entry. Embassies, consulates, and many private facilities maintain a "safe haven" within the premises. It is the most secure location in the building and is designed to withstand attempts at forced entry for long enough to hold out until help arrives. The access points need to be reinforced and able to withstand considerable abuse. The door to this room must be strongly reinforced at the least. A better option is to use a door specifically designed for this purpose. The Rav-Bariah Company makes a line of excellent doors that are rated to withstand attempts at forced entry from 5 to 60 minutes. Some of these doors, such as the Forced Entry Models 9310 or 9315, are high-security steel doors rated to withstand a 60-minute attempt at forced entry. The door shown on the right in Exhibit 6.1 is the best choice for securing such a safe haven. This is the Rav-Bariah Forced Entry Model 9315. It also provides ballistic protection against rounds fired from military rifles. The construction is of reinforced steel, and it has a high-security four-way lock. It also may be ordered with various accessories, such as a high-security Mul-T-Lock cylinder, double cylinder protector, and protective cover plates and handles. Remember that the walls of the safe haven must also be reinforced. There are many ways to accomplish this. Construction with steel mesh will make it difficult for attackers to cut their way into the room. Steel plates or Kevlar will provide ballistic protection against rounds fired through the wall. Another very effective way of constructing a ballistic barrier is to fill the wall with common "pea" gravel. Members of the Irish Republican Army used this technique quite effectively while fighting the British in Northern Ireland. They filled ammunition cans, roughly the size of a large shoebox, with gravel and stacked them up to form a barrier. Testing by the Federal Bureau of Investigation ballistics-testing laboratory proved this technique's effectiveness. An eight-inch barrier of pea gravel provides protection against high-powered rifle rounds. The densely packed and irregularly shaped gravel is as effective as many commercially produced ballistic barriers and may be a lot cheaper to implement.

The secure room also should have some way of calling for help other than the telephone line to the residence. An emergency radio or cellular phone is the preferred method. In addition, your home should be stocked with drinking water and food in the event that the security situation makes it necessary to remain indoors over the course of several days.

The foregoing items all relate to physical security. Remember, physical security is the primary concern. Make forced entry a very difficult proposition for an assailant. There is no such thing as impregnability. Given enough time and the right tools, any place, including heavily fortified positions, can be breached. If you ever travel to Israel, a trip to the mountain fortress Masada will convince you of that fact. Masada was a masterpiece of Herodian construction. Located 2,000 feet above the Dead Sea (Yam Hamelach), it was accessible only through a narrow winding trail known as the Snake Path. The narrow and torturous path allowed defenders to kill attacking soldiers as they attempted to breach the walls. Almost 2,000 years ago, the Roman legions of Vespasian besieged Masada. After numerous attempts to overcome the city failed, the Romans simply built an enormous ramp on the far side of Masada, which allowed for a conventional mass attack by legionnaires. Masada, once thought impregnable, quickly fell. The point is that you cannot stop a determined attempt at entry. All you can do is delay it. Fortunately, that is all that is required for general security concerns. Make entry look difficult, and you have greatly decreased your chance of being targeted for break-in. Make it even harder actually to accomplish, and you have brought the odds down still further. If it takes the bad guys time, they will most likely abort rather than risk identification and arrest.

ALARM SYSTEMS AND VIDEO MONITORING

Once physical security issues are addressed, it is appropriate to examine what additional steps may be taken to further enhance security. The next step is to see what types of technological solutions are appropriate for the location. The most common security technology is a simple alarm system wherein sensors are affixed to all points of entry. When the alarm is set, a complete electrical circuit is formed. Any attempt to open a door or window "shorts" the system and sets off the alarm. The alarm may be localized, with a siren that goes off when the system is breached. Other systems are wired into a central station that receives the alarm and may dispatch police or security units as necessary. Notification to the central station also may be accomplished through the use of cell phone technology. The system generally uses a telephone land line to make contact, with the cell phone serving as a backup. In many Third World countries, where phone service is unreliable, cell phone backup is a necessity. The added benefit to this system is also that it still works if an intruder is skilled enough to cut the phone lines before attempting a break-in.

Technology has greatly increased the number of options for alarm systems. Infrared motion detectors, infrared beam perimeters, and glass-break alarms are common. Security systems may be accessed through the Internet as well. If you are away from home and are using a security system with this type of remote access feature, you can connect to the Internet and actually interact with your security system. Perhaps you merely want to check the status of the system to ensure that all is well. If your system uses a video camera system, you can monitor the cameras from your computer. Other systems allow you to turn on lights or bypass a particular system or zone. After this point, security becomes quite James Bondian. Certain perimeter systems sense vibration, sound, and the pressure of footfalls. Some perimeter systems can distinguish between a bird landing on a fence and a person attempting to climb over it. These "smart fences" make any attempt at intrusion virtually impossible. There are three ways to get past a fence: You can climb over it, cut through it, or tunnel underneath it. The products of some fence companies can not only detect any such attempts but also have an incredibly low number of false alarms. Once these fences go up, a perimeter is established that is virtually impossible to cross without being detected. That is the mission. These fences are not designed to be unbreachable barriers; they are merely an enhanced alert system. In extremely hostile areas, smart fences can be doubled, with razor wire in between plus other impediments against attack.

Video cameras and infrared technology also provide further enhancement to the security of a residence or other facility. The presence of camera systems is, by itself, a deterrent to entry or assault. Closed circuit cameras tell potential intruders that they are expected. Furthermore, in addition to the fact that the residents may well be alerted to the presence of the assailant or thief, criminals realize that if they continue with their plans, the camera will record them. Even if they think they can be successful, they must weigh the likelihood of success with the risk of later identification and capture.

Cameras also enhance access control ability. For example, a restricted access gate or door with a closed circuit TV (CCTV) camera monitoring the entrance allows the resident or guard the ability to visually confirm the identity of individuals before they are granted admittance. In addition, cameras allow you to observe areas around the house that you cannot see. Attackers or burglars always try to avoid areas from where they can be seen. They have the advantage in this regard if they have been watching your movements and patterns of activity. For example, if they know you generally leave the house at 8:00 A.M., they do not need to wait to attack you outside the front door where they would be likely to be observed. They will wait on the side of the house, for example, out of your direct view because they know you will walk right past them on your way out. Properly positioned cameras afford you the ability to watch the entire outside area or perimeter. In addition, the mere presence of cameras tells potential assailants a great deal. It tells them that you are a security-conscious person and that you might not be as easy a target as you appear.

NEIGHBORHOOD WATCH

Another excellent and easy way to enhance security is by cultivating good relations with your neighbors. It is often said that good fences make good neighbors. Allow us to make this observation as well: Good neighbors make good fences. People who know you are apt to also know when things look a bit out of place. If, for example, they know you are away on vacation and see the lights on in your house, they will most likely call the police on your behalf. We all know this from personal experience. We have neighbors, and we know the people who should be at their homes and who should not. Your neighbor also has a different vantage point from yours from which to make observations. Agents and police officers routinely conduct surveillance on criminal suspects. In the Drug Enforcement Administration (DEA), we would sit in our cars for hours and sometimes days while watching bad guys. Unless you are completely inept, you would never park in front of the target's home. The goal was always to try to find a place where you could make observations and not be seen by the subject of the surveillance. So you would park down the block or on an intersecting corner. The subject rarely realized that he was being watched. However, we were routinely scrutinized or even questioned by the people who lived in the house we were parked in front of. Many times neighbors called the police, and sector cars would pull up in response to calls about a suspicious vehicle parked in front of a home. On several occasions we even had neighbors calling the target of the surveillance and discussing the suspicious cars out front. Sometimes these people obviously intended to alert the criminal that the cops were around. More often than not, though, the person who called had no idea that his neighbor was a crook and was concerned about the presence of an unfamiliar vehicle in the neighborhood. For our purposes in enhancing security, this type of interaction is exactly the type of behavior we want to encourage. Talk to your neighbors. If you are living in an area with other Americans or foreign nationals, you might discuss taking the responsibility to watch out for each other. It is a good practice that can be a valuable asset.

Another benefit of having a relationship with your neighbors is being able to look out for each other's property while you are not home. Many people living abroad make long trips back home to be with family. Alert and conscientious neighbors can keep an eye on things until you return. They can (and should) be asked to pick up and collect your mail while you are away. A big pile of mail in your box or at your door can attract unwanted visitors.

AVOID PREDICTABLE PATTERNS

In later chapters, we discuss the importance of varying your routine while traveling to and from work. Potential attackers like predictable targets. If they know where you are at a given time during the day, you will become a very attractive target for them. While driving, you must learn to travel on different roads between the office and your residence. However, you must extend this procedure even to the actions you take while in your own building. Ilan recounts the murder of an Israeli diplomat some years ago. This individual lived in a high-rise apartment building not far from the Israeli embassy in Brussels. He was a creature of habit and would leave the house and return home at the same time each day. In addition, because he lived so close, he would leave the office at the same time each day and return home for lunch. His attackers quickly learned his routine and were even able to follow him into his building and learn which floor he lived on. Because his schedule was so predictable, his attackers felt that he was an easy target for assassination. One assailant simply waited for him on the floor of his apartment outside the elevator door at the time he was expected to arrive home for lunch. The diplomat got off the elevator at the expected time and was shot to death by the waiting assailant. From the terrorists' standpoint, this was a simple operation, made so by their target's failure to adhere to one of the most basic security rules: Avoid a predictable routine. This type of operation would have been far less attractive to the attackers had their victim varied his routine, perhaps having lunch in the office on occasion or traveling at different times. Another practice that we also recommend is to vary your routine even as you enter the lobby of your apartment building and take the elevator to your floor. Make it hard for someone watching you to figure out what floor you live on. It is a simple matter for someone in the lobby watching you enter the elevator to figure out your floor by watching the floor indicator. We strongly recommend that you follow the same procedure for the final portion of your trip home, namely the ride in the elevator, as you do for the trip between your place of work and your residence. By this we mean vary your route home even within your building. Don't always take the elevator directly to your floor. Ride it one or two floors above or below on a regular basis and take the stairs the rest of the way. Not only will this provide you with a bit of extra exercise, it also will throw off anyone attempting to determine where you live by watching the elevator lights or even by taking the elevator up with you. When David used to follow suspects into an elevator in an attempt to learn where they were going, he would walk in and press the button for the highest floor. Thus he was guaranteed to learn where the subjects of the surveillance would get off. Listen to the little bell inside your head. If you don't like the looks of someone riding the elevator with you, don't get off at your floor. If the little bell is really ringing at the prospect of getting into an elevator alone with a suspicious character, then do not go in at all.

By the way, elevator assaults are also common with muggers and sexual predators. A favorite trick of the New York City hoodlum is to wait for a potential mugging victim to enter the lobby and get into the elevator. If you've ever ridden an elevator in New York, you will realize that they were not built for speed. As the doors close, the attacker sprints up the stairs to the second floor and presses the button, causing the elevator to stop at that floor. Then the attacker performs what is known in New York as the bum's rush, charging in and attacking, often brutally, in order to rob the victim of his or her wallet, purse, or jewelry. There are not many options in this situation. Many times victims realize that they are in for it. They felt that something was wrong as they entered the elevator but did so anyway. They may helplessly watch the attacker run for the stairwell as the doors close, effectively sending them into harm's way. What can be done? Think for a moment what you would do. It isn't a bad exercise to learn to get your self-thinking in a defensive mode. You are in the elevator and, as it closes, you realize that this is exactly the scenario we just described. You know that you are trapped in the elevator and that on the second floor the door will open and you will be attacked. What do you do? Obviously, if you are armed, this would be a good time to draw your weapon. However, since this is not going to be the case with the vast majority of folks, you have only your wits to protect you. The first thing you should do is try to hit the DOOR OPEN button before the elevator starts its ascent. If the door opens, you can get off the elevator and scream for help. You may still be attacked if the assailant realizes what you have done. This is a better choice, however, because you are more likely to encounter help in the lobby rather than in the elevator on the second floor. If the door will not open, hit the EMERGENCY STOP or ALARM button. If the elevator stops then, with an alarm going off, you can be certain that the bad guy is not going to get in. If you hit the ALARM button, the effect may very well frighten the assailant away. If the elevator has neither of these options, you have no other choice than to prepare to fight for your life. Never assume that you will avoid assault by simply handing over your valuables. If that happens, you are lucky to have lost nothing but some money or property. However, if it does not, prepare to take whatever action is necessary to make sure you go home that night.

ADDITIONAL RECOMMENDED MEASURES

For home or apartment security, another good option is to consider getting a dog. This is not suitable for everyone. You may be allergic or your schedule may not be conducive to caring for an animal. Maybe you are just not a "dog person." Nevertheless, if you have a dog, you have gone a long way toward enhancing your personal security. Dogs are living burglar alarms with teeth. The sound of a dog barking at the presence of an unfamiliar person is the last thing attackers want to hear. In addition, if intruders try to get in while you are out, they have to factor in the delay that dealing with a dog will cause. If it is a big enough dog, they also may need to factor in the loss of a limb.

Make it a habit always to ask who is at the door before you open it. Never assume it is the person you are expecting because Daddy always comes home at six o'clock. The people who will try to harm you and get into your home probably know that, too. They will capitalize on your complacency if you let them. If you have children, make sure they adhere to this rule. No exceptions. Also, pay attention to the sound of the voice of the person who responds to your challenge. A common way to gain entry is to grab a person who is expected and force that person to knock and talk.

Never leave the door open or unlocked. Many of us unlock the door a few minutes before we expect a family member to get home from work. This is a common practice that must be avoided. On the sitcom *Seinfeld,* every time Jerry buzzed in George or Elaine through the downstairs door, he immediately unlocked his door and left it partially open. Don't do this. A very common technique used by burglars or home invaders is to walk down the hall inside of apartment buildings and randomly try to open doors. Invariably, they will find unlocked doors.

Try to avoid receiving deliveries at home. That is tough to do if you are expecting the delivery of your new dining room set. But try to have routine packages and mail delivered to the office. We discuss mail and package handling procedures in Chapter 11.

LOOK BEFORE YOU GO

When you leave the house, make sure you first look out of the windows, peephole, or cameras and observe the area outside of your home. Pay attention to the street. Are any unfamiliar cars parked there? Before you leave, open the door and look down the street. Pay attention to your surroundings, and make it a point to vary the time that you leave your home. Another simple measure to take is to utilize lights on timers when you are away from home. Most people have seen the movie *Home Alone.* In that movie, Joe Pesci, the leader of a two-man burglary team, has all the timers on the block figured out. True, the lights-on-timers method is low tech and commonly known to burglars. However, like a good bowl of chicken soup when you are sick, while it may not help, it won't hurt either.

LIMITING ACCESS TO THE HOME

Remember, these security enhancements will not help if you are willingly admitting persons posing a security risk to your home. Most people understand that they should deny access to unexpected visitors or unverified workers. Sometimes, however, that same level of diligence seems to lapse in regard to the employment of domestic workers. Hiring the right domestic employees can make adapting to life in your new home much easier. Conversely, if you get the wrong one, you are opening yourself to the risk of becoming the victim of property crimes or even crimes of violence. These people will have virtually unrestricted access to your home. They must be screened with exceptional care. The best way to hire a domestic household employee is through recommendations of a friend or other trusted person who has utilized his or her services in the past. Even an individual recommended by someone you know should be required to produce other references, preferably from Western families that they have worked for in the past. References should be checked. Often the local embassy has a list of household workers who have been employed by embassy employees and have been found to provide satisfactory services. In any event, interview all applicants carefully and evaluate their suitability to fit your needs. Just because someone else had a positive experience with a particular employee does not mean that person will be acceptable to your individual situation. A veteran DEA agent of our acquaintance is married to a Thai woman who is an unmatched expert in finding and hiring the perfect person to work in their home. She is a direct person and clearly communicates her needs and expectations to applicants during the interview. If the person is hired, there are never any surprises. If you know anyone with that type of ability, by all means bring him or her in to give you advice and perhaps even handle the interview for you. By the way, if people don't work out and you need to terminate their services, do the smart thing. Tell them their services are no longer required as of that moment. Do not allow them even to finish out the day. Once you fire them, they are gone. You should, however, send them on their way with a nice severance package, depending on how long they stayed with your family. At least two weeks' salary is generous or a full month if they were with you for longer than a few months. Even if they have hard feelings about being fired, a fair separation agreement tends to smooth things over. Avoiding the animosity of a domestic is worth the few extra dollars it may cost you. Under no circumstances should you allow people to work in your home after you have fired them.

Pay particular attention to the use of the telephone in your new home. It is always preferable to have your home phone number unlisted and unpublished. Just as in the United States, no one who answers the phone should give his or her name or his or her family's name. Children should be discouraged from answering the phone; if they do, they must be directed never to speak with someone they do not know. Telephone scams are common in every country. Beware of people posing as official personnel, such as police or utility employees from the phone corporation.

Another good practice to follow is to avoid being picked up or dropped off by local car service drivers at your exact residence. Both of the authors make this a habit even here in the United States. You never know who will be operating the cab. Ilan was very sensitive to this practice while working as an agent at the Israeli embassy in Washington, D.C. On one occasion, a livery service driver picked up Ilan and his wife at the airport. Ilan noticed that the driver was from a country with unfriendly relations to Israel. Rather than expose his Israeli accent, he chose to let his wife talk to the driver and had the driver drop them off several blocks away from their home. If you get into a cab and you feel uncomfortable for any reason, do not get brought directly home. Perhaps you have an argument with the driver during the trip or suspect he is from a country with no sympathy for persons of your nationality. Whatever the reason for your discomfiture, it is a good idea to keep your address unknown and ask to be dropped somewhere else.

WARDEN SYSTEMS

A final and very important point to follow is for you to maintain close ties to the embassy or consulate in your country of residence. Local embassies are beginning to operate e-mail service to Americans residing in their area of responsibility. Simply subscribe to the service and you will receive security updates as they become available. An example of such a listing is shown below; it is from the U.S. Embassy in Germany. Expatriate Americans residing in Germany can subscribe to this service.

All Americans in Germany are invited to join a new public service of the American Embassy in Germany. This new service allows you to receive up-to-date public announcements and travel warnings that may have a direct impact on your safety and security.

U.S. embassies and consulates overseas traditionally use warden systems to transmit important public announcements and travel warnings to Americans abroad. Public announcements are a means to disseminate information about terrorist threats and other relatively short-term and/or trans-national conditions posing significant risks to the security of American travelers. In the past, public announcements have been issued to deal with short-term coups, bomb threats to airlines, violence by terrorists and anniversary dates of specific terrorist events. Travel warnings are issued when the State Department decides, based on all relevant information, to recommend that Americans avoid travel to a certain country.

Traditional warden systems rely upon the efforts of dedicated volunteers to spread the word among Americans living in the area. The newly created e-mail service provides an efficient way for the Department of State to quickly contact Americans in Germany.

This service will be used for official purposes only. Most messages broadcast will directly relate to your safety or security. Recent public announcements concerning the possibility of terrorist threats targeted against Americans are an example of the new service's usefulness. We may also, upon occasion, use the service to transmit information of general interest to Americans in Germany, including announcements concerning taxes and voter registration.

We urge you to sign up for this valuable service as soon as possible. To subscribe to the new service, simply go to our sign-up page, *or send an e-mail to* GermanyACS@State.gov *and put the word SUBSCRIBE in the subject line.*

Check with your local embassy and find out if it offers a similar service. If it does or if one is being contemplated, make sure you subscribe to the service. In addition to security updates, these sites also provide additional service-related information to American citizens. Do not fail to subscribe to whatever informational services the local embassy or consulate may provide. Often this will be the fastest way to receive updates about the local security situation.

Exhibit 6.2 is a sample checklist that will help you address each of the points we have discussed.

Exhibit 6.2   Travel on Assignment: Personal Awareness Form

Employee name: _____

Street address: _____ City: _____

Phone number: _____

Other members of the household (include names and relationship)

_____

_____

(continues)

Exhibit 6.2   Travel on Assignment: Personal Awareness Form *(Continued)*

The employee lives in: ☐ House   ☐ Building

☐ Building with controlled access

License plate number: _____

Where does employee park his/her car: ☐ In closed garage   ☐ On the street

General Recommendations

- Keep a low profile. Dress and behave conservatively.
- Request that the phone company does not list your phone number.
- Arrange any meetings with unfamiliar people in a familiar/public area.
- Try to vary regular travel routes by changing travel times or using different roads.

House Checklist

- Check the following:
  - *Windows*—Look for solid windows and frame. Slide windows can be opened easily; therefore, make sure there are working locks on the window.
  - *Sliding Doors*—Make sure the locks work properly.
  - *Doors*—Make sure outside doors have an eyepiece large enough to see a significant area in front of the door. All doors to the outside should have dead bolts.
  - *Roof*—Most houses have ducts for the vent, cooling system, and fireplace. Make sure that these exit points are locked.
  - *Lights*—Thieves hate bright lights. Install bright lights around the house and keep them on all night.
  - *Yard*—If you have a fenced-in yard, have a sliding bolt lock on the side gate. Have sensor lights that will go on when motion is detected around the house. Cut tree limbs that could be used to climb to the roof or upper-level windows.
  - *Fire Prevention*—Be sure that there is a fire alarm system and a fire extinguisher. Keep a first aid kit at home.

- *Additional Measures*
  - Consider adding a video camera, intercom and alarm system to strategic places around the house. These devices can significantly increase your security.

○ Create good relations with your neighbors. Good neighbors watch out for each other and may notice suspicious people or events when you are not at home.

○ Consider getting a dog.

○ Be careful when you or a family member opens the door. Never open the door to a stranger and try to avoid receiving deliveries at home.

○ When you leave the house, quickly look through the windows to check the surrounding area for any unusual movement.

○ If you travel, create the illusion that you are at home. Use timers to turn lights on and off in different areas of your house throughout the evening.

Car

- Check the car every time that you do not have direct eye contact with it.
- Park the car in an area that is well lit.
- Keep all doors locked while driving.
- **Don't leave valuables on your seats when you park.**
- Travel using different roads.
- Suggested roads for daily travel routine:

  Option 1: _____

  Option 2: _____

  Option 3: _____

- Choosing a driving road:
  ○ Drive on a main road.
  ○ Travel roads with more than one lane.
  ○ Prefer roads that are close to a police station.
  ○ When driving, use the rearview mirror to detect any cars that may be following you.
  ○ Pay attention to any unusual objects on the road (road blocks, cars stopped on side roads).
- Use public transportation from time to time.

Mail and Delivery

- Try to avoid receiving deliveries at home.
- Consider an item suspicious if it has:
  ○ Powder or any substance leaking from it.
  ○ A threatening message on the envelope or letter.
  ○ An excessive amount of postage.

(continues)

Exhibit 6.2   Travel on Assignment: Personal Awareness Form *(Continued)*

○ A handwritten address.
○ An incomplete or illogical return address.
○ An uncommon return address.
○ A lopsided or unusual feel (e.g., powdery feel).
○ A strange odor.
○ The size and weight are not proportionate.
○ An oil stain on the envelope.
○ The envelope is torn or opened.

Travel

- Stay at reputable hotels and motels. Don't put your life in jeopardy to save a few dollars.
- At the hotel, locate the nearest fire escape before you need it. Check the windows and doors to make sure they are secure.
- Ask for a second story room at a hotel. Ground-floor rooms are more susceptible to break-in.
- Don't open the door to anybody unless you are familiar with him or her. Talk through the door without opening it (those chain guards on the door are not very effective).
- Avoid rest stops except when they are crowded.
- In metropolitan areas look for a hotel in a busy area.
- Avoid mass transportation at night. Don't try to save a few dollars and take the subway at night in unfamiliar territory. Spend the extra money and take a taxi.
- Separate your cash into two portions. Keep some of the money in your wallet and the rest in a belt pouch or separate pocket. If you have a purse, carry it in front of you, over your shoulder and across your chest. Hold onto it with your hands.
- Make a copy of your passport in case the original is lost or stolen. Keep the copy in a safe place.
- When renting a car, make sure that your car has emergency roadside equipment.
- When flying, try to get a nonstop flight.

In Case of Emergency

- Know police station locations and phone numbers.
- Know hospital locations and phone numbers.

- When traveling abroad, know the embassy or local consulate location and phone number. Check in with the embassy or local consulate when you arrive at your destination.
  - *Keep all these numbers near a phone or within reach.*
  - *If you have children, make sure they know the phone numbers.*

CHAPTER 7

Vehicle Safety Measures

ALMOST EVERYONE DRIVES A CAR in the United States. Often the American love of driving remains while living or traveling abroad. It allows us to be more independent and relieves us of the dependence on local forms of mass transit. Unfortunately, it also provides terrorists or common criminals with another avenue of attack. This chapter will teach you how to be less vulnerable during an attack—whether at home or abroad. The rules are simple and easy to follow.

Let's begin with one important premise: You are vulnerable while in your car. Attack can come in many forms: car bombs, road bombs, drive-by shooting, ambush, roadblock, and carjacking, to name but a few. You must appreciate the dangers that driving abroad may present and learn to minimize those risks. Before we go into detail about specific security-related issues, we want to make it clear that the greatest danger to Americans who are driving overseas is traffic accidents. It is estimated that at least 200 Americans die each year in traffic accidents overseas. In fact, traffic accidents abroad kill far more Americans each year than disease, violence, or terrorism. According to the Association for Safe International Road Travel (ASIRT), "the chances of being killed on the roads in countries to which many Americans currently travel is from 20 to 70 times higher than in the United States."[1] All internationally bound Americans should consult ASIRT. It provides excellent analysis of road and travel conditions around the world as well as detailed information about the road conditions, driver behaviors, patterns of traffic, seasonal hazards, night travel, medical care, and traffic safety statistics. A visit to its website (*www.asirt.org/index.htm*) is highly recommended.

VEHICLE PREPARATION AND SELECTION

When driving abroad, the absolute first step to take is to make sure that whatever car you drive is reliable. Most parts of the world do not have AAA (Automobile Association of America) or roadside assistance. Your vehicle must run well and reliably. Maintenance is an absolute necessity and becomes far more important than it is in the United States. You must be sure that oil is changed, belts are changed periodically before they exhibit excessive wear, and that your car undergoes frequent engine inspections. If you are renting a car, select one with low mileage and from a reputable company. Rent a make and model common to the country. Avoid choosing a vehicle that would clearly mark you as being affluent or a tourist, but do select one with the best crash rating available. Since, as we've said, more Americans abroad are killed in traffic accidents than are the victims of terrorism or street crime, you need to make sure they are equipped with seat belts and air bags as well.

Is there anything about the rental car that will identify it as such to an interested observer? In the past it was common in the United States to issue license plates that clearly identified the cars as being rentals. (The situation is less common today.) Are there markings of that sort on the vehicle you are renting? Recall our earlier discussion about the way predatory criminals in the United States looked for the license plates that indicated that the vehicle was a rental. This is equally true, and perhaps even more so, abroad. As we have repeatedly noted, to a criminal in a developing country, an American tourist or resident is far more likely to have something worth taking than a local citizen. In many countries, most locals cannot afford to rent a car; affluent tourists and foreigners are the predominant car renters.

In certain parts of the world, cars that are available for rental lack many desirable options. From a security standpoint, it is a good idea to have power locks and windows, because they afford greater control over access to the car. Not all cars have this feature; try to rent one that does. Drive with the doors locked and, whenever possible, with the windows closed. Make sure the climate control system works. If you are in a country in Southeast Asia with no air conditioning, you will be miserable. You will also be placed at greater risk if you need to drive with your windows down because the air conditioning doesn't work or is nonexistent.

SECURE YOUR VALUABLES

It is always sound advice to secure your valuables and not leave anything worth stealing in plain view even when you are in the car and driving. Many people have enough sense not to leave their wallet, camera, or other items that will attract the attention of a would-be thief in a parked car. You must get in the habit of securing your valuables even when you are driving. Often criminals post themselves at heavily trafficked intersections and observe the interior compartments of vehicles as they pass. Once they see an item of interest, it is a simple matter for them to smash the window, grab the object, and disappear into the crowd before you even have time to react. Thieves on motorcycles or motor scooters routinely drive in between lanes of traffic. How difficult would it be for someone on a moped to reach into your open window, grab your purse or wallet on the seat next to you, and escape? Professional thieves make their living doing this every day. Furthermore, by having some item of value visible in the car, you also may attract the attention of a nonprofessional who may seize on the opportunity that you have presented. You can easily prevent these crimes of opportunity. Remember, in many parts of the world, the monthly salary of a factory worker putting in a fifty-hour work week equals what you may pay to have dinner with your spouse at a fancy hotel restaurant. Your brand-new digital camera on the front seat is equal to several months' wages. Don't tempt locals with unnecessary displays of affluence.

RECOGNIZE A SETUP

In case this point isn't already obvious, you should never pick up hitchhikers or stop for any reason in an area that is not populated and well policed. Often female hitchhikers induce cars to stop. Then the drivers are victimized by the hitchhiker's companions who were hidden nearby. Do not offer to give a ride to anyone whom you do not know well. Criminals have unlimited numbers of ways to deceive motorists into stopping and provide them a chance to strike. These techniques are common wherever there are criminals; that means *everywhere*. A technique that is often tried at night in the United states is called the "stop sign bump." Criminals select a motorist. Perhaps the car is a valuable model; if a sexual crime is being attempted, the driver is a female driving alone. When the targeted vehicle approaches a stop sign and comes to a halt, the criminal's car gently moves up close behind and lightly "bumps" the target vehicle. In almost every case, the driver of the "accidentally" struck vehicle stops and gets out to check the damage, exchange license and insurance information, or yell at the inattention of the driver who just hit him or her. That is exactly what the bad guy is counting on, and that is when he will strike. If this happens to you, do not stop on the road. Drive to the nearest area of safety, such as a police station or hospital, and stop there.

Often the bad guys pose as good Samaritans themselves. A few years ago in Long Island, New York, a series of sexual assaults were perpetrated by a man who prowled the highway looking for females driving alone late at night. The assailant would pull alongside the victim's car and start shouting that there was something wrong with her tire. The man was clean cut and well dressed and seemed so sincere and concerned. The driver would pull off the road to check what was wrong, with the "good Samaritan" pulling in behind and offering to provide assistance. That is when the women were raped. Do not stop anywhere you would be vulnerable to attack. Drive to a safe place and then check your tire. Sometimes criminals pose as injured victims themselves. Concerned drivers who stop to offer assistance are assaulted.

Contact the local embassy or consulate for information to prepare yourself against local crimes involving vehicles or otherwise. A particular country may have recently experienced a rash of carjackings that follow a particular pattern. Being forewarned is truly being forearmed. Learn how the criminals operate and you can protect yourself through vigilance and proper avoidance measures. Another thing for you to always bear in mind: Criminals frequently work in groups. Just like a pickpocket who uses an accomplice to "accidentally" bump the victim while the pocket is being picked, thieves, robbers, carjackers, and the like also use others to distract or deceive the victim.

VEHICLE SAFETY CHECK

We mentioned before how important it is to be aware of your surroundings and to change your routine frequently. These are things we can control.

Unfortunately, there are other things we can't control. We can't watch our car all the time or always park it in a secure parking area. Criminals and terrorists who might want to attack us know that well and may try to use your unattended car as a tool to fulfill their goal. Although we can't watch the car all the time, the minimum we can do is to check it before we get in. The following discussion deals with the necessity and method of checking your vehicle.

It is good practice to always give your vehicle a quick safety check anytime you are going somewhere. Do this prior to your trip, in a safe area. Check the tires for wear, low pressure, or flats. Check the spare tire as well. Also examine fluid levels as well as the condition of the engine belts. In many areas of the world, the danger of becoming a bombing victim is all too real. Therefore, it is necessary to physically examine the vehicle for an explosive device. This may seem to be an inconvenience, but to quote one of Tom Clancy's characters in *The Hunt for Red October,* "There is no extravagance in the pursuit of safety." When should such an "extravagant" inspection be made?

PARKING

Where will you park your car? Do you have a garage or secure lot at your residence? Is parking at work secure or accessible to the general public? If at all possible, avoid parking on the street and use established and trustworthy parking garages. Obviously, if you must park on the street or in an unsecured lot, you are going to be exposed to greater risk. If you are tired of your brand-new laptop, just leave it in your car. You will be shopping for a replacement in short order. In addition, although ordinary crime statistically presents greater danger to you than acts of terrorism, using secure parking facilities will enhance your security in that regard as well. Although car bombs can be attached to a vehicle quickly and unobtrusively, generally would-be bombers require a bit of privacy to affix them. Perhaps your attacker wants to disable your vehicle by tampering with your engine or electrical system or by slashing your tires. These types of activities are far easier to accomplish on a dark lonely street or quiet public garage than inside a secure private lot. Where you leave your car definitely impacts the level of scrutiny that you must give to it. As we have noted, the general rule is that you must check your car every time you do not have direct eye contact with it. If you are, for example, working at the U.S. embassy and park in a secure lot guarded by vetted security personnel, you probably can skip the intensive inspection. If, however, you are parking anywhere where potential assailants can approach the vehicle unhindered, you need to give it at least a cursory examination. Before you discount the importance of this practice, remember why terrorists often select car bomb attacks. Because the car is usually used by the same person, generally on a regular schedule, the car is a perfect choice for a successful method of attack. People who want to hurt you know that at some point they will be able to find you in the driver's seat at a specific time and in a specific location. This can be a deadly combination. Just because you may not be a particularly high-profile target, don't assume that you will not be attractive to a terror group operating in the local country. The purpose of terror is to terrorize. A stated goal of many terrorist organizations is the murder of Americans anywhere in the world.

CAR BOMBS

Car bomb attacks occur all over the world. Even the United States has its share of car bombings every year. While David was an agent on Long Island, a Suffolk County Narcotics detective named Dennis Wustenheuff was killed by a car bomb in the driveway of his home. The U.S. Department of State, Office of the Coordinator for Counterterrorism, documented a pattern of car bomb attacks in South Africa for the year 2000. During that year there were nine car bomb attacks in the city of Cape Town. These bombings targeted not only South African government officials but also restaurants and nightclubs with Western affiliations. Government officials noted that the trend was characterized by larger bombs and more sophisticated remote detonation devices. South African authorities blamed the attacks on the People Against Gangsterism and Drugs (PAGAD), a militant Muslim organization.

Ilan has trained Israeli diplomatic personnel over a number of years in the proper techniques used to check a vehicle. Often when he starts to discuss the issue, students commonly say, "This is a waste of time. I am not a mechanic, and if someone put a bomb in my car's engine I will never find it." Ilan privately agreed with that argument and decided to research actual car bombings to evaluate the effectiveness of the program he was teaching. He spent several years analyzing many attacks that involved placing a car bomb on a vehicle. To his surprise, he found that in almost all of the incidents, loss of life could have been prevented easily. In almost all of the incidents he reviewed, the attacker placed the bomb somewhere it would have been very easy to find if the driver had been trained where to look and had made a car inspection a routine precaution. Why is this so? Can't expert bombers hide an explosive in a place that can't be readily observed?

To address this point, we need to remember a few facts. First, criminals and/or terrorists have a limited amount of time in which to operate and to install a bomb. Terrorists generally gain access to the car while it is parked in a public place. They need to work quickly because a passerby might observe them while they are attempting to place the device. Even terrorists get nervous and worry about the risk of detection and arrest. Consequently, assailants try to limit the amount of time they are exposed to reduce their risk of getting caught. Second, criminals and terrorists both assume that people are not checking their cars anyway. Therefore, why risk detection by doing something that is complicated and time consuming like opening the car's hood and planting the bomb inside the engine compartment? That would only increase their risk of exposure without greatly enhancing the success of the mission. One of the easiest ways to bomb a vehicle is to place the explosive in a crumpled-up brown paper bag and to put it under the car. The bag looks like just another piece of trash, perhaps the remnants of someone's lunch. Bombers wait for the victim to return to his or her vehicle and then remotely detonate the explosive. Often they use a cell phone for this purpose. Cell phones operate on batteries. Devices that use batteries cause electrical current to flow. It is easy to redirect this current to an electronic detonator. All bombers have to do is call the number of the phone attached to the bomb, and it will detonate.

How do you check your vehicle? You do not need any special skills to prevent an attack. All you need to do is to learn which areas of your vehicle are likely spots for a bomb to be placed, then devote a few minutes to examining these vulnerable points each time your car has been out of your direct eye contact. Once you learn where to look, it will be very easy to find anything that is unusual

The four points on your vehicle that are most vulnerable to a bomb placement are: behind the tire, on top of the tire, under the car, and in the trunk or engine compartment.

Bomb behind the Tire

A common technique used by terrorists attempting a car bomb assassination of a particular individual is to hide the explosive device behind the tire as you are facing it (see Exhibit 7.1).

In Exhibit 7.1, a bomb is simply placed behind the wheel closest to the driver's seat. We have wrapped the "bomb" in white to allow you to clearly see what we are describing. Don't expect a real bomb to be so noticeable! The triggering device may be a simple wire that your car pulls as you drive away. Or a simple pressure switch can be attached to the explosive and stuffed under the tire. The weight of the tire keeps the switch depressed. When the

Exhibit 7.1   Bomb behind Tire (left) and Bomb behind Tire Close-Up (right)

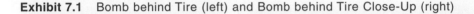

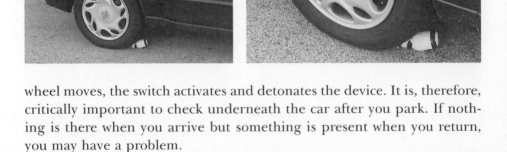

wheel moves, the switch activates and detonates the device. It is, therefore, critically important to check underneath the car after you park. If nothing is there when you arrive but something is present when you return, you may have a problem.

Bomb on Top of Tire

In Exhibit 7.2, the bomb has been placed on top of the driver's side wheel. Before you think that a bomb like this is easy to spot, consider the situation of a dark-colored device placed on top of the tire in the evening. Even this somewhat amateurish attempt will succeed most of the time. People returning to their cars at night after having dinner out usually do not spend much time checking their cars. The areas on top of or behind the front tires or wheels and underneath the car are not immediately visible unless someone squats down. While attackers can install a bomb behind any of the tires, statistics show that in most instances, terrorists generally place the device behind the front tire closest to the driver's seat. This is not surprising because the closer the bomb is to an intended victim, the less explosive is required and, hence, the smaller the bomb can be. This is important for several reasons. First, a smaller device is less likely to be observed. Second, often terrorists can acquire only a small amount of explosive material. If a group is contemplating multiple bombings, it will need to be somewhat parsimonious with its supply of C4 or whatever explosive material they are using.

Exhibit 7.2   Bomb on Top of Tire

This method of placement is also quite desirable because it can be done quickly, without the attacker being exposed for very long. This technique is so quick to accomplish that it can be used on a vehicle parked on a public road or openly accessible parking area. The method of detonation is generally a simple triggering device. As soon as the vehicle moves, the trigger (or the pin on a hand grenade) is pulled and the device is detonated. Although this method is very common because of the relative ease with which the bomb can be rigged, it is also very easy to detect the device. All we need to do is to take a quick look behind the tires, paying extra attention to the area behind the tire that is closest to the driver's seat. Remember, this positioning will change between left- and right-hand drive cars.

Bomb under the Car

The technique of simply placing a large explosive device under a car is probably the method chosen most frequently by terrorists in a bombing attempt on a vehicle. Attackers who possess sufficient quantities of explosive materials have used this method quite frequently. The reason for this is very simple. With enough explosive material, the attackers can assemble a bomb that is large enough to destroy the car completely and thus ensure the target's death. Also, it is very easy for the attackers to install this type of bomb, because it doesn't need to be attached physically to any part of the car. Attackers can prepare the bomb at home and then merely place it directly under the car (see Exhibit 7.3). The attackers are exposed for only a very short time, and therefore their risk of detection and capture is very low. Usually, this type of device is detonated with either a remote control or a timing device. It is, therefore, critically important to check underneath the car after you park, and again when you leave, to be sure that nothing has changed.

In Exhibit 7.3, the bomb has been put inside a light-colored box, which was placed under the car. The bomb could easily be mistaken for a pizza box that had fallen to the ground. If you were parked near a pizza shop, you might ignore it. Terrorists are counting on you to accept the most plausible explanation there is. Don't forget, though, that dark boxes placed at night might be invisible unless you make a thorough search every time.

Exhibit 7.3   Explosive in Box beneath Car

As mentioned before, it's very easy for attackers to plant the bomb in this manner, but it is also easy for alert drivers to prevent this kind of attack. Just as the attacker can place a bomb under the car, the target can look under the car and see the bomb very clearly. One note of caution, however: Remember the paper bag trick. During your inspection, if you see a crumpled-up bag that is larger than a balled-up piece of sandwich wrap, suspect it. Remember to check the area under the car after you park. As mentioned above, be suspicious if you notice something when you return.

Bomb inside the Trunk or Engine Compartment

Placing a bomb inside the trunk or engine compartment is less popular with terrorist attackers because it requires that the car be broken into prior to the placement of the explosive. However, if it can be accomplished without detection, it is an excellent way for a bomb to be placed (see Exhibit 7.4). If attackers can gain access to the trunk, they can pack a large quantity of explosive material inside. The unsuspecting driver may drive it into a targeted facility. Since this type of bomb takes more time to install than the ones already discussed, the attackers will need to operate in a closed or secluded place where nobody can see them. It may also be accomplished in a parking garage where you leave your keys with the attendant.

Exhibit 7.4   Bomb inside Trunk

While the risk for the attackers is higher and requires them to be more sophisticated in their techniques, this method has been used when the objective has been to deliver a bomb into a secure facility. It is easier to have a bomb driven into a secure location inside a car familiar to the security force than inside one that is not. For example, an employee driving to work each day in the same car will likely pass through security without inspection. In most government facilities, even secure locations, security generally either wave through familiar vehicles driven by recognized individuals or perform a perfunctory check of a picture ID. Neither of us has ever had our vehicle inspected by security anywhere. Once we have shown our ID, we have always been waved right through the guard gate. The same is true for thousands upon thousands of federal agents, intelligence analysts, military officers, and others with unfettered access to sensitive facilities. As a rule, agents and military personnel are not given instruction in the methods of securing their private or issued vehicles. It would not be especially difficult to place explosives in an agent's car and have the agent unwittingly deliver it inside a sensitive facility.

However, since the object is to bomb a facility, the attackers use a large amount of explosive material. Therefore, it is easy to find when you open the trunk of the car. Furthermore, even without checking the trunk, aware and alert drivers can simply feel the extra weight in their trunk by the change in the handling characteristics of the vehicle.

It is somewhat more difficult to find a bomb that has been placed in the engine compartment, but a little training can solve that problem.

Whenever we check inside the trunk or under the hood, we need to be aware to the possibility that the attacker has attached the bomb to the hood or the trunk and rigged it to explode when the hood or trunk lid is raised beyond a certain point. In either case, we should open it very slowly and not all the way at once, as Exhibit 7.5 shows.

As shown in Exhibit 7.5, generally a long length of wire, with a fair amount of slack, is attached to the trunk lid or hood. The simplest method of detonating the device is to use the opening of the trunk or hood to pull the wire taut, thus triggering the bomb or pulling the pin on a hand grenade. The slack is present because the bomber must be able to affix the bomb to the vehicle and attach the wire to the lid without setting it off. The bomber tapes the bomb in place and partially closes the lid or hood. Then the bomber ties the detonation wire to the lid or hood. You can understand the need for slack in the wire if you try to imagine installing this bomb and not pulling the detonation wire during the installation process. Because there is slack in the wire, by carefully opening the lid or hood by inches and looking underneath, you should be able to see any trip wire before you cause the bomb to explode. The attackers can also easily disable the engine to ensure that the hood gets opened by the target as he or she tries to diagnose the engine trouble. Just as electronic trunk release buttons on a keychain will allow a trunk to be safely opened and inspected, there are also electronic remote opening features for hoods as well. Some security-conscious individuals also place double-locking devices on the hood and trunk as an added precaution, or indicators in strategic areas of the car to detect whether anyone has been in the trunk or under the hood. Every James Bond fan will remember 007's trick of moistening a long hair and sticking it between two folding closet doors. If the hair is disturbed, it is clear that someone has

Exhibit 7.5   Bomb inside Engine Compartment

been in the closet. You can use a small piece of strategically placed tape or thread to detect an unauthorized entry into your vehicle. It is also a good idea to have a small flashlight on your key chain. Do not rely on a flashlight that you keep in your vehicle for use during an inspection of your vehicle. You should begin your inspection before you are even near the vehicle, as it is easier to see under the car while you are some distance away. If you notice something and it is dark, you need to have a light with you. There are many good, small lights available on the market (see Exhibit 7.6).

Exhibit 7.6   Small Flashlight on Key Chain

ROADSIDE EMERGENCY EQUIPMENT

It is also a good idea to keep a basic roadside emergency kit in your vehicle. The basic equipment is the same as you should maintain in your personal or work vehicle at home. Make sure you have an inflated, *full-size* spare tire. The emergency "donuts" that usually come with a vehicle are not suitable. You may need to drive a long way over poorly maintained roads before you can get to a service area where your tire can be repaired or replaced. The "donuts" are not recommended for more than 25 miles and limit the speed at which you can travel. Make sure there is a functional jack and lug wrench. If your car has locking lugs on the tires, make sure the key is in your car.

You will also need a basic tool kit that includes an adjustable wrench, slotted and Phillips head screwdrivers, pliers, duct tape or PVC tape, booster cables, water-resistant flashlight, extra batteries stored in a waterproof plastic container, a siphon pump, one can of tire inflator, and six road flares. An excellent piece of equipment that you should also consider is a rechargeable jump starter. This is a battery with which you can jump-start your vehicle in the event your battery fails and no one is around to give you a boost. Many of these units have a built-in compressor that allow you to inflate a tire under emergency roadside conditions. You must also expand this basic kit to include items specifically required by the environment in which you will be traveling. For example, in very hot climates, you will need to bring extra coolant for your radiator as well as an ample supply of drinking water. In cold weather, stow aboard an ice scraper, a small folding shovel, emergency candles, waterproof matches, and gloves. A small first aid kit consisting of Band-Aid strips, gauze pads, and adhesive tape is also a good idea.

If you are traveling cross-country, a compass is an indispensable item. Nowadays a global positioning system (GPS) system is even better and can allow you to pinpoint your location to within several feet on a map. Depending on the country that you are in, the GPS may be able to provide you with the same type of detailed driving instructions that you can get in the United States. If not, the system still can tell you your location and direction and show it on a map. Prices for serviceable GPS systems have fallen a great deal, and units are now available at very reasonable prices. One of our own company's services is the installation of satellite tracking in a vehicle as well. This device allows for your own corporate security staff to locate your vehicle at any time. This device also allows for instant, two-way messaging to summon help if an emergency arises in undeveloped areas. Information on this service is available on our website at *www.globalsecuritygroup.com.*

NOTE

1. Association for SAFE International Road Travel (ASIRT) *www.asirt.org/Index.htm.*

CHAPTER 8

Principles of Route Selection

ATTACKS ON INDIVIDUALS WHO ARE DRIVING their vehicles are common with both terrorists and common criminals. An individual traveling by car can be quite vulnerable. If the bad guys have spent any time at all watching you, they will know exactly when and where you will be most vulnerable and act against you at that moment. We have discussed the basic principles of route selection in Chapter 7, in the context of vehicle safety. We've decided, however, to devote a separate chapter to teaching Americans living abroad how to drive in a manner calculated to enhance their safety. This subject is taught in virtually every intelligence academy throughout the world. The goal is to reduce the number of agents and operatives assaulted, kidnapped, or assassinated. One of the most important ways you can increase your level of security is to carefully select the roads you drive on, whenever possible. Knowledge of the principles of route selection will enable you to do this and are generally broken down into a short summary known as "the 10 rules."

1. Be alert in and around your car.
2. Avoid "choke points."
3. Avoid one-lane roads.
4. Watch the car in front.
5. Watch the car to the rear.
6. Avoid predictable patterns of travel.
7. Beware the "box."

8. Avoid heavily trafficked roads.

9. Use roads with "safe havens."

10. Use well-lit roads.

Most, if not all, disciplines and fields of studies have their own unique rules. Many of them merely state the obvious in order to make an instructional point. Take, for example, firearms training. There are many rules that are common to the discipline of firing a weapon in anger. However, the initial rule that is somewhat wryly stated is "The first rule in a gunfight is to have a gun." The parallel of this rule as applied to driving security is "Pick your road." You must understand that security is a daily concern and that part of your new "security mind-set" will be to consciously select roads to drive on that place a would-be attacker at a disadvantage. It is no different from a general selecting the most advantageous terrain for a battle.

In August 2002, CNN obtained a copy of a tape showing the type of training that Al Qaeda terrorists undergo. A review of those tapes can provide many valuable security lessons. One example that is directly on point for this discussion is the section showing how Al Qaeda terrorists assault a moving vehicle in order to kidnap the occupant. The clip shows several terrorist vehicles following the target. The vehicles box the victim's vehicle in, and the assault is initiated. In seconds the victim has been pulled from the vehicle and is thrown into one of the terrorists' cars. Had the objective been merely to kill, the attack would not have even taken that long.

The tape reveals a great deal about the terrorists' level of training as well as the types of operations they are training for. The first thing that is readily apparent is that the team on this tape is organized and has thoroughly drilled the techniques they are practicing. They execute their assignments with military precision. They have an assault team as well as perimeter security. The operation is well coordinated, and the teams communicate with hand-held radios. They also use different vehicles for different purposes. They use pickup trucks to secrete the assault team and motorcycles for the perimeter security team. They handle their prisoners quickly and efficiently. Once the assault is completed, they signal the command to withdraw by using the car horn. As they withdraw, they also detonate an explosive device with maximum effect after their teams have left the area. However, perhaps the most frightening element in the video is the fact that the assault team is giving commands in English. Even more to the point, the "victim" role players are pleading with their captors in English. Whom do you think they are preparing for?

PROTECTING AGAINST CAR ATTACKS

How can anyone protect themselves from this type of attack? Certainly there are ways. One way is an effectively armored vehicle and security personnel in lead and chase cars. However, since most of us do not have the luxury of that level of security, we must act so that we never get to the point where we will be the target for that type of assault. To do this you need to follow the recommendations of this chapter religiously. While doing so is no guarantee that you will not be attacked, it certainly will lower your chances of being the victim of this type of assault. It is vitally important never to deviate from these procedures for any reason.

Be Alert

The first rule to keep in mind is to be alert for anything unusual even before you enter your vehicle. Think about it. You are about to drive someplace in a foreign country. You really don't know the rules and generally can't yet spot things that are out of the ordinary. You might have already been targeted for a robbery, carjacking, kidnapping, assault, or assassination. So you pay extra careful attention to your vehicle and to the vehicles and individuals in close proximity to your car. Remember that you are particularly vulnerable while you're getting into your car. The next time you are in a busy parking lot, take a few minutes to observe people as they walk to their cars. Few people bother to look around and see if anything looks unusual, suspicious, or out of place. Watch as they insert their key into the door lock. No one looks around before they do it. While they are placing the key into the lock, where is their focus? Of course it is on the door lock, where they are trying to insert the key—a proposition that is even more difficult if they are burdened with packages that they have not set down. One veteran Drug Enforcement Agency (DEA) agent used to choose that exact moment to take pictures of the bad guys. He would walk up close to the subject's vehicle and snap the picture the instant the key went in. He always got great close-up shots and was never caught. People were just not paying attention and were easily distracted.

Choke Points or Bottlenecks

The second rule is to avoid choke points or bottlenecks. Let's begin by discussing this concept as it is critical while planning safe routes of travel. The concept of any choke point or bottleneck is central to avoiding an ambush or other assault. A choke point is any point through which you must pass to get to a location known to your potential attackers. For example, say the travel time between your home and office is approximately 40 minutes. Your home is located in a secure neighborhood, and there are several roads that you can take to get to work. However, along the route there is a bridge that you must cross regardless of the route you choose. Or it may be that no matter which side street you take from your residence, they all funnel into one street or avenue that you must take for you to reach your destination. That is a bottleneck or choke point (see Exhibit 8.1).

Exhibit 8.1   Choke Point Diagram

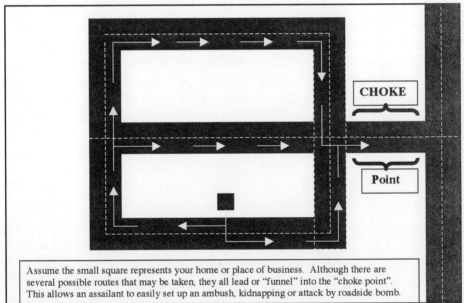

Assume the small square represents your home or place of business. Although there are several possible routes that may be taken, they all lead or "funnel" into the "choke point". This allows an assailant to easily set up an ambush, kidnapping or attack by roadside bomb.

Why is the choke point or bottleneck significant? The obvious reason is that it allows potential assailants the ability to stage an ambush and/or roadblock with relative ease. Whether their goal is kidnapping or assassination, they will know where to find you on any given day. If you are not being driven in a security motorcade with advance and chase vehicles, you will be completely vulnerable to attack. You must, therefore, avoid choke points, at least those that you must cross on a regular basis. This means that you must consider your travel options when you are selecting a place to live.

Avoid One-Lane Roads

The third rule has a similar reason behind it. Your preference should always be to drive on a road with a few lanes rather than one. The reason is simple: Narrow roads or single-lane roads are easy to block and afford a potential attacker an easy place to set up an ambush. Roads with multiple lanes allow a potential target to escape; criminals and terrorists tend to avoid planning an ambush on such roads. However, roads with several lanes allow for other types of attack, which we discuss below.

Watch the Car in Front of You

The fourth rule is always to pay attention to the vehicle directly in front of you, especially if you are on a one-lane road or come to stop sign or traffic light. The reason is clear. On a single-lane road, it is possible to create an effective roadblock by merely having a car stopped in front of you. The same is true if you're following closely behind a vehicle as it comes to a place where you will normally expect a vehicle to stop, such as at a red light or stop sign. In the United States and abroad, many tactical enforcement teams use this technique during the arrests of potentially dangerous criminals who are driving a car. This is the scenario: There is one car directly in front of you and one behind you. The car in front comes to stop sign and slows to stop. This is what you would expect any car to do, so no alarm bells start to go off. The car behind you slowly pulls up close to the rear of your vehicle. Again, it is doing what you'd expect any ordinary car and driver to do. If the attackers are experienced, they probably will put the lead car in reverse and begin to back slowly into your vehicle. It is unlikely that your first reaction will be to think that you are being attacked. Your natural reaction is to wonder what the driver in the car in front of you is doing. Perhaps you even have time to blow your horn. While your attention is fixed on the vehicle backing into you, several armed individuals quickly exit the car that has moved up within inches of your rear bumper, effectively pinning you between them (see Exhibit 8.2). Suddenly, you have armed agents on you. Terrorists have learned this technique and they practice it.

Exhibit 8.2   Two-Car Blocking Method: Stop Sign or Light

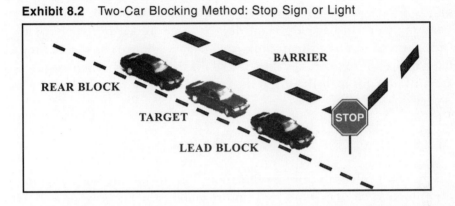

Before you can react, armed attackers are outside your window screaming and pointing their weapons at you. You also can expect the windows of your vehicle to be smashed and for you to be pulled from the car at gunpoint. In a situation like this, we can't teach you any correct tactical response to allow you to escape unscathed. Even if you were armed, which is unlikely on foreign soil, and are very well trained, there is little that you can do in this type of situation. The only technique that we have seen taught in counterterrorist schools that might help is to attempt to defeat the ambush by ramming the blocking vehicle. However, in order to perform this technique successfully, you need room to generate speed and maneuver. Always keep enough distance between your car and the car in front of you to take these actions if necessary. Ramming escape techniques are taught at some professional driving schools, and you might want to consider taking one of their courses.

Watch the Car behind You

The fifth rule is basically just a reminder to use your mirrors while you are driving. If you are being targeted, you will be followed. Unless you have been targeted by an extremely well trained surveillance team, you'll be followed by individuals driving a car directly behind you. Check your mirrors frequently and pay attention to who is behind you. Chapter 10 discusses this issue in greater detail.

Avoid Predictable Travel

The sixth rule is to vary your route between home and work. We discuss this further in the next chapter, but the idea is to make it harder for someone to follow you. Remember: If you are being followed, those who are watching you will have a certain degree of paranoia. If you try to act in such a way as to make them think you are surveillance conscious, they will likely move on to an easier target. Even if they do not switch targets, you are still making it difficult for them to follow you and easier for you to detect their presence.

Beware the Box

The seventh rule is to beware of the box. This technique is a common tool for enforcement personnel and, unfortunately, the bad guys as well. On a two-lane road, assailants in several vehicles will attempt to box you in by placing a vehicle in front of you, behind you, and to your side and forcing you to stop (see Exhibit 8.3).

In this exhibit, three blocking vehicles surround the target's car. Since the barrier prevents escape in that direction, all that attackers need to do is to block the front, the rear, and the open side. This is a coordinated maneuver that requires all three blocking vehicles to slow down at the same time and force the target to stop. If the technique is poorly executed, the target may be able simply to drive out of the box and escape. If, however, the cars slow in a coordinated manner, escaping may prove difficult.

Exhibit 8.3   Three-Car Blocking Method: Alongside Barrier

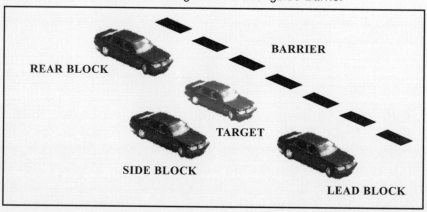

Difficult, but not impossible. In addition to the ramming techniques described below, several methods taught in antiterror driving schools teach student drivers how to defeat this trap. Again, the countermeasures must be learned from professionals in a well-respected school. The techniques also must be practiced on a fairly regular basis.

Another version of the same attack may be carried out by four blocking vehicles on wide, multilane roads with no hard barrier separating the two directions of travel (see Exhibit 8.4). As you can imagine, this attack is even more difficult to execute well. If you have ever seen some of Fox Television's *Scariest Police Chases,* you will know that even trained professional police officers sometimes have a hard time coordinating a stop in this manner.

All of these techniques require some coordination and prior practice on the part of the bad guys. And, as the Al Qaeda training tape obtained by

Exhibit 8.4   Four-Car Blocking

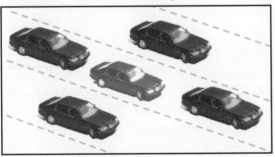

CNN show, the bad guys do practice. If you haven't accepted that reality by now, we recommend that you watch the tape, which shows armed Al Qaeda members practicing the exact scenario we have just described. Even so, if you are alert you can see this coming and drive out

of it. As we have said, even if you do get boxed in, if you are driving a car with some mass and horsepower, you can still defeat this maneuver by using techniques that are taught in professional driving schools. Realize that you will probably be shot at during your escape. We would rather risk being shot while trying to escape than to be taken by captors.

Avoid Heavily Congested Roads

The eighth rule is, whenever possible, to try to avoid roads where it is likely that you will be stuck in traffic. This is easier said than done, as traffic is a reality all over the world. If the road conditions in your country of residence are such that you will encounter heavy traffic in the same place and time on a daily basis, you must pay particular attention to vary your routes of travel. Stop-and-go traffic makes it very easy for you to be assaulted or kidnapped. Remember, the motorcycle is the traditional vehicle used in assassinations. A motorcycle allows the assailant to approach the target quickly, even in heavy traffic. Escape is also a simple matter on a motorcycle, even during the local rush hour.

More Rules

The ninth rule merely states that it is better to drive on a road with a police station on the way than one without a police station. The simple reason is that if you do need police assistance, they are nearby. This is also true of other safe havens, such as hospitals and the embassies of friendly countries.

And finally, the tenth rule tells you to travel on well-lit roads whenever possible. Light is always a deterrent to crime; it allows you to see the road ahead of you and makes it safer for you to drive.

EMERGENCY VEHICLE OPERATION

A final point for anyone considered to be a high-risk target or someone living in a dangerous region: Don't merely consider taking an emergency vehicle operations course (EVOC); take one immediately followed by a course in antiterrorist driving techniques. The average citizen can learn many things in three to four days of training. An EVOC program will teach you the basics of high-speed driving. You will learn to take corners and turns safely and at high speeds. Emergency braking techniques, lane changes, and high-speed backing are taught and form the basis for the antiterrorist driving course to follow. This course teaches students to defeat the types of vehicular attacks commonly used by terrorists and criminals. Typically you will be taught how to defeat a roadblock, how to escape an ambush, the pursuit intervention technique (PIT) maneuver, and how to reverse direction from either a standstill or at high speed. Even apart from the obvious advantage of learning how to defeat an attack against you while you are in your vehicle, such a course will improve your overall level of safety during normal driving as well. Remember, common traffic accidents are the single greatest cause of death for travelers under the age of 35 as well as for travelers in good health of any age. You have a far greater chance of being killed in a car accident than you have of becoming the victim of terrorism or criminal violence. It is a skill you should seriously consider acquiring. If you have a driver, bodyguard, or security detail, have them undergo training. If you are relying heavily on locally hired drivers, their training is critical. This point is made more clearly in the following analysis.

ANALYSIS OF A CAR ATTACK IN PAKISTAN

Here we analyze a tragic attack that resulted in the murder of five people, four of whom were Americans. Such incidents should be reviewed to prevent the loss of any more innocent lives, especially when the deaths could easily have been prevented. The incident occurred in Karachi, Pakistan, on November 12, 1997. Although we feel uncomfortable Monday morning quarterbacking this incident while the families of the victims are no doubt still keenly feeling their terrible loss, we believe that not doing so and ignoring the practical value of the lessons that can be learned is to render the victims' deaths meaningless. If another family might be spared the loss of their father, mother, or child, then the lessons learned from this tragedy may have some positive meaning.

While we discuss this situation, bear in mind the rules that we have just described. While we do not have all the facts relative to this attack, it is clear that the failure to follow basic vehicle security rules 1, 5, and 6 (and quite possibly more) contributed to the murders. On November 12, 1997, at approximately 8:00 A.M., four employees of the Union Texas Petroleum (UTP) Company were picked up at their hotels by a Pakistani driver employed by their company. The local driver was operating a blue four-door Nissan station wagon. Three of the men were staying at the Hotel Pearl Continental; the fourth was lodging at the Sheraton. As the vehicle left the hotel area, it was followed by a red Honda Civic with two or three men inside. Apparently, the Civic had fallen behind the Nissan in traffic and the driver had to weave in and out of traffic aggressively in order to catch up. Surprisingly, the driver of the Nissan either did not notice or was not alarmed by the presence of a red vehicle pursuing them. Law enforcement and undercover agencies generally do not choose red vehicles as surveillance vehicles because they are very easy to pick out and remember. In this case, the red color of the vehicle made no difference. The driver of the Nissan failed to be mindful of traffic behind them, violating rule 5, even though the vehicle was brightly colored and was being driven erratically. At approximately 8:10 A.M., the red Civic caught up to the Nissan, cut it off, and forced it to stop One or two assailants, armed with AK-47 assault rifles, exited the Civic and first killed the driver by firing through the windshield. The driver's murder ensured that the vehicle would not be able to escape. The terrorists then moved to the sides of the Nissan and executed the four Americans by firing through the windows. A third assailant may have been firing from inside the Civic.

There can be no doubt that the four employees of UTP had been under surveillance before the attack. While the reported account of this incident says nothing about such surveillance, it is inconceivable that such an attack could have been planned and executed without the gathering of prior intelligence through physical surveillance. Apparently neither the driver of the Nissan nor the four UTP employees detected the presence of that surveillance. Chapter 10 discusses how to determine whether you are under surveillance as well as countersurveillance measures at length.

Another security lapse was the failure of the driver and his passengers to vary their patterns of travel by altering the route they took and their times of travel. No effort was made to avoid predictability, in violation of rule 6. In addition to the violation of several vehicle-related security rules, other mistakes were made. The first and most easily correctable mistake would have been to use a properly armored vehicle while transporting employees in a high-risk area like Karachi. Information relative to the selection and use of such armored vehicles is provided in Chapter 9. It is sufficient for this discussion, however, to note that a properly armored vehicle could have provided sufficient protection against the 7.62×39 mm rifle rounds fired by the terrorists. In addition, a properly trained driver would have measurably increased the chances that this attack could have been prevented. Numerous EVOC and antiterrorist driving courses teach a variety of specific techniques to use while operating an armored vehicle; such courses are designed to defeat this type of assault. Proper observational skills are taught during the antiterror phase of such training, which is invaluable. In addition, the courses also teach how to defeat a vehicular roadblock. Defeating a roadblock is not a difficult thing to learn during hands-on instruction. All you need is a vehicle of sufficient weight and enough room to generate some speed. In the case being examined, we have a four-door station wagon being blocked by a Honda Civic.

If you are alert and the blocking vehicles are not well positioned, you may be able to escape the ambush. Keep in mind that you can learn how to perform this type of maneuver in any professional antiterrorist driving school. As with any skill, learned techniques must be practiced on a regular basis for them to work. Another good habit to begin right now is to never roll up too close to the vehicle directly in front of you. Make sure when you stop you can see the rear tires of the car ahead of you. Make this a constant practice, and you will always maintain enough room between you and the car in front of you to allow you to react in case of attack.

Our recommendation is to try to attend schools that have instructors with prior experience as law enforcement or intelligence officers for the Secret Service, DSS, or CIA. There are also several emergency driving schools whose non-agent instructors have taught for well-respected academies such as the Federal Law Enforcement Training Center (FLETC) or the Secret Service Academy in Beltsville, Maryland. By getting training yourself or having your drivers trained, you can significantly improve your chances of surviving even a well-planned and coordinated attack. You will learn to evade and escape. Furthermore, you'll learn how cars can be used as weapons. Your car is a several-thousand-pound object moving at high speed. Simply crashing into the blocking car, perhaps repeatedly, can disable and possibly kill the attackers. Needless to say, running over an armed terrorist will put him out of business permanently. One point to remember if you are driving in an armored vehicle is that the protective armor adds a great deal of weight to the car or SUV. While the suspension systems of such vehicles are enhanced to accommodate the added weight, the handling characteristics will be dramatically different from a regular vehicle. If you are planning to take a driving course, you will need to use your own armored vehicle or find a school that has such vehicles in its fleet.

The attackers in the UTP case were members of the Mutehida Qaumi Movement (MQM), a radical Islamic group. The timing of the attack, just one day after a Pakistani national named Aimal Kansi was sentenced to death in Fairfax, Virginia, for the murder of two Central Intelligence Agency employees at CIA headquarters in 1993, led investigators to link the two events and term the killings in Karachi a terrorist act of reprisal. Subsequently, two Pakistani nationals were arrested, tried, and convicted of the crime in Pakistan. Other MQM members who were involved have not yet been arrested and remain at large. In November 2002, Kansi was executed for his crimes by the state of Virginia. More such attacks in retaliation are expected by the U.S. Department of State. If you are truly concerned about being attacked in this manner, you will need to armor your vehicle and learn counterterrorist driving techniques. By taking these actions in combination with adherence to other basic rules of vehicle safety and route selection, you can dramatically reduce your chance of being targeted. While these measures may seem extreme, there is no other way to defend against this type of attack. The next chapter provides further information on protecting your vehicle and yourself with armor.

CHAPTER 9

Protective Equipment

MUCH OF THE INFORMATION PROVIDED in this book deals with prevention. The authors strongly believe in the premise that appropriate security protocols will allow most people to avoid becoming the victims of terrorism or criminal acts. Awareness, foreknowledge, and proper planning are central to achieving the goal of increasing the level of personal safety. However, since no security measures are completely foolproof, there is also a need to be well prepared in the event of attack. Body armor, vehicle armor, and gas masks are only some of the equipment that can dramatically increase your chances of surviving an attack.

BODY ARMOR

The production of bullet- and explosive-resistant products is a multibillion-dollar industry. Police agencies and military organizations have been using bullet-resistant technology for over 100 years. In fact, the concept of personal protective armor is thousands of years old. Since early man began using stones and clubs in combat, there has been a need to protect against the effect of such weapons. During various eras in human history, armor has undergone many evolutions. Early man used animal skins. Later humans fashioned shields out of wood and made bronze breastplates and suits of armor. Today the materials used are called Kevlar, Twaron, Spectra-shield, Zylon, and boron carbide. These products are our modern equivalents to suits of armor and armored chariots.

Since the invention of gunpowder and its subsequent use as a propellant to push a lead ball down a steel pipe at sufficient velocity to cause injury and death, humans have sought ways to protect themselves against such projectiles. In the late 1800s silk was used to create thickly padded vests that were able to defeat the slow-moving bullets of that era. Legend has it that the Archduke Franz Ferdinand was wearing such a vest at the time he was assassinated, which was the proximal cause of World War I. It was not until the 1960s that protective vests made from Kevlar began to see use in the law enforcement community.

The threats that we are concerned with are small arms and explosives. Proper selection and use of protective equipment can substantially increase the chances of surviving an armed attack of this nature. Different types of armor are designed to protect the user against a particular level of threat. For example, soft body armor (SBA), the flexible armor worn by police officers, is capable of protecting the wearer against bullets fired from most commonly encountered handguns. The armor will not provide any protection against rounds fired from a high-powered rifle. While it may seem that soft armor is inadequate for use by police, analyses of shooting incidents involving U.S. law enforcement officers indicate that officers are most likely to be shot at by criminals using handguns. A small number of cops are killed by rifle fire, to be sure. But the type of armor required to stop rifle bullets is much heavier and rigid. Armor of this type could not be worn for any length of time because of its weight and rigidity. A cost-benefit analysis is therefore appropriate. Hard armor cannot be worn for long periods, and it is very unlikely that a street cop will come under rifle fire. Furthermore, since it is possible to provide substantial levels of protection against the likely threat, which is assailants using handguns, soft armor is an appropriate choice. Police tactical units that have a greater likelihood of responding to a crime involving a criminal using, for example, an assault rifle generally opt to use hard-armor plates in conjunction with the soft body armor. Hard armor works well as an adjunct on a tactical vest that will likely be worn for short periods of time. It is not suitable for covert use and cannot be worn under clothing. It would not, for example, be appropriate for an executive needing a protective vest that could be worn under a suit. A lightweight vest designed to provide a lower level of protection but affording greater comfort and flexibility would be the appropriate choice under those circumstances.

The first stage in choosing the appropriate SBA for a high-profile business executive or other individual at risk is to identify the most likely threat that may be encountered. As you will see in this chapter, identically rated vests actually vary greatly in the level of ballistic protection they provide. Some are suitable as low-level protective garments worn inconspicuously under clothing while others are more appropriate for use in the type of tactical armor worn by SWAT teams. Let us first focus on concealable armor. There are several brands of soft body armor suitable for use under a suit. A new material, Zylon shield, has allowed for the development of truly concealable armor providing great protection. Many other lightweight materials can be manufactured into concealable vests as well, but they do not equal the performance of Zylon shield. Woven Zylon (not Zylon shield) is marvelously light and flexible but provides only a minimal level of protection against multiple rounds fired into the vest. Zylon shield is a bit stiffer but provides an impressive level of protection. It is also very expensive. This product can be quite useful for those who have good reason to believe that they may be a target for assassination and want to wear an inconspicuous ballistic vest under their clothes. Remember: This type of armor provides protection against common handgun rounds only.

How can a business executive, celebrity, or correspondent going into harm's way select the appropriate product? The first step is to conduct a risk assessment. First of all, is the individual in question likely to be targeted by an assassin using a handgun? If so, what type of weapons and ammunition are common to the region? Many commonly available handgun rounds overseas will easily defeat the ultra-light armor that could be worn beneath clothing, with the possible exception of Zylon shield. The Russian Tokarev round passes through many types of armor with ease. The same is true of steel-core 9-millimeter (mm) rounds. In many instances, all the armor would likely do is to partially deform the bullet as it passed through the vest into the wearer's body.

The intended wearer also needs to consider the actual amount of *effective* coverage a vest will provide. How do you know how to purchase the right vest? What standards do vests need to meet? How are they tested and how can consumers know they are purchasing the best available product? In the United States, vests have been certified and rated according to standards established by the National Institute of Justice (NIJ) for more than 25 years. The NIJ sets the performance standards and establishes the testing protocols. Soft body armor protective levels are designated I, IIA, II, IIIA, III, and IV. The categories are established based on the level of protection that the vests are designed to provide; each successive level provides protection against greater ballistic threats (see Exhibit 9.1).

Exhibit 9.1   NIJ Standard for the Ballistic Resistance of Police Body Armor

---

1. PURPOSE AND SCOPE

The purpose of this standard is to establish minimum performance requirements and methods of testing for the ballistic resistance of police body armor
intended to protect the torso against gunfire. This standard is a revision of NIJ
Standard-0101.02, dated March 1985, clarifying the labeling requirements,
acceptance criteria, and backface signature measurement procedure. The
scope of the standard is limited to ballistic resistance only; the standard does
not address threats from knives and sharply pointed instruments, which are
different types of threat. In addition, the standard does not address armor that
incorporates inserts, or variations in construction of the ballistic panel over
small areas of the torso, for the purposes of increasing the basic level of protection of the armor (whether ballistic or blunt trauma) on localized areas.

2. CLASSIFICATION

Police body armors covered by this standard are classified into seven types,
by level of ballistic protection performance.[1] The classification of an armor
panel that provides two or more levels of ballistic protection at different locations on the ballistic panel shall be that of the minimum ballistic protection
provided at any location on the panel.

   As of 1987, ballistic-resistant body armor suitable for routine full-time
wear throughout an entire shift of duty is available in types I, II-A, and to a
limited extent type II (depending largely upon the climate) which will provide
protection from common handgun threats. Type III-A, which will provide protection from 9 mm submachine guns and 44 Magnum handguns using the test
rounds, and types III and IV, which will protect against high-powered rifles,
are normally considered to be special purpose armor most appropriate for
use during tactical operations. See Appendix A.

---

[1] The ballistic threat posed by a bullet depends, among other things, on its composition,
shape, caliber, mass, angle of incidence, and impact velocity. Because of the wide variety of
cartridges available in a given caliber, and because of the existence of hand loads, armors
that will defeat a standard test round may not defeat other loadings in the same caliber. For
example, an armor that prevents penetration by a 357 Magnum test round may or may not
defeat a 357 Magnum round with higher velocity. In general, an armor that defeats a given
lead bullet may not resist penetration by other rounds of the same caliber of different construction or configuration. The test ammunition specified in this standard represent common
threats to law enforcement officers.

2.1 Type I (22 LR; 38 Special)

This armor protects against 22 Long Rifle High Velocity lead bullets, with nominal masses of 2.6 g (40 gr) impacting at a velocity of 320 m (1050 ft) per second or less, and 38 Special round nose lead bullets, with nominal masses of 10.2 g (158 gr) impacting at a velocity of 259 m (850 ft) per second or less. It also provides protection against most handgun rounds in calibers 25 and 32.

2.2 Type II-A (Lower Velocity 357 Magnum; 9 mm)

This armor protects against 357 Magnum jacketed soft point bullets, with nominal masses of 10.2 g (158 gr) impacting at a velocity of 381 m (1250 ft) per second or less, and 9 mm full metal jacketed bullets, with nominal masses of 8.0 g (124 gr) impacting at a velocity of 332 m (1090 ft) per second or less. It also provides protection against threats such as 45 Auto., 38 Special +P and some other factory loads in caliber 357 Magnum and 9 mm, as well as the threats mentioned in section 2.1.

2.3 Type II (Higher Velocity 357 Magnum; 9 mm)

This armor protects against 357 Magnum jacketed soft point bullets, with nominal masses of 10.2 g (158 gr) impacting at a velocity of 425 m (1395 ft) per second or less, and 9 mm full metal jacketed bullets, with nominal masses of 8.0 g (124 gr) impacting at a velocity of 358 m (1175 ft) per second or less. It also provides protection against most other factory loads in caliber 357 Magnum and 9 mm, as well as the threats mentioned in sections 2.1 and 2.2.

2.4 Type III-A (44 Magnum; Submachine Gun 9 mm)

This armor protects against 44 Magnum, lead semi-wadcutter bullets with gas checks, nominal masses of 15.55 g (240 gr) and impacting at a velocity of 426 m (1400 ft) per second or less, and 9 mm full metal jacketed bullets, with nominal masses of 8.0 g (124 gr) impacting at a velocity of 426 m (1400 ft) per second or less. It also provides protection against most handgun threats, as well as the threats mentioned in sections 2.1 through 2.3.

2.5 Type III (High-Powered Rifle)

This armor protects against 7.62 mm full metal jacketed bullets (U.S. military designation M80), with nominal masses of 9.7 g (150 gr) impacting at a velocity of 838 m (2750 ft) per second or less. It also provides protection against threats such as 223 Remington (5.56 mm FMJ), 30 Carbine FMJ, and 12 gauge rifled slug, as well as the threats mentioned in sections 2.1 through 2.4.

(continues)

Exhibit 9.1   NIJ Standard for the Ballistic Resistance of Police
                   Body Armor *(Continued)*

2.6 Type IV (Armor-Piercing Rifle)

This armor protects against 30 caliber armor-piercing bullets (U.S. military designation APM2), with nominal masses of 10.8 g (166 gr) impacting at a velocity of 868 m (2850 ft) per second or less. It also provides at least single hit protection against the threats mentioned in sections 2.1 through 2.5.

2.7 Special Type

A purchaser having a special requirement for a level of protection other than one of the above standard threat levels should specify the exact test rounds and minimum impact velocities to be used, and indicate that this standard shall govern in all other respects.

As you can see, a level IA vest is designed to meet a lower threat level than a level IIA vest. For reasons unknown, the NIJ uses the designator "A" to indicate a lower level of protection within a category. Thus, a level II vest provides greater protection than a level IIA. Each gradation indicates effective performance against particular ballistic threats and velocities. In addition, blunt trauma, or back face deformation, is also measured and factored in to differentiate performance between the levels. Blunt trauma is simply the amount of crushing force that the round impacting the vest will cause to the wearer. The standard adopted by the NIJ is that blunt trauma greater than 44 mm, as measured in the test medium, is likely to cause death or serious injury to the wearer even if the round does not penetrate the vest. Often a vest prevents penetration but does not sufficiently disperse the energy of the bullet that will be absorbed by the wearer. Excessive blunt trauma will render a vest unacceptable against a particular ballistic threat. Besides protecting against bullets, vests that protect against blunt trauma can save lives in auto accidents. Many police officers have survived auto accidents because they were wearing protective vests. Just as the armor protects against the blunt trauma associated with a bullet impact, it also provides blunt impact protection from the effects associated with a car crash.

HOW SOFT BODY ARMOR IS CERTIFIED

In the United States, the NIJ standards are well known and most police officers, the biggest consumers of SBA, are generally aware of SBA's intended function. Many police departments and agencies rely completely on the NIJ standards and procure vests based on the NIJ rating alone. The question is: Are these standards sufficient to allow agencies or individuals like you to select the product that will provide the best level of protection? The answer is no.

The basis for our conclusion may be found in the testing protocols established by the NIJ itself. This procedure, as well as other important information, may be found in a book published by the NIJ entitled *Selection and Application Guide to Police Body Armor.*[1] This guide provides a good overall look at body armor in general. However, it also makes many erroneous conclusions and reveals that the NIJ's own testing standards are inadequate.

The NIJ claims that "No documented fatal injury has ever resulted from a round of ammunition penetrating body armor that NIJ had approved as protection against that level of threat."[2] However, this statement is rendered almost meaningless once it is analyzed more deeply. All it means is that no vest ever failed to meet the standards the NIJ has arbitrarily set. There are many cases of vest penetration. In fact, the Federal Bureau of Investigation (FBI) was among the first law enforcement agencies to reject the NIJ's rating system after an agent wearing a vest was murdered. On May 29, 1995, FBI Special Agent William Christian was ambushed and shot to death while attempting to apprehend the killer of a corporal in the Prince George's County Police Department. He was shot at point-blank range and was struck numerous times, both in the area of his vest and around it. Although the wounds inflicted on Agent Christian in nonprotected areas were fatal, the investigation revealed that one of the rounds that struck his vest had penetrated his torso. This raised alarm bells, and the FBI initially concluded that the vests were defective. Not so, said both the NIJ and the manufacturer. The round that penetrated Christian's vest was very close to another round that had also struck the vest. *The vest was neither designed nor required to provide protection against multiple impacts striking the armor in close proximity.* What, then, are vests expected to do? An examination of NIJ standards and test practices will explain.

Prior to testing, vests are secured to clay blocks and are shot with the indicated test rounds. The NIJ claims that it chose clay as a backing material for a variety of reasons, but the main one seems to have been that clay deforms when it is hit, creating a depression allowing blunt trauma to be easily measured. The ballistic panel is held flat against the clay and does not replicate the curvature it exhibits while worn by a human being. The test panel is shot six times in specific locations with the test round and assessed for penetration (see Exhibit 9.2).

Each of the six test shots must be what is termed a fair hit, which is defined by the NIJ as "a bullet which impacts the armor at an angle of incidence no greater than five degrees plus or minus from the intended angle of incidence, *no closer to the edge of the armor part than 7.6 cm (3 in) and no closer to a prior hit than 5 cm (2 in),* at an impact velocity no more than 50 ft (15 m) per second greater than the minimum required test velocity."[3] Nothing in the literature available from NIJ explains why this standard was chosen. For example, a round of ammunition that strikes the vest within 4.9 centimeters (cm) of a previous hit and penetrates is deemed an "unfair hit" and does not result in a failure of the vest for rating purposes. An impact that strikes the vest even the slightest bit less than three inches from the edge is likewise deemed to be "unfair" and does not disqualify the sample. Think about that. The NIJ does not require that a vest stop a bullet 2.99 inches from any edge! While briefing the Drug Enforcement Administration (DEA) Safety and Equipment committee several years ago, David demonstrated the inadequacy of this standard by measuring points three inches from the edge of the issued SBA and then connecting the dots with a grease pencil. What you get is a postage-stamp-size area that the NIJ certifies as ballistically effective. *The vest is not required to be effective outside that area.* Now consider that fact in conjunction with the designs of most vests sold for undercover use. These are the designs that are most likely to be suitable for the executive looking for additional protection that can be worn under clothing. The vests are scooped out low under the chin and armpits, providing limited coverage for the user's body. Most salespeople point this out as a benefit, citing the wearer's comfort. The NIJ itself also promotes these "comfort" standards, contending that officers or others are less likely to wear uncomfortable vests. This may be true, but comfort also must be balanced against protective ability. The available data tell us where vest design needs improvement.

Exhibit 9.2   Test Shot Pattern

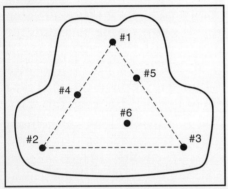

EFFECTIVENESS

Another troubling test parameter is the NIJ's decision to exclude penetrations of test rounds impacting less than two inches from a prior hit. Why two inches? Once again, it is an arbitrary standard. We can state from personal experience that most vests will fail if they are subjected to testing above and beyond what the NIJ requires. Of course, there must be some cutoff for testing purposes. At some point, a round striking in close proximity to a prior hit will penetrate, especially in lighter-weight armor. Similarly, a round on or very close to an edge will take the path of least resistance and travel around the SBA into the wearer's body. There must be sufficient material to disperse the energy of the bullet. But two inches between shots and three inches from an edge? The standard that David adopted while creating the testing protocol for the DEA was one inch from the edge and one inch between shots. While this standard is still subjective, it works in favor of the individual wearing the armor. In addition, besides the obvious point that requiring a vest to be effective against multiple, closely grouped impacts provides more protection for wearers, it also allows the tester to get a feel for the sample being tested. Once the vest is stressed a bit more beyond what the NIJ requires, it will either demonstrate its superior design or it will fail utterly. During one testing phase at the DEA, David tested nine different vests from a variety of companies. Each sample was rated and certified as level IIIA by the NIJ. Only one vest out of nine passed David's more demanding protocol. The other eight, including tactical vests worn by officers in departments in major metropolitan areas, failed. They were shot through with alarming ease. Only through testing can those responsible for vest selection get the necessary "feel" for the right choice.

What is the correct approach? In our estimation, the standards set forth by the NIJ do not reflect the needs of the end user, the person who is relying on the product to stop a round. Standards will always be subjective. But it is the responsibility of individuals to decide what type of protection they require and what tradeoff relative to comfort versus level of protection they are willing to make. They must make this determination on the basis of science and available data. Standards will also vary depending on application. Vests for patrol officers to wear during a full shift or for executives to wear beneath their suits must be more comfortable than vests worn for only short periods. If you are considering the purchase of tactical vests for your security staff or bodyguard force that will be worn for generally shorter periods of time, you can obtain a product of heavier construction that is better suited to withstand multiple impacts and blunt trauma. The same is true if you are a reporter covering the news during a war or in dangerous situations. One caveat, however: Just because a vest has a tactical design does not mean that it also has a tactically adequate ballistic package under the impressive looking exterior. Several years ago, the DEA purchased $400,000 worth of tactical vests for its clandestine lab units. They were purchased in complete reliance on their NIJ rating and were not tested independently. David, who had just finished research and development on a more demanding test standard that reflected real-world needs, decided to shoot these new vests according to that new protocol. The vests were impressive looking, level IIIA-rated tactical armor. During the testing process, several rounds penetrated the armor, so the vest failed the test. A retest, requested by management, also resulted in failure, and the vests could not be issued to agency personnel. This was an expensive lesson. The vests sat in storage for a few years and were ultimately distributed to local law enforcement agencies with the notice that they had failed the more stringent DEA test parameters.

These purchasing problems are not confined to the Department of Justice. A major department in New York State purchased extremely lightweight vests for its officers without testing. Subsequent to the purchase, the DEA was contacted and asked to provide the testing data relative to this vest. Unfortunately, the DEA had rejected this particular vest after it failed during two separate trials. The vests are now being worn by thousands of uniformed and plainclothes police officers. The time to evaluate a vest's performance level is before procurement. Set standards for SBA and then test to see if a particular vest measures up. For the corporate user, this will not be an easy task. An executive at risk is not in a position to conduct ballistic tests on body armor. It will, therefore, be necessary to talk to an expert in the field in order to identify the appropriate SBA for the circumstances.

DETERMINING YOUR SOFT BODY ARMOR REQUIREMENTS

How should standards be established? The first step is to determine the threat that you are facing. For law enforcement officers, the best approach is to look at what the trend has been in law enforcement over the last decade. The best source of this type of information is the Uniform Crime

Reports compiled by the Federal Bureau of Investigation (FBI). Little more than 10 years ago, the most common threat to law enforcement officers was the .38 caliber revolver. Officers generally were shot one time at extremely close range. However, this statistic is no longer true. The prevalence of 9 mm semiautomatic weapons has changed the dynamic. Today officers are more likely to be shot multiple times, also at close range, with a weapon firing 9 mm hardball ammunition. We believe that this trend will also apply to private sector end users as well. How does this fact affect the type of SBA that you should consider wearing?

The most obvious concerns are obviously the higher velocity (and hence greater penetration) of the 9 mm bullet as well as the greater likelihood of being hit with multiple rounds. An assailant is now likely to be armed with a handgun carrying 16 rounds and will empty it, firing without regard to the constraints followed by law enforcement officers and protective personnel. The NIJ does use the 9 mm hardball round at a velocity of 1,400 feet per second as the standard while testing level II and IIIA vests. However, the NIJ does not test the armor for effectiveness against multiple hits in rapid succession. This is an unacceptable fatal flaw in the testing process. *Vests behave differently when hit by multiple rounds in rapid succession.* David has personally shot dozens of level IIIA vests of different manufacture. While many perform adequately when hit by multiple rounds fired one at a time, most completely fail when hit by rapid semiautomatic fire or short bursts with a submachine gun (SMG). The reasons are complex. Armor works by dissipating the energy of the rounds as they strike the vest. In some SBA, the effect of rapid fire overwhelms the armor's ability to dissipate the energy and results in penetration. In other cases, the armor, especially the ultra-lightweight vests made from Zylon or lightweight hybrids, exhibits tremendous bunching of the ballistic material when it is shot. The material is pulled toward the point of impact, causing large gaps in the coverage area. Often successive rounds strike the vest in an area that suddenly is devoid of ballistic material, and the rounds easily penetrate the nonballistic vest shell. The recommended protocol calls for a three-round burst fired from an SMG. All three rounds must fall within a three-inch-diameter circle.

What is the appropriate standard for use by a corporate executive seeking armor to wear under clothing? Obviously, such a vest must be lighter and thinner than SBA worn by police officers or security personnel. Everyone wants lighter body armor. The trend in the industry is to design and market vests that are thinner, lighter, and more flexible than ever.

There is a downside to this. *In general, lighter, thinner, and more flexible vests provide a corresponding loss of protection.* The lighter the vest, the greater the likelihood that it will fail under extreme conditions. There are vests that are, in our opinion, too light and flexible to provide good performance for security personnel or for a backup team of bodyguards operating in an extremely dangerous environment. That is not to say that ultra-lightweight vests do not serve a useful purpose. They do. They are ideal for use by executives or other VIPs to wear under clothing. It is just necessary to understand that these ultra-lightweight vests have limitations. Don't get lulled into a false sense of security by virtue of the fact that you are wearing soft body armor under your clothing. The actual size of the protected area is smaller than you think, and performance against multiple shots striking you in close proximity to each other will not be good.

SELECTING THE RIGHT DESIGN

No available body of data deals with actual field performance of SBA or other protective products used by civilian wearers. We must, therefore, look at the data that are available: the statistics obtained from the use of SBA by law enforcement when we try to determine which product type or design is suitable for our own individual needs. A look at these statistics is extremely useful in assessing the type of standard to set as far as design and coverage area is concerned.

Between 1992 and 2001, 643 police officers were killed in the line of duty, of whom 307 (52 percent) were wearing SBA at the time they were murdered and 594 were killed by assailants using a firearm. Further analysis of total number of slain officers wearing SBA provides a great deal of insight into how body armor should be designed and selected. Of the 307 killed while wearing SBA, approximately half died as a result of being shot in the head. This statistic, while tragic, cannot help us analyze the effectiveness, or lack thereof, of a particular vest design. (It does, however, make a strong case for issuing bullet-resistant helmets to law enforcement officers.) It is necessary, therefore, to limit our analysis to the 114 officers killed while wearing armor as a result of being struck in the torso. The largest number of officers in this group were killed when rounds entered above the level of their vest. This includes shots to the neck or the region of the collarbone, which accounts for 36 (31.6 percent) of the officers slain. Thirty-two officers (28 percent) were killed when they were struck by rounds to the shoulder and armpit area. Nineteen officers (17 percent) were killed by rounds that entered between the side panels of the vest or in the armpit. Eight officers (7 percent) were struck below the level of their vest, and 19 (17 percent) died when rounds penetrated their vest.[4]

How can these figures help citizens in the private sector select the proper armor for their personnel or themselves? By studying these statistics, we can learn where vests are failing. The obvious conclusion is that the more of the individual's body that is covered by armor, the better. These figures tell us that, while we need to consider the comfort with which the vest can be worn, we must always tip the scale toward having more coverage rather than less. NIJ comfort guidelines recognize this fact but do not emphasize the point strongly enough.[5] Executives should select vests that come up as high under the arm as possible, and the top edge of the vest should reach the collarbone. Wrap-around should be front over back and should overlap by at least two inches. The vest also must be an appropriate length, preferably covering the navel. Remember, length and overlap is of great importance because any *vest will fail if it is struck close to an edge.* If an executive or celebrity is seeking a vest that is truly concealable under clothing, then it may be necessary to choose a design with somewhat less coverage. A very good design for this application is the Extreme ZX by American Body Armor. It is lightweight and flexible and provides a good level of protection as a concealable vest (see Exhibit 9.3). Remember, regardless of which model of concealable armor you select, make sure you do not buy a vest with excessively wide armholes or too generous a scoop in the neck.

Exhibit 9.3   Model Extreme ZX by American Body Armor

Photo courtesy of Armor Holdings, Inc.

ENVIRONMENTAL CONCERNS AND SPECIAL THREATS

Consider what climate-related effects may be unique to your environment. Where are you located? Are your vests likely to be subjected to extreme heat or cold? Will the wearer be perspiring heavily or working around water? Vests perform differently under different conditions. In Bangkok, Thailand, or in Saudi Arabia, temperatures routinely reach above 100 degrees. Some vests do not perform well at such temperatures. These vests also may become saturated from perspiration if they do not have water-repellent features. Some vests that are otherwise satisfactory will fail when saturated with water.

The existence of special threats must be considered as well. If you are working in a country where there is a great availability of armor-piercing or steel-core rounds, you have to factor that in to your decision-making process. As mentioned above, the Russian Tokarev round easily passes through most SBA. Is that weapon available to the bad guys operating where you will be working? These concerns should be addressed as part of any corporate risk assessment.

TACTICAL ARMOR AND RIFLE-RESISTANT PLATES

The next level of available armor products is commonly known as a tactical vest. As the name implies, the purpose of the tactical vest is far different from the function of concealable body armor. It is worn over clothing and is heavier and more restrictive than concealable armor. It also provides the wearer with a much greater level of protection. More of the wearer's body is covered; the armor is thicker and includes functional ballistic collars, shoulder panels, and groin protectors (see Exhibit 9.4). Few manufacturers seem to understand the proper function of groin protectors, by the way. Besides the obvious area that is in need of protection, groin protectors also need to be wide enough to protect the femoral artery from harm. A severed or lacerated femoral artery will kill you in a matter of minutes. While David was in the DEA, he spent a great deal of time designing an

Exhibit 9.4   Author David Katz wearing a Protech Body Barricade Tactical Vest

effective panel that provides the appropriate level of protection to that area. A properly designed tactical vest also provides superior levels of protection against bursts fired from a submachine gun, provides better protection than SBA near the edges, and also is effective against rounds striking the vest in close proximity to each other. Furthermore, the vest carrier, which is the garment that holds the ballistic panels, also can be fitted to hold hard armor plates. These plates are generally worn over the center of the body in the front, thus protecting the heart, and in the rear protecting the spinal cord. The types of plates must be selected carefully depending on the specific types of ammunition common to a particular area or country. In Exhibit 9.1, the hard armor begins with the designation level III. Remember, IIIA is actually lower than III and is designed only to provide protection against common handgun rounds. Level III plates provide protection against some rifle rounds but not all. For example, a level III plate will stop an ordinary jacketed lead bullet fired by an M16 rifle (.223 caliber or 5.56 mm) or an AK-47 (7.62 × 39 mm). The problem is that much of the ammunition for these weapons is not standard. The M16 ammunition issued to our soldiers and allies abroad is a mild armor-piercing round designated the M855 or SS109. For the AK-47 there are many types of rounds with steel cores or jackets. These rounds will pierce level III plates as well as the level IIIA armor beneath it and enter the wearer's body. Someone familiar with relative ballistic performance and body armor and the type of ammunition used by the potential assailants should be tasked with selecting the hard plates to be used.

RBR Tactical Products, Inc. offers excellent tactical vests that are very well made. Specifically, the stitching (which has a great deal to do with a vest's ability to stop a round) is among the best in the industry. The design of the throat piece and shoulder harness also has proven to be quite effective in preventing penetrations to those areas (see Exhibit 9.5).

Exhibit 9.5 RBR Tactical Vest

Photo courtesy of RBR Tactical Products, Inc.

VESTS FOR CORRESPONDENTS

What individuals in the private sector will need this type of protection? One obvious use is by the literally hundreds of correspondents reporting from war zones or where the risk of terrorist attack is great. TV footage from Iraq, Afghanistan, and the West Bank shows many reporters clad in flack jackets and wearing ballistic helmets. While from watching such footage it is largely impossible to determine the type of ballistic materials under the vest carriers, it is easy to evaluate the design of the carrier itself and determine if the level of protection provided to the correspondent is sufficient. More often than not, the designs provide insufficient amounts of coverage. In addition, the design of virtually every collar or throat guard is seamed and not fashioned out of a solid continuous piece of ballistic material. A seamed collar is worthless if it is struck. A round or bullet or shell fragment will take the path of least resistance and go right through the unprotected seam into the wearer's body. Even a small laceration to the carotid artery will likely prove fatal absent immediate medical care. Vests must be designed to provide as much coverage as possible and more than just "cosmetic" protection to vital areas. Vests need to have pockets to accommodate hard armor that is capable of defeating military rifle rounds. Hard-armor plates (see Exhibit 9.6) should cover the vital organs of the chest in both the front and back of the vest.

Correspondents need to become more familiar with ballistic vests and need to use the equipment appropriate to the threats they are likely to

Exhibit 9.6   Rifle-Resistant Hard Armor Plates from Armor Holdings, Inc.

Photo courtesy of Armor Holdings, Inc.

encounter. The first thing they need to do is realize that the vest carrier (the garment, usually ballistic nylon, taffeta, or Nomex, which contains the ballistic panels) should serve to identify them as members of the press and not as combatants. If you are a reporter, you should avoid using the same type of armor as those in the conflict. To do so is to risk becoming a target yourself. In the same manner that law enforcement agencies have POLICE clearly displayed on their vests, you should have the word PRESS on your vest in large, bold letters. Consider having it written in English as well as the local language.

Before you order your equipment, you need to research the weapons used in the conflict. Do this for *both sides* in the conflict. This point is critically important as you may find yourself on the receiving end of both hostile and "friendly" fire. The differences in the ammunition used could prove fatal to you if your hard armor is not resistant to any round you are likely to find in use where you are going. For example, in Afghanistan, the Taliban and Al Qaeda favored the AK-47 rifle. American troops carry the M16. Many types of hard armor will stop rounds from one but not from the other. Make sure yours stops all available varieties of both rounds. The soft armor in the carrier must be effective against all handgun rounds with superior ballistic effectiveness near the edges. It also should be tested against multiple-round bursts and have a seamless collar. The groin protector should be squared off like an apron and cover the groin and the femoral arteries in both legs.

It is imperative to understand that the soft body armor in the vest will not stop bullets fired from any military rifle. It will, however, provide protection against shrapnel. The hard plates are what will defeat a rifle round.

OTHER USES OF TACTICAL ARMOR

Tactical vests also have great use while moving a VIP through a potentially dangerous area by motorcade. Even armored vehicles can be breached, and there is always the chance that the person being protected (known as the principal) will need to be evacuated from a stopped car or one that is burning. A tactical vest, with appropriately designed and selected armor plates, is the best choice for that type of situation. Additional armored products, such as helmets and shields, are also indispensable and are discussed below.

Any team using a counterassault vehicle to protect the principal's vehicle should also utilize tactical vests. In the event of an armed attack, the counterassault team will engage the assailants long enough for the principal to be evacuated. Also, if your company is operating in a region where an armed incursion into your facility is a real possibility, management should consider training some of the security staff in hostage rescue methods, such as establishing a defensive perimeter. These individuals, besides needing proper training in the use of the appropriate weaponry, must be outfitted with tactical body armor.

BALLISTIC HELMETS

In addition to SBA and rifle-resistant plates, other protective products should be considered for certain applications. The first indispensable item in this category is a ballistic helmet. If you recall from the analysis of the law enforcement shooting fatalities, more than half the cops killed in the line of duty were shot in the head. Anyone facing any potential risk of being caught in a firefight is at the same risk. For war correspondents reporting from regions where artillery is falling nearby, it is critical that they wear an appropriate helmet. Reporters often are right in the middle of battles, bombings, or sniper situations. David Miller of Fox News was scant yards away outside of Jerusalem in 2001 as a sniper shot and critically wounded an Israeli soldier. If you report on this type of action, you know the dangers without us having to tell you. What you may not know is how effective the armor that you are relying on to save your life actually is.

Exhibit 9.7   Bolt-Free RBR
                     Ballistic Helmet

Excellent ballistic helmets are available from RBR Tactical Products, Inc. The helmet shown in Exhibit 9.7 is a new design, which does not use bolts to secure the suspension system.

This is a level IIIA helmet, which can be upgraded to defeat rifle rounds by the addition of a special insert. These helmets are the product of choice of the best law enforcement and military tactical units in the world and are suitable for use by war

Photo courtesy of RBR Tactical
Products, Inc.

correspondents, VIPs during an evacuation, or trained private security teams. Several of these helmet designs accommodate earpieces worn both by special operations operatives and reporters.

SPECIFIC RECOMMENDATIONS

To our knowledge, our company, Global Security Group, LLC, is the only private consulting company that will do a threat assessment and identify, through ballistic testing, the appropriate armor products to meet the perceived threat. However, before we make specific product recommendations, we offer this caveat. Technology in the field of ballistic armor is advancing at a rapid pace. It is likely that even within the short space of several years more effective products will be available that will be lighter, stronger, and more flexible. That being said, in our opinion the best ballistic product available today for use in soft body armor is a material known as Zylon shield. Zylon shield differs from woven Zylon, which we do not recommend. Zylon shield was successfully tested by both the FBI and DEA and was rated as the most effective ballistic package for its combination of strength and lightness. It was accepted as the gold standard for vests used by the DEA regional enforcement teams as well as the FBI's elite hostage rescue team (HRT).

The exact number of Zylon shield plies in the armor used by the DEA and HRT is confidential. This product is available to civilian purchasers and is ideally suited for use as the ballistic material in both concealable and tactical armor. For procurement information, see Appendix B on this book's website (for website access details, see page iii).

Realize, however, that older technology continues to be quite effective. If weight is not a critical factor in your selection process, then Kevlar, providing it is enclosed in a waterproof package, is still a good choice.

OTHER BALLISTIC EQUIPMENT

Other items worth considering are ballistic shields and bomb blankets. Both have very specific uses in tactical operation and also can provide cover during an evacuation or rescue. Bomb blankets are effective to shield an area from the effects of a bomb blast and also can be used to provide emergency cover if an area comes under small arms fire. Protech

Inc., now a division of Armor Holdings, makes the gold standard for both these products.

ARMORED VEHICLES

Armor Holdings has extended its acquisition of superior armor products through the purchase of O'Gara & Hess, the finest maker of armored vehicles in the world. O'Gara & Hess have produced armored limousines used by the President of the United States since the 1940s. The first such vehicle was produced for President Harry Truman. Currently, O'Gara & Hess provides armored vehicles for over 60 heads of state. The company also provides excellent products for corporate VIPs in need of armored vehicles. In the United States, the company is headquartered in Ohio. It also maintains facilities in France, Mexico, Brazil, Colombia, Italy, and Switzerland.

If you are considering the purchase of an armored vehicle, you must do a great deal of research prior to selecting the appropriate product. You must carefully analyze the location where the vehicle will be used as well as the nature of the threat. If your concern is to be protected against handgun-wielding assailants, carjackings, and smash-and-grab robberies, you may opt for an armored vehicle protected against handgun rounds only. While vehicles with this level of protection will not defeat rifle fire, they do have the attractive advantage of looking and handling virtually identically to their nonarmored counterparts. The added weight in armor and ballistic glass is between 300 and 500 pounds depending on the size of the base vehicle. O'Gara Handgun Protection vehicles are built in Fairfield, Ohio, and are certified to defeat most commonly available handgun rounds, including the .38 super, 9 mm automatic, UZI submachine gun, .357 Magnum, and .44 Magnum. Optional security modifications include electric dead-bolt locks, locking fuel caps, satellite telephone, dual battery system, global positioning satellite (GPS) tracking system, and an inside trunk release. Options in the more heavily armored models include everything from underbody grenade protection and fully armored roofs to armored gas tanks and batteries. O'Gara & Hess can armor a wide range of vehicles. Exhibit 9.8 shows an example of a vehicle fitted with ballistic armor.

What level of protection is appropriate for your circumstances? The first step in making the best choice about the level of protection you need in your vehicle is to get a professional risk assessment of the likely threats that may be encountered. Failing to procure such an assessment may have tragic results. As we've discussed, even the government—though you would assume that it would be in a position to make informed selections—often picks the wrong product. The DEA has an extensive presence in the cocaine-producing countries of South America. As you might imagine, this is a hazardous assignment. The DEA decided that the agents needed to have their vehicles armored to reduce the danger from local drug traffickers as well as communist rebels. Millions of dollars were spent to armor the vehicles. Unfortunately, the individual in charge of procurement did not analyze the threat the agents were facing. In Colombia and Peru, for example, the bad guys favor AK-47 assault rifles. The armored vehicles

Exhibit 9.8   Armored Vehicle by O'Gara & Hess

Photo courtesy of Armor Holdings, Inc.

purchased by the DEA were designed to provide protection against handgun rounds only and were insufficient to meet the threat. On one occasion, several armed men carrying assault rifles stopped a car driven by an agent and his girlfriend. They ordered the couple to exit the vehicle. The agent, aware that the vehicle armor would not stop the bullets fired by their weapons, complied. Fortunately, they both survived the encounter. However, had the vehicle been appropriately armored, they could have simply driven away from their assailants. Similar cases have occurred in Israel with tragic results. On one occasion at least, terrorists using machine guns attacked an armored school bus. The armor was not designed to defeat rifle rounds. Bullets penetrated into the interior of the bus and several people were killed.

Different regions in the world pose markedly different risks. For example, in the United States, handguns pose the most common threat. In many other parts of the world, assailants are more likely to be armed with rifles. Every vehicle that will be used where there is a threat from shoulder weapons should be capable of defeating rounds fired from such weapons. Most terrorists abroad will use AK-47 rifles, which fire 7.62 × 39 rounds.

Armor-piercing ammunition is likely. Or they will use the American-made M-16 rifle firing 5.56 mm rounds. Again, light armor–piercing ammunition is commonly available. Vehicles should be capable of stopping such ammunition as an absolute minimum in protection.

O'Gara & Hess also builds vehicles that provide protection against an armor-piercing projectile from a military assault rifle. The added level of protection requires the use of a substantially greater amount of armor and ballistic glass. Not every vehicle can accommodate this added weight. The company has several decades of experience in engineering rifle-protected vehicles that not only provide substantial levels of protection but are also able to be driven with a high level of performance and handling.

Specialty threats also must be considered. Have the local terror cells ever used a rocket-propelled grenade (RPG) during an attack? How about mines or explosives? Vehicles can be armored against those threats as well. The downside is heavier weight and greater cost. Remember, any armor can be defeated. Shoulder-fired missiles and enough explosives can stop a tank. They can certainly stop an armored car. Currently, O'Gara & Hess offers an explosive-resistant vehicle that provides protection against TNT, pipe bombs, grenade attack, and land mines. We suggest that anyone in need of such a vehicle contact the company or a professional security-consulting firm with expertise in this area. O'Gara & Hess, as well as our own company, have expert staff who can analyze the anticipated threat and recommend the correct level of armor protection. These companies can armor virtually any vehicle that may be appropriate to the specific needs of the client. Exhibit 9.9 presents a chart detailing the various levels of protection offered by O'Gara & Hess.

GAS MASKS AND ESCAPE HOODS

Several additional products critical for surviving certain types of attacks are not related to armored products. Gas masks and escape hoods are indispensable kinds of protective equipment that are the only means of countering an attack using gas or biological weapons. The appropriate mask or hood also allows wearers to survive in an atmosphere rendered toxic during a fire. We briefly discuss the products available to the civilian market to prepare you to meet either danger.

Law enforcement SWAT teams have long used gas masks during tactical operations where CS (o-chlorobenzylidenemalononitrile) gas was deployed.

Exhibit 9.9   O'Gara & Hess Levels of Protection

THE O'GARA CATEGORIES OF PROTECTION

The degree of protection you need must correspond with the level of threat you may potentially face. Our goal is to provide you with complete confidence to travel freely. The O'Gara Categories of Protection are designed to help you determine the kind of protection you need by matching your threat level as well as your vehicle preference.

Handgun Protection

Surrounded by lightweight vehicle armor, these vehicles are engineered to withstand multiple hits from weapons such as handguns and submachine guns. O'Gara offers handgun protection conversions in different levels of ballistic protection for over 20 popular brands of cars and sport utility vehicles.

Features:
- Lightweight perimeter protection
- Multi-layered ballistic glass
- Operable front windows
- Computer armor (where necessary)
- Protected battery
- Run-flat tires
- Warranty

Optional Security Modifications:
- Underbody grenade protection
- Locking fuel cap
- Protected fuel tank
- Dual battery system
- Inside/outside intercom
- Luxury upgrades
- Public address system and siren

* additional options available upon request.

Assault Rifle/Armor Piercing Protection

For those facing immediate, consistent, high-level threats, assault rifle/armor piercing protected vehicles from O'Gara are available in several levels of ballistic protection from AK-47 ball ammunition up to high-caliber armor piercing ammunition.

Features:
- Operable front windows
- Computer armor (where necessary)
- Protected battery
- Run-flat tires
- Protected fuel tank
- Roof protection
- Underbody grenade protection
- Proper reinforcements at brakes and suspension where necessary
- Warranty

* optional security modifications available upon request.

Explosion Resistant Vehicle Protection

Working in conjunction with the Royal Canadian Mounted Police, O'Gara has developed a highly effective explosion resistant protection system for selected sedans and SUVs. Capable of defeating threats from TNT, pipe bombs, multiple grenades, land mines and other blast threats, these vehicles provide a higher level of blast protection than any previous system. Even with this exceptional level of protection, each vehicle retains the comfort and performance sought by discriminating automotive buyers.

Courtesy of Armor Holdings, Inc.

These masks also are widely used by the clandestine laboratory investigations units of the DEA and other law enforcement teams required to enter illegal drug labs. Often these labs produce toxic fumes that can kill or seriously injure law enforcement officers required to enter such places. Today, however, the law enforcement community has had to prepare for even more horrific possibilities. The real danger of terrorist attack using weapons of mass destruction has forced police officers and federal agents to procure and issue protective masks certified to protect the wearer against the nuclear, biological, and chemical (NBC) threats more commonly faced by the military.

This scenario is not without precedent. On March 19, 1995, followers of the Japanese AUM Shinrikyo (Supreme Truth) cult leader Shoko Asahara brought quantities of sarin, a deadly nerve toxin, into the Japanese subway system during the morning rush hour in lunch boxes and closed soda cups. The terrorists left the sarin on the subway and punctured the containers as they exited the car. The release of the gas killed 12 and injured over 5,000 people. The chilling fact of these attacks was that sarin is such a deadly agent that it could have easily killed thousands, had the cultists developed a better technique of dispersing the agent. It has been well documented that Saddam Hussein used sarin as well as mustard gas against his minority Kurdish population. Pure sarin is colorless, odorless, and volatile, and a highly lethal compound. Its pathogenic mechanism is to inhibit the enzymatic action of cholinesterase (ChE), producing excessive amounts of acetylcholine that, in turn, cause signs and symptoms mainly in muscarinic, nicotinic, and central nervous system structures. What this means is that sarin is a potent nerve agent. It may be absorbed through any part of the body, but it is most effective as a weapon when it is released into the atmosphere and is breathed by the intended victims. Military journals describe the effect of sarin exposure. The first sign of exposure may be a reaction at the point of contact: localized sweating, muscular twitching, and severely constricted eye pupils. Other initial symptoms include a runny nose accompanied by tightness of the chest with shortness of breath and dimness of vision. In more severe exposure, headache, cramps, nausea, vomiting, involuntary defecation and urination, twitching, jerking, staggering, convulsions, drowsiness, coma, and respiratory arrest may be seen. Mohammed Atta, the operational leader of the September 11 attacks, spent time inquiring about obtaining a crop duster. The terrorists could have easily used a crop duster to spread sarin over a densely populated area, killing many thousands.

The issuance of gas masks effective against NBC agents is universal in Israel. Every Israeli man, woman, and child has a government-issued mask and is familiar with how to seal a room in the home to provide a measure of safety in the event of this type of attack. NBC-rated masks are available to the public in the United States as well. Generally they are large, bulky devices and do not lend themselves to easy and unobtrusive storage. The other alternative is the new generation of protective masks and hoods that perform the same task and come in small, convenient foil packages. The level of protection provided by these hoods varies. Some provide virtually the same level of protection against NBC threats as the standard military-issue masks. Others provide lesser levels of protection; these are generally smaller and lighter as well. Some hoods are merely filtration masks; these filter out particulate matter, such as soot and smoke, but will not protect you against toxic fumes or biological hazards.

The escape masks are designed to protect against specific threats. The Duram Personal Escape Mask provides short-term protection against biological and chemical threats. The Duram Smoke Hood filters out toxic gases associated with fires and also filters out carbon monoxide. These lightweight masks are disposable and they come packaged in compact foil pouches.

The Duram Personal Escape Mask is an emergency evacuation mask you can carry in your pocket, designed to provide respiratory protection and reduce health risk and mortality rate associated with the inhalation of toxic air. It is pocket sized and weighs less than 150 grams (around five ounces). It is a one-size-fits-all device and accommodates long hair, facial hair, and glasses. The filtration system uses specially impregnated activated charcoal to remove toxic gases, and it has a five-year shelf life.

Exhibit 9.10   Duram Personal Escape Mask

Photo courtesy of Duram, Inc.

Exhibit 9.10 shows the Duram Personal Escape Mask. It is certified to provide protection against ABEK-type gases and chemical weapons such as ammonia, carbon tetrachloride, chlorine, sarin nerve gas, hydrogen chloride, hydrogen sulfide, nitrogen dioxide, sulfur dioxide, capsicum spray (pepper spray used by law enforcement), tear gas, smoke, and a variety of other toxic gases and fumes. This mask is also rated to provide protection against biological and chemical threats. This product is already in widespread use among law enforcement, military, and civilian clients, including the FBI, the United States Marine Corps, the Royal Canadian Mounted Police, McDonnell Douglas, Monsanto Chemical, Nestlé, Carlton Hotel line, Hilton Hotels, and the Italian navy, to name but a few.

CHILDREN'S MASKS

One item of extreme importance that must be considered when providing protection for an entire family is how to provide respiratory protection for infants and small children. Filtration masks most commonly are not what are termed a "positive pressure" or "over pressure" mask. That means that most of the masks used for emergency escape or to provide protection against NBC attack are not pressurized and have no flow of air into the mask without the respirations of the user. You need to breathe through the mask. The vacuum created brings the contaminated air into the filter, where it is cleaned before reaching your mouth and lungs. The difficulty is that it is sometimes hard to inhale with sufficient force to breathe easily. Certainly it is impossible for small children and infants to do so. Therefore, a pressurized system must be used with children and infants.

The best such products that we have seen are made by the Israeli firm Supergum (see Exhibit 9.11).

In Supergum's excellent and relatively inexpensive systems for use by children, the pressure

Exhibit 9.11   Child's Mask (left) and Infant Protective Suit (right)

Photos courtesy of Supergum, Inc.

is created through a small battery-operated device and is reusable as long as it is cared for properly. The mask has a positive, pressurized flow of air that allows children to breathe normally. The claustrophobic feeling of wearing a hood or mask is unavoidable. Parental assurance and comfort is the only way to overcome this. Adults with respiratory problems also will need pressurized systems as they lack the ability to breathe with enough sustained forced. For infants, a completely enclosed protective environment that surrounds the child's upper body is available; it allows the child to feel more comfortable and move the upper body freely while wearing the mask. These masks provide clean air over-pressure protection to children. The infant model comes in a convenient storage and carry case. Both units will operate at peak efficiency for 10 hours in a contaminated environment. Both also provide protection against NBC threats and allow wearers to drink safely while wearing the mask or module.

FIREARMS

Besides discussing protective measures, it is necessary to briefly discuss defensive measures. In most countries, foreign nationals are not authorized to possess a firearm. In some countries, however, resident Americans can own weapons for sporting purposes. The question of whether to own a weapon for self-protection is an emotionally charged one. In addition, should an American use a firearm to kill a would-be attacker in the home, adverse legal consequences may ensue. Unless the individual has a high level of firearms proficiency and clearly understands the local law regarding the use of deadly physical force, the decision is simple: It is probably preferable to engage the services of a local and vetted guard service that can provide armed guards if necessary. In many countries, the cost of hiring such a service to protect a neighborhood or apartment complex is very reasonable, even more so when the cost is shared among a group of families and individuals.

If you are an executive and you are considering the addition of armed security personnel to protect your facility, you have a much bigger job ahead of you. It is insufficient merely to hire locals with weapons and feel as if you will be well protected. All security personnel need to be well trained; armed security guards need an even higher level of training. Not only will you need to follow all local laws relative to the establishment of such a guard force, but your company will need to make a commitment to hiring the best instructors available to teach the staff to become proficient with firearms and tactics. Remember that these skills are perishable; if training and retraining are not conducted on a regular basis, these skills will degrade dramatically. If, however, the conditions in the host country or the sensitivity of your facility require such a force, then the time and money spent training them is worthwhile. A well-trained staff can serve as a bodyguard detail, repel an armed attack, or conduct a hostage rescue. Don't trust functions of that level of importance to untrained employees.

If you need to equip such a force, you will need to consult with local authorities relative to the nature of the proposed guard unit and any legal limitations local law will put on them. Often there exist legal restrictions on the types of weapons that may be used, even by authorized individuals, in the host country. Restrictions may be placed on the caliber and type of weapons you can consider. If you can select weapons for your security staff, we suggest the following.

Most law enforcement agencies have adopted the Glock pistol as the standard sidearm for their police officers. Both of us favor the Glock because of its simple design, ease of handling, and reliability. Qualified instructors can teach individuals to become acceptably proficient in the use of Glock pistols in a relatively short period of time. In the United States, the trend in law enforcement is toward the .40 caliber Glock pistol. This represents an upgrade from the 9 mm cartridge more common abroad. Either caliber is acceptable. Overseas, however, you will find .40 caliber ammunition difficult to obtain.

Unquestionably the world's leader in the production of shoulder weapons is the firm Heckler & Koch. Virtually every elite tactical team in the world uses their products. The 9 mm MP-5 is still the mainstay for units seeking a compact submachine gun. However, in our estimation, shoulder weapons should fire, at a minimum, a rifle round such as the .223 caliber (5.56 mm). If your facility is attacked, it will not be by terrorists using handguns. The bad guys use rifles and so must your security force if it is to provide a strong deterrent.

NOTES

1. U.S. Department of Justice, Office of Justice Programs, National Institute of Justice, *Selection and Application Guide to Police Body Armor,* NIJ Guide 100-87.
2. Ibid., p. 40.
3. *Ballistic Resistance of Body Armor.* NIJ Standard 0101.3, section 3.5.
4. U.S. Department of Justice, Federal Bureau of Investigation, Uniform Crime Report, 2002.
5. NIJ Guide 100-87, pp. 38–39.

CHAPTER 10

Countersurveillance

MOST TERRORIST OPERATIONS ARE NOT CONDUCTED at random or haphazardly. Virtually all terrorist attacks are preceded by a preoperational stage where intelligence is gathered about the intended target. Typically, terrorists compile lists of potential targets that they believe will further their political goals. Potential targets include military installations, economic centers, civilian population centers, and selected individuals. Many of their targets are selected for their country of origin, with citizens of the United States and Israel being the most desirable. The exact selection procedure itself is unclear. One thing that is clear, however, is the fact that terrorists do not commit resources to an attack until they have acquired extensive information relative to the likely success or failure of a strike—even small-scale operations like an individual assassination or kidnapping. Basically, they are conducting the terrorist equivalent of a feasibility study.

The tragic murder of Lawrence Foley, an American diplomat in Amman, Jordan, on October 27, 2002, provides an unfortunate reminder of this fact. Mr. Foley was shot to death as he left his home. According to an Associated Press wire service report, he had been under surveillance by his assailants for some time before they struck. The report quoted a Jordanian police official who stated, "The killing appeared to have been carried out by professionals who had been following Foley for some time to determine his schedule." As this crime occurred during the writing of this book, we do not have any further information as to this claim. However, certain things may be reasonably inferred from the event and historical precedent. Mr. Foley was a career diplomat. He was 60 years old and was a senior administrator for USAID (United States Agency for International Development). His current duties involved helping the Jordanian people develop projects that were for the sole benefit of the citizens of Jordan. What possible motivation would a terror group have in killing such a man, apart from the fact that he was an American diplomat? The answer is, most likely, that they had no specific reason for murdering Mr. Foley. In all probability, the goal of the cowardly terrorists was to kill anyone associated with the embassy of the United States. Over the course of time, the terrorists conducted surveillance of embassy personnel and selected a target based on the opportunity he afforded. This means they would be looking for a target with a regular and predictable schedule; someone without a security detail and who did not appear to be overtly conscious of the presence of surveillance. Mr. Foley, quite simply, was murdered because the terrorists felt that attacking him would expose them to the lowest level of risk.

As we mentioned in the introduction to this book, a radical Islamic website has published a guide titled "How to Kidnap American Citizens." A large section of this "guide" is spent discussing the ways in which intelligence may be gathered on prospective targets before an attempt is made. This "gathering of information" refers to physical surveillance of the intended victim. Terrorists will spend months and even years researching their targets and potential methods for attack. They have become quite adept at doing their homework. They use the Internet extensively to search for photographs and building blueprints. They access public documents. They pay for information in much the same way as our government and law enforcement agencies pay informants. However, there is no substitute for getting direct information and ascertaining the facts on the ground. Extensive use of surveillance is an integral part of this process of intelligence gathering. Terrorists use many of the same methods as do those in the law enforcement and intelligence communities. They rent apartments with a direct line of sight to a potential target. They photograph and follow potential targets of a kidnapping or assassination. Common criminals also conduct a type of surveillance, although on a far less elaborate scale. Such criminals who are contemplating a burglary will watch the location first, sometimes for only minutes or sometimes for several months. In law enforcement terms, this is referred to as "casing" a prospective target. Some criminal organizations and individuals conduct extensive surveillance of individuals or locations for purely criminal purposes.

You will recall from an earlier chapter our mention of some organized criminal groups in Russia that stake out the Moscow airport looking for affluent foreigners to victimize. Typically, one or more individuals on foot watch passengers as they deplane. It isn't very difficult to identify those with money, especially those who ignore the general rule about not appearing too flashy or well to do. Someone working at the airport may do the foot surveillance. Flight attendants, who have a great deal of time during a long flight, may even be the ones making the initial evaluation of the target's potential value. It is then a simple matter of following the subject to the hotel. A local taxi driver may be directed to pick up that person; thus the group will know exactly where he or she is staying without multiple car surveillance. In any event, the person has been identified as a target for robbery. The goal may be to wait several days until the person goes out on the town and then conduct a simple mugging. Or perhaps the criminals will just identify the hotel and room, wait for the person to go out, and then enter the unoccupied room and steal whatever valuables have been left there. In any case, the same principles of surveillance detection apply whether the perpetrators are terrorists or common criminals.

SURVEILLANCE IS COMMONPLACE

Surveillance of Americans and Western Europeans living, working, or even traveling abroad has long been common. Frequently it has been associated with surveillance conducted by the foreign intelligence officers looking for activities inconsistent with the subject's stated reason for being in the country. While this is still true, more recently terrorists and common criminals conduct surveillance in advance of an attack or criminal act.

Because of this reality, the State Department provides a short block of instruction on countersurveillance for government employees overseas as part of the Security Overseas Seminar. In addition, the State Department also has recognized the importance of educating nongovernmental employees abroad. To this end, the State Department has published a document entitled *Security Guidelines for Americans Working Overseas*. It provides a great deal of valuable information, including the importance of being aware of your surroundings in order to become aware of possible surveillance. While this is good advice, the document devotes only two pages to the subject of target recognition and provides few specific details about exactly how this should be done. Common methods of surveillance and the things that you might observe that would indicate that you are being targeted are not explained.

WHAT IS SURVEILLANCE?

What exactly is surveillance? Surveillance is really nothing more than gathering information, generally from physical observation or the interception of telephone, fax, and e-mail or radio communication. The specific purpose of surveillance is to compile intelligence relative to the movements, associates, and activities of the target of the surveillance. In law enforcement, the purpose of surveillance is to acquire evidence or intelligence, usually to support a criminal prosecution of the subject. In special circumstances, law enforcement does not use surveillance as an end to a prosecution but rather to amass intelligence information on suspected foreign agents, organized crime, or other subversive domestic groups. Terrorists and/or criminals conduct surveillance as a prelude to committing a crime or terrorist attack.

Surveillance can be conducted in several ways. There is both physical surveillance and technical surveillance. Physical surveillance generally refers to watching the movement and activities of the subject of the surveillance. The surveillance can either be mobile or stationary but is generally both. Mobile surveillance refers to actively following someone on foot, in a vehicle, or both. The purpose is to track subjects' movements: determine where they go, routes of travel, what they do, and whom they meet. A stationary surveillance refers to a fixed location from where the surveillant can watch the subject. It may be done from an adjacent building, a parked vehicle, or even from a fixed position on foot.

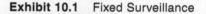

Exhibit 10.1   Fixed Surveillance

Exhibit 10.1 shows a typical setup for a fixed surveillance point using a parked car as the "point" or "eyeball." Notice the number of intervening cars between the target and surveillance vehicle. This gap makes it less

likely that the target will detect the surveillant's presence. The curvature of the street also works to the advantage of the surveillant as it allows for the observation of the entire driver's side of the vehicle from a position of cover. Notice also that this street is one-way only. The point vehicle needs only to alert other surveillance operatives that the subject is in the vehicle and is departing. Other units can be waiting farther along the subject's known or anticipated route in order to pick up the mobile surveillance away from the subject's residence.

DETECTING SURVEILLANCE

Let's discuss the common ways that you may be followed or otherwise become subject to surveillance. By understanding the technique, you will become sensitive to what to look for and be able to detect all but the most sophisticated attempts at surveillance.

How do you know if you are being followed? The first thing to be mindful of is your level of awareness. If you are wandering around in condition white (see color code definitions in Chapter 2), you will be oblivious to the presence of even the most ineptly run surveillance. Pay attention to your surroundings. That is the single most important thing to do. The central rule in detecting whether you are the subject of surveillance is: *If you see the same individual or vehicle, separated by time and distance, at least three times, you can assume you are being followed.*

Surveillance is an art, not a science. Its object is to observe someone without being detected. The greater the skill of the individual or individuals conducting the surveillance, the more difficult it will be to realize that they are there. We will discuss a physical, mobile surveillance first— following someone, either on foot or in a vehicle. A discussion of this technique will make you understand the point about surveillance being an art. It will also give you a basic understanding of standard surveillance techniques.

METHODS OF SURVEILLANCE

Let's assume for a moment that you are the subject of terrorists' surveillance. Perhaps you are a prominent businessperson and have been selected as a possible target for a kidnapping. They decide to follow you to evaluate your level of security and select the best time and place to grab you. If you have been following the advice given thus far, you should appear quite alert and aware of what's going on around you. As mentioned earlier, this fact in and of itself may persuade the bad guys to look for an easier target. But say they begin to follow you. Typically, the surveillance will begin from a location that they associate with you. If their intelligence has allowed them to identify your residence, they might begin from there. If not, then they are likely to try to get to you from your place of business. The initial stage of the surveillance would begin with someone watching you from a stationary point—perhaps inside a car parked down the street from your home or from an apartment nearby that offers them a good vantage point from which to observe you. Remember, they do not need to be physically close to you. By using a decent pair of binoculars, they can stay quite a distance away if they have a clear field of vision. If your home, for example, is located in an area where there is only one road that you can possibly take, they don't even need to watch you at your home. They can station someone at an intersection that you must pass and begin the surveillance from there. Incidentally, this stage offers you your first opportunity to detect their presence. Even if you have only lived in a place for a short while, you will begin to focus in on things that seem unusual or out of place. An unfamiliar vehicle, for example, parked on your street might be an indication that you are being watched.

Assume you enter your vehicle and begin to drive somewhere. If you are being followed and you are cognizant of your surroundings, you will have your second chance to pick up on their presence. Doing so will depend to a great extent on the number of people following you and their level of skill. Remember, surveillance is an art. The bad guys need to see you while attempting to avoid being observed in turn.

The easiest surveillance to detect is single-unit surveillance, especially if the person following you is not particularly adept. You drive down your street. Immediately, a car that was parked along your block starts up and pulls into traffic behind you. If the person is operating alone, he or she will need to keep you in sight at all times. The car will stay behind you and match your speed. When you turn, the car will turn. If the person tailing you is completely inept, he or she will "lock on your bumper"—be right behind you at all times. If you change lanes, the other car will as well. Obviously this type of behavior should be easy for you to notice. You look into your side and rearview mirrors and mentally note who is behind you. If a vehicle makes more than a few moves that match yours, then it is time to pay closer attention to it. It is easy to confirm whether a vehicle is following you or not by doing a few simple things. We discuss those techniques below.

A lone individual attempting to follow you may be more successful if he or she is skillful at surveillance. A competent person will not lock on your bumper but will stay behind you at a discreet distance. The person will follow you from an offset position rather than to your rear. For example, say you are on a highway traveling in the left lane. The surveillance vehicle is behind you, a few cars back, shielded by other vehicles in the right lane. The driver can observe you, and you are less likely to pick the tail up when the car is not directly behind you. If you begin to change lanes and prepare to exit, the person is perfectly positioned in the right lane to turn off without changing lanes and then follow you onto the ramp (see Exhibit 10.2).

Exhibit 10.2   Point Vehicle Following from the Offset Position

TEAM SURVEILLANCE TECHNIQUES

The preferred technique of mobile surveillance is the use of a multiple vehicle surveillance team rather than a single car. Here's how it typically works. You leave your home. An individual in a stationary spot alerts the other team members that you are on the move. As you begin to drive, someone in the stationary vehicle radios your vehicle description and direction to the rest of the team. A second car can then easily pull in behind you in a fluid and unobtrusive way. The rest of the team members follow at a distance and prepare to assume the point position, as directed by the individual leading the surveillance. For example, say you are driving your vehicle down a busy street. In traffic, it is easy for someone following you to blend in with the other cars on the road and avoid detection. Suppose, however, that you make a turn onto a small and lightly trafficked road. The lead car may turn with you and maintain the point. However, now you are driving in a quiet area with little traffic. It becomes easier for you to notice a car following you, so the lead car's driver becomes more cautious. The lead car will stay with you until the driver feels the need to break off to avoid detection. Perhaps the lead will stay in contact until you are ready to make a turn. Now the lead car must choose whether to turn with you again or not. If the lead car decides to break off you to avoid being detected, the driver then radios the next car in line (commonly called the alternate) and tells it to make the turn. The lead car goes straight and a new vehicle with a different face behind the wheel assumes the point position. This procedure is repeated frequently, with surveillance cars switching off to avoid having the same car follow for too long.

The more cars that are used, the harder it is to spot their presence. Harder, yes, but certainly not impossible. How can you pick up on the presence of surveillance vehicles if multiple vehicles are used? There are several ways. First, if you pay attention to the cars around you, you may notice the same car reappearing behind you at regular intervals. Remember, this technique is only as good as its operators. For example, one member of the surveillance team may linger with you for too long because his or her alternate is caught too far back in traffic to help out. The team has alternates but one car is forced to remain the lead car. The driver may lock bumpers or take too many turns with you because he or she has to or else risk losing contact with you. If this happens, you will have the opportunity to pick up on the surveillance.

Other group surveillance methods require a higher level of training and a larger number of surveillance vehicles. For this reason these methods are more likely to be utilized by professional intelligence officers or specialized police units. These techniques are used by premier American law enforcement agencies such as the Drug Enforcement Administration (DEA) and Federal Bureau of Investigation (FBI). Agencies or groups that are superbly trained will use advance vehicles, chase cars with multiple alternates, stationary surveillance points, and cars running along parallel streets.

The system shown in Exhibit 10.3 is extremely effective because prepositioned vehicles cover every possible route that the target can take.

The wide coverage makes it unnecessary to take turns with the target. Think about it; if you are driving and there is one car behind that mirrors your movements, you will take notice. Poorly trained teams or individuals use this technique and allow you to identify their presence quite rapidly. Trained teams make identification much more difficult because they keep placing different cars behind you. It is even more difficult if the team members can stage themselves in positions along your route and

Exhibit 10.3   Moving Box Surveillance

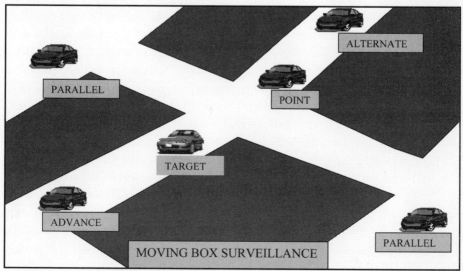

simply alert other team members by radio that you have just passed a particular location. Teams using 6 to 10 cars will be hard to detect. If a team augments its surveillance with electronic tracking devices, it may be almost impossible to detect. However, once again, all it takes is a little human error to blow the whole surveillance. You still have an advantage because you know what is usual for your surroundings. Keep alert. Remember the rule: If you see the same car or individual three times separated by time and distance, you are being followed. Again, it is difficult, if not impossible, to conceive of terrorists or common criminals using some of the more sophisticated surveillance techniques. If you are the subject of an elaborate and well-trained surveillance team, it is far more likely that you are being targeted by the host country's intelligence service.

The next type of mobile surveillance is foot surveillance. Again, your ability to detect the presence of security is contingent on many factors.

How many people are on the street? Is there anything particular about the appearance of the person following you? Unusual dress or physical characteristics will obviously help you figure out that you are being followed. You would be far more likely to observe Dennis Rodman following you than you would Dennis Franz. By the way, this cuts both ways. Remember the advice in Chapter 2 about dressing and behaving conservatively? If you are sporting pink hair, you are not exactly going to blend in. That is, unless you are in certain neighborhoods in Los Angeles, New York, or London.

Foot surveillance techniques can closely follow the techniques used in a mobile surveillance. A team is more effective than a single-person surveillance operation. One person follows on foot, not too closely behind you. The person may be following in an offset fashion by walking behind you on the other side of the street. When you turn, the tail does not but rather allows the alternate to pick you up. Once again, the technique is only as good as the individual operative's skill level. The exact same mistakes that allow you to identify a mobile surveillance hold true on foot. It is also likely that anyone following you will need to remain in radio contact with the other team members still in their respective vehicles. Years ago, agents in law enforcement agencies like the DEA and FBI used miniature microphones either clipped inside their lapel or built in to an earpiece, allowing the operative to use the same piece of equipment to transmit and listen to the response or other radio traffic. Today, with the prevalence of cell phones, it is no longer necessary to use clandestine microphones to transmit while following someone on foot. It is commonplace to see people walking down the street and talking on their cell phones. This will not be something that will catch your attention. However, if the cell phone activity is coupled with other patterns of behavior consistent with someone conducting surveillance, it may indicate that you are being followed by a team using both vehicular and foot surveillance techniques.

TECHNICAL SURVEILLANCE

The most effective surveillance is conducted by combining physical surveillance techniques with technical surveillance. This allows for the most complete acquisition of information with the lowest probability of detection. Surveillance conducted in this manner by a professional and well-trained team can be extremely difficult to detect and defeat.

Technical surveillance is a broad term that refers to the use of electronic or optical equipment to gather information. The range of such equipment is vast, including cameras, listening devices (bugs), tracking transmitters, infrared and microwave radiation, parabolic microphones, cell phone tracking, and wiretapping. While these devices do not replace the need for physical surveillance, they certainly provide a substantial addition to the effort. The use of eavesdropping equipment, for example, can allow people to gather information that would otherwise have been impossible. The use of a simple video camera can allow a particular location to be monitored by a signal transmitted to a point remote from the actual site of the surveillance. Generally, both stationary and mobile surveillance techniques are used in tandem. However, if the subject appears to be surveillance conscious—that is, takes precautions to avoid being followed—then a stationary surveillance method may be used exclusively. This method also may be utilized quite effectively with technical surveillance techniques such as a wiretap.

Let us assume that a stationary surveillance is set up on the residence of Subject A in conjunction with a wiretap on Subject A's phone. The wiretap intercepts a call where Subject A arranges to meet someone at a particular location later that day. Stationary surveillance may then be set up at the location of the anticipated meeting. This technique avoids the necessity of following Subject A from his or her residence to the meet location. Where possible, the goal of the surveillance would be to follow Subject A. That would allow the surveillance team to see where Subject A went before the meeting. Perhaps Subject A went to another location and removed a package that would be transferred at the meeting. A thorough surveillance technique would try to see if that is, in fact, what happened.

It is quite common in the DEA and other law enforcement agencies to keep a subject under constant surveillance even while a wiretap is operative. The telephonic intercepts may not provide all the information that is needed. For example, in the case of narcotics law enforcement, a wiretap may reveal that the subject is going to meet someone to conduct a drug transaction. If the subject is a supplier, for example, it may be clear from the intercepted conversations that he or she is going to deliver a large quantity of drugs to a customer. It is common for drug dealers to keep their supply of narcotics in a safe location known as a stash house. If the location of the stash house is unknown and it is believed that the subject will go there before the meeting, surveillance will try to follow the subject from the residence to find where the drugs are being stored. If those following you believe you are going to stop somewhere of interest to them, they will combine a wiretap with a full-court surveillance, meaning they will combine the technical surveillance with an aggressive physical surveillance. Remember, tapping a phone is far easier in many countries than it is in the United States. In addition, it is not all that difficult to place a transmitter in a vehicle or other location to eavesdrop on your conversations. Cell phone and cordless phone calls can be intercepted with simple equipment available at Radio Shack.

Surveillance is frequently augmented with video cameras and micro-wave transmitters. This is a bit high tech for the average criminal or poorly trained terrorist, but it is certainly within the grasp of well-funded and well-trained terror groups. Needless to say, if you are being targeted by an intelligence service of a foreign country, expect them to rely heavily on such devices. It is also quite easy to place tracking devices on your vehicle, which gives the opposition the luxury of being able to track your movements without needing to put a physical surveillance team on you. Actually, that is not entirely accurate. It is still important to keep a surveillance team on the subject even when tracking devices, or "bird dogs," are being used. The advantage to using a tracking device is that it allows the team to keep well behind the target. The device will provide the team with the target's direction. By measuring the signal strength, the team will gain a rough estimate of how far ahead the subject is. Some of the better devices, including those that make use of cell phone cell sites or the global positioning satellite (GPS) system, actually provide information that seems like it came from something "Q" developed for James Bond. These units actually can place the target on a map accurately to within several feet. They also can measure the target's direction of travel and speed, and show which intersection he or she is approaching. Obviously the use of this level of technology makes detection all but impossible. That is the bad news. The good news is that it is extremely unlikely that any terrorist cell, no matter how well funded it is, will have this type of equipment. And even if the terrorists do have such equipment, there is always the human factor to consider. A mistake by surveillance operatives can compromise even the most elaborate operations. In fact, even a competent team keeping mistakes to a minimum can be observed and compromised by an alert subject. In law enforcement parlance this is referred to as "burning the surveillance" or simply "getting burnt."

What should you do if you believe you're being followed or monitored? The general rule is to avoid making it obvious to those watching you that you are aware of their presence. This is recommended for a number of reasons, the first being your own personal safety. We certainly recommend that you appear to be an alert and cautious person to anyone trying to follow you. You will remember the story of the army sergeant in Chapter 2 who was crossed off a terrorist hit list because he seemed to be surveillance conscious. Being aware may very well mark you as a difficult target, and you may be passed over for an easier subject. However, if you do detect surveillance, here are a few pointers:

- Do not change your routine. Continue about your business.
- Stay in well-lit and populated areas only.
- Do not stare at the people following you or attempt evasion unless you have reason to believe an attack on you is imminent.
- Calmly proceed to a safe haven like the U.S. embassy (or an embassy of a friendly nation), a hospital, or a police station.
- Contact the Regional Security Officer as soon as possible.

The reason not to show that you are aware that you are being followed is that you do not know how they will react. Therefore, it is prudent not to provoke any reaction. It is conceivable—not likely, but possible—that you are being followed in order to be assassinated. Any action you take may cause those following you to attempt to kill you rather than allowing you to escape. Perhaps you are being followed by the country's intelligence service or by local police. Alerting them to the fact that you have become aware of their activities may cause an unwelcome reaction. You may be taken into custody for interrogation or you may receive a beating. A friend of ours works as an agent for the Diplomatic Security Service. He has stories about other agents finding surveillance devices in hotel rooms they were staying in while in Russia. More than a few agents tore out such devices only to have their clothing or tires slashed later in response. The message being delivered is "You know the game and you need to play by the rules." Go about your business and remain calm.

What is the correct response when you realize that you are being followed? The U.S. State Department recommends that you contact the embassy or consulate immediately. We both agree with this approach. There is really no other option under these circumstances. The embassy regional security officer will decide whether the local authorities need to be notified or whether to handle it in-house. This decision will depend on several factors, most important of which is the level of mutual cooperation between the embassy and local authorities. In some countries, the relationship is less than cooperative, and, as mentioned, it may well be that the local police or intelligence agencies are the ones following you. This is particularly true in many developing nations, where corruption is rampant and the police sometimes are working for the bad guys. The embassy will know whether that is likely and will proceed accordingly.

How can you check for the presence of people following you? Remember, your goal is to identify that you are being followed without tipping your hand. During David's tenure with the DEA, he participated in hundreds of surveillance operations. Sometimes the surveillance would get burnt. Targets wouldn't do anything to tip their hand but later would confide to an informant or an associate on a wiretapped line that they were being followed. Occasionally a bad guy would write down a license plate number and get a Department of Motor Vehicles (DMV) check done on it. DEA vehicles were "flagged" with the local DMV, and the state authorities would notify the agency if someone ran the plates. On rare occasions a target would try to confront a surveillance agent or simply wave, acknowledging the agent's presence. The object for our purposes is to figure out that you are being followed without the surveillance team realizing that you have observed them.

Many techniques are effective for picking up the presence of people following you. Counterespionage schools and schools specifically designed to teach criminals to watch out for surveillance exist. Years ago, Colombian cocaine traffickers began mandating that their workers abroad attend these schools to prevent them from getting arrested in possession of million of dollars in cash or drugs. In schools operated by expatriate Americans, Cubans, Israelis, and Russians, students were trained to drive in a manner designed to frustrate surveillance.

The premise of these techniques is actually quite simple: Do things that are unusual and see if anyone does the same thing. For example, one such technique is called "squaring the block." Drive to an intersection and turn right (or left). Drive to the next intersection and make another right (or left). Repeat the process twice more, and you are back where you started, going in the same direction. This is generally an unusual move to make. Look in your rearview mirror. Is anyone doing the same thing? If so, you may be being followed.

Another method is to drive into a store parking lot and see who follows you in. Does the same vehicle leave when you do? (Remember that if multiple vehicles are used, someone else in another vehicle may follow you out.) If you are on a highway, try to vary your speed. Does anyone seem to slow down or speed up with you? By the way, one of the most effective ways to compromise surveillance is by driving on a highway *below* the posted limit. In point of fact, most people routinely break the speed limit. If you are driving at an almost painfully slow speed, most people will pass you. See who does not. It is very difficult to slow down enough to stay behind someone under those conditions. Surveillance operatives often have the lead car pass and exit the highway when possible. The alternate stays comfortably back to allow for distance to be eaten up slowly if it must eventually pass the subject. The more effective method is to use a helicopter to stay with a subject looking for "a tail." Another effective method is to use tracking devices. If the folks on you are this sophisticated, then you have a problem.

Use your rear- and side-view mirrors. Notice cars around you, especially cars that seem to mirror your movements. If you are able, jot down their license plate numbers. Pay attention, and detecting surveillance is not all that difficult to do. Remember, your goal is to detect the presence of surveillance without doing anything to indicate that you are aware that you are being followed. There are many more aggressive ways to "burn" surveillance. Let your tail follow you down a one-way street. Radically change speed or change lanes repeatedly. Exit a highway and then immediately reenter back onto the same road. Double back along your route. There are many other such methods that, while they are very likely to reveal whether you are being followed, you should avoid. You need to be very low key and select only those techniques that don't advertise the fact that you are checking to see if you are being followed.

While you are being followed, you are at risk. Stay calm, try to confirm your suspicions, and do nothing to confront or antagonize the people who are tailing you. You have the advantage as long as the bad guys believe they are still invisible. Once they realize that you know they are there, they can change from surveillance to assault, if that is their ultimate purpose.

If you find yourself the subject of surveillance, you need to start to "what-if" the situation. If you are attacked, where can you go for help? How far is it to the embassy or consulate? Are the local police likely to assist you?

The first and best choice, when possible, is to drive immediately to the embassy, where you will be safe and where you can speak with the regional security officer or a subordinate. That person will advise you what to do and will notify whatever local authorities he or she deems appropriate. If the officer believes that you are in imminent danger, he or she will assist you in safely leaving the country if necessary.

CHAPTER 11

Receipt of Mail and Packages

FOR NUMEROUS REASONS, TERRORISTS HAVE LONG USED attacks via the mail or other package delivery systems. The mail allows for the attack to be delivered by unwitting third parties, while the attacker remains safely anonymous. Letter and package bombs have claimed hundreds of lives and maimed hundreds more all over the world. One individual or a group of individuals can target multiple subjects in widely disparate areas without risking capture. In the case of explosives, the detonation not only causes injury to the person opening the package but also results in partial or complete destruction of the evidence. The packages often find their way directly to the intended target and, if well concealed, are impossible to detect until it is too late. Furthermore, terrorists are not the only ones to use this method to attempt to kill or injure others. Disgruntled employees, deranged individuals, and even jilted lovers have been responsible for many such attacks.

Cases involving the use of the mail system for terror are usually difficult and require a long time, even many years, to solve. Remember the Unabomber case. The bomber, Ted Kaczynski, terrorized the country for years, sending bombs to unsuspecting victims in order to promote his bizarre agenda. Simple investigation did not lead to his capture. After years of fruitless attempts to solve the case, the Federal Bureau of Investigation (FBI) behavioral scientists agreed to one of the bomber's demands, to publish his "Unabomber manifesto" in the national press. The FBI, armed with an extensive psychological profile of the subject, gambled that someone would recognize the content or style in the manifesto and alert the police. This is exactly what happened; Kaczynski's brother turned him in after reading the published piece. The recent anthrax scare has yet to be solved. Five people died as a result of exposure to anthrax spores sent through the mail. While their deaths were tragic, the number of dead could have been much greater. This type of attack will continue to be used to inflict terror for as long as there is a system of mail delivery.

BASIC PROTECTIVE MEASURES

How can individuals protect themselves against this type of attack? Within the borders of the United States, there are postal inspectors dedicated to helping police the mail system. The government is working hard to procure the necessary technical equipment to monitor the mail and detect explosives, poisons, or biohazards before they are delivered. While you are living overseas, unless you live in a country like Israel, such safeguards are unlikely. Once again, you are left with the necessity of taking personal responsibility for safeguarding yourself from attacks that use this delivery system.

Let's talk about some of the basic commonsense measures that are the first level of defense against a letter attack. First of all, while living abroad you should make every effort not to receive mail, packages, or deliveries at home. We discuss the issue of deliveries later on, but whenever possible, have mail and packages delivered to an alternate location, such as your place of business. For government employees this is automatic. Each member of the embassy staff uses the Army Post Office (APO) as a mailing address. Mail is scanned with x-rays and, in some cases, explosive detection equipment and is sorted within the embassy. The mailroom staff is trained in proper handling procedures and is better able to identify suspicious items. However, individuals in the private sector do not have the luxury of having trained governmental employees screen their mail. Private industry is beginning to realize just how vulnerable it is to this type of attack and has begun to address some of these issues in private mailrooms. We encourage this trend. If, during a threat assessment, we see flaws in a company's mail-handling procedures, we design company-specific measures to fix them. Still, companies are slow to implement necessary security changes. And, unfortunately, security is often ratcheted up after an attack occurs but usually slackens as the memory of the incident fades. As a result, each individual needs to be his or her own safety inspector.

Most of the measures dealing with the receipt of mail and packages are based on common sense. First rule; trust your instincts. They usually are right. If you get an item that for any reason seems suspicious or makes you uncomfortable, *do not open it.* Carefully place it aside and calmly consider your options. (We discuss what those options are below.)

The easiest way to separate mail is to look at the return address. A letter or parcel from a familiar sender is not a threat (with the possible exception of an ex-wife or ex-husband). The same is true regarding expected packages. For example, if you order something from the Eddie Bauer catalog and two weeks later you receive a package from Eddie Bauer, it is safe to assume that the package is legitimate and you don't need to call the embassy to x-ray the package. You can include most periodicals and other items that you subscribe to in the same "safe" category. Those are the easy items. Now what about the rest? For example, you receive a box with a return address that is unfamiliar to you. You don't recall ordering anything so you pay a bit more attention to the type of package. You notice it is from a U.S. location and a company name is on the box. So you call information in the United States or check the Internet to get the name of this company and its number. If you learn that it is something that your spouse ordered and forgot to tell you about, you have solved the mystery.

What types of mail or packages should set off alarm bells and have you calling the embassy for guidance?

The best set of general guidelines has been set forth by the United States Postal Service. Few people realize that the Postal Service has its own investigative division of armed postal inspectors. Many of these inspectors are experts in recognizing explosive devices disguised as letters or packages. Below is a listing of some of the recommendations of the Postal Service and other governmental agencies about how to detect a mail bomb.

Restrictive Endorsement

A mail bomb may include the words "Private" or "Personal" or "To be opened by addressee only." The reason for this is obvious. The bomber wishes to ensure that the intended victim, not the secretary in the office or someone else at home, opens the package and thereby sets off the explosive. This is particularly significant if the package comes to the office where the addressee is not in the habit of receiving personal mail. Other wordings, such as "Fragile," "Rush," or "Handle with Care," are also common in mail bombs.

Suspicious Lettering on the Envelope

Obviously, if the envelope is addressed with letters clipped from a newspaper or magazine, you will pay attention to it. That is unusual enough to get anyone to notice. Equally as significant, though a bit more subtle, may be the incorrect spelling of the name and/or title of the addressee. In addition, the handwriting may be distorted or smudged.

Return Address

The return address may be nonexistent or fictitious, or the return address may be delivering a message as well. For example, an industrialist accused of releasing toxic substances into the environment might receive a letter with a cemetery plot as a return address. This type of return address is particularly significant and should cause your alarm bells to work double time.

Physical Signs

A package or letter containing an explosive may have protruding wires, aluminum foil, or oil stains. The package itself may feel stiff and look lopsided. It may have an excessive amount of wrapping and an obviously irregular shape. The package may feel as if it has liquid sloshing around. Mail bombs generally also have excessive postage. There may be a strange odor coming from the package or even an electronic buzz. A ticking sound from inside the package is more common in cartoons, but if that type of sound is coming from a letter or package, and you are not expecting a mail order cuckoo clock, don't open it.

Postmark

Check the postmark and compare it with the return address. There should be a general correlation between the two. For example, if the return address says John Smith, 123 Main Street, Anyplace USA, and the postmark is from Yemen, you might want to think twice.

Contents Difficult to Remove

Once you open the package, you may feel some pressure as you are removing the contents. This might be indicative of the triggering device pressing against the inside of the container. Once the contents are removed, the pressure holding the trigger down is released and detonation occurs.

DOS AND DON'TS

What do you do if you receive a package or letter that you suspect may contain a bomb or hazardous substance? The first thing to do is remain calm to allow yourself to think clearly. In case it is not obvious, *DO NOT OPEN THE ITEM*. Similarly, do not attempt to open a portion of the package and try to observe the contents. If it is a bomb or biological weapon, any tampering may cause it to detonate or release the toxic substance. Put the package or letter down in an open area. Do not place it in a drawer, cabinet, or other confined space. By confining the object, you can actually enhance the explosive force. Also, if flammable or explosive gases are leaking from the object, you need to allow for as much ventilation as possible. If the package is put into a small space, the concentration of the gases may quickly reach what is termed an "explosive atmosphere." Isolate the item and open the windows. This will allow the dangerous gases to vent and lessen the chance of explosion.

Do not submerge the object in water. Many chemicals explode on contact with water. In any event, water will probably not disable the device anyway. Water may short out electronic detonators with unfortunate results. Leave the package unmolested and evacuate the area. If you are in a country with an efficient and trustworthy police force, contact them. Otherwise, contact the embassy or consulate and ask for instructions.

DELIVERIES AT HOME

The issue of package delivery presents other issues to deal with as well. Apart from the potential for danger in a delivered package, there is also the possibility of being assaulted by the delivery person. By the way, this is true for anyone unknown that you open your door for: repairmen, inspectors, or installers of any kind. Ordinary criminals pose as individuals for whom you would normally open the door. In the United States, thousands of people are robbed, raped, or worse every year because they open their doors for people they don't know. Overseas you are at a greater disadvantage. In the United States, you at least have an idea what the person reading the gas meter should look like. Abroad you probably will have no idea. Americans know that the FedEx delivery person will be driving a marked truck and be in uniform. Even in the United States, where official mail carriers use personal vehicles, they will still be in uniform. If they are not, you need to ask a lot of questions before opening the door. What is the standard uniform and vehicle for delivery people in Thailand? What about Jordan, Malaysia, or Russia? This is why you should avoid receiving deliveries at home. Get them at work. If they must be delivered to the home, always make sure that you are expecting a delivery before opening the door. If not, with the door closed, ask the delivery person for his or her office number and verify whether the individual is legitimate. Do not accept deliveries if you don't know who sent them and certainly don't open the door for anyone you are not expecting. Always ask to see identification and ask for the number of their employer.

RECEIPT OF MAIL AND PACKAGES AT THE OFFICE

As we mentioned before, you should try, if at all possible, to have your mail and parcels delivered to you at work. This generally will reduce the danger of you being victimized by someone gaining entry to your home by posing as a delivery person. But how can you avoid having a mail bomb or letter containing a biohazard from smoothly passing through the office mailroom and getting delivered to you at your desk? Is there a way to make office mailrooms your first line of defense to protect against this type of attack?

The answer, of course, is yes. You just need to systematically apply the commonsense steps you would take at home to the office. In combination with policy and procedures to handle mail properly, mailroom employees need to be taught what to look for and how to determine which items get delivered immediately, which need greater scrutiny, and which get rejected. Businesses are more likely to be able to afford technical equipment that will allow for rapid assessment of a suspicious package. Items such as X-ray machines and explosives detection equipment are available and may be purchased for the mailroom. All of the companies that manufacture this type of equipment provide instruction to their customers in the field. They will train your staff in the proper use of the machines and enable them to detect threats that would be otherwise impossible to observe. In addition, it is also possible, and relatively inexpensive, to separate the air space in the mailroom from the building's ventilation system. This will prevent the contamination of the entire facility in the case of an attack with a hazardous chemical or biohazard such as anthrax. Exposure would be contained and would not spread beyond the mailroom. This precaution may be implemented quickly, and it dramatically reduces the number of individuals exposed in the event of such an attack. If you are an executive in your firm, you should make it a priority to establish such a plan in your place of business. If you're not an executive or manager, you need to bring this issue to the attention of management or the appropriate decision maker.

We have included a basic mailroom protocol to assist you in understanding the steps to be taken to properly secure your mail facility. However, implementation of an effective screening system requires a comprehensive methodology tailored to the unique needs of your facility. In addition, the system is only as good as the people operating it. Laziness, incompetence, poor training, and human error can cause the system to fail. Therefore, a truly effective screening system also should include personnel selection criteria, training guidelines, and an ongoing evaluation process. It also should provide a mechanism for reporting and correcting lapses and failures. Exhibit 11.2 is a sample mailroom screening protocol.

Remember, sometimes a package will display several of the warning signs listed in the exhibit; sometimes it will display only one or two. Sometimes bombers are cognizant enough of screening procedures to pack a bomb or biohazard bearing none of the warning signs. As a general rule, however, there will be at least some indication that the package or letter deserves to be given a greater level of scrutiny. Exhibit 11.1 shows an otherwise innocuous-looking package bearing a restrictive endorsement. Notice,

Exhibit 11.1   Innocent-Looking Package Requiring Special Handling Procedures

Exhibit 11.2   Mailroom Protocol

General

Letter or package bomb incidents have occurred at businesses, universities, government offices and installations, and private residences. The motivation for this kind of attack could include revenge, insurance fraud, and political or environmental terrorism directed against a person or organization.

Using Mail as Bomb Delivery Method

Mail or package service can be a desirable tactic for terrorists or criminals for several reasons:

- Sending a bomb through the mail allows the attacker to strike a specific target from a distance.
- The mail or package can reach any target at any time.
- The attack is delivered by an unwitting participant—the postman or parcel delivery person.
- It is very difficult to identify a suspicious item; it may appear to look like any other piece of mail.

All of these factors make a mail attack desirable as there is a reduced risk of capture and increased probability in the success of the attack.

Create a Plan

The main goal of a mail bomb security plan is to detect the weaponized letter or package before it reaches the intended recipient. Therefore, companies need to have a well-established screening procedure to limit the risk. A mailroom protocol together with common sense and good judgment can achieve the goal of reducing the level of vulnerability to this type of attack.

Important Elements to Include in the Plan

- While creating a plan, you must differentiate between business mail, regular mail, and nonregular mail. Business mail and regular mail are received on a routine basis from other businesses, clients, or customers. Nonregular mail gets the greatest degree of scrutiny.
- When dealing with packages, it's important to create a way for employees to notify security or mail personnel about the anticipated arrival of a package. The employee needs to provide information such as the recipient's name, department, and phone number as well as the name of the sender, the package contents, and its anticipated size.

(continues)

Exhibit 11.2 Mailroom Protocol *(Continued)*

- Security personnel and any person who processes the mail need to be familiar with suspicious signs and to be trained regularly. The following list presents different warning signs for letter and packages that have occurred in previous incidents:

  Address

  - A handwritten address or one that is poorly typed
  - An incomplete or illogical return address
  - An uncommon return address
  - Foreign return address on a package, indicating it was not sent by a local business
  - No return address
  - Unusual manner of delivery (during nonwork hours or by a person not belonging to a parcel service).

  Sense and Feeling

  - The size and weight are not proportionate.
  - A lopsided or unusual feel (e.g., powdery feel).
  - A strange odor.
  - The envelope feels stiff, rigid, or contains heavy cardboard, metal, or plastic that prevents the envelope from bending.
  - Sounds (ticking, buzzing, clicking) or other strange noises coming from the package.

  Visual

  - The envelope is torn or opened.
  - There is an oil stain on the envelope.
  - Powder or any substance is leaking from it.
  - A threatening message is on the envelope or letter.
  - An excessive amount of postage is on the letter.
  - Wires are protruding from the envelope or package.
  - Envelope or package is sealed with excessive amount of tape or string.
  - Misspelling of common words, address, name, all of which might suggest difficulty with English.
  - The letter or package uses company titles but no reference name.
  - Markings such as "Personal," "Confidential," or "Private."

• The plan is not finished when routine procedures are implemented. It must include procedures for an emergency situation. When a piece of mail has been determined to be suspicious, the primary concern should be your personal safety and the safety of other employees. Remember, your job ends when you discover a suspicious package. At that point, the responsibility belongs to law enforcement professionals who train for this kind of situation.

When You Discover a Suspicious Letter or Package:

  ○ Remain calm.
  ○ Set the item down.
  ○ Don't move the item or carry it outside.
  ○ Evacuate the area.
  ○ Notify security, management.
  ○ Notify law enforcement.

too, the lack of a return address. The package may very well be legitimate and pose no risk at all. However, an effective and well-operated screening system would certainly identify this package as deserving of additional attention.

Mail bombs, unfortunately, do not require a great deal of sophistication to build and send. Exhibit 11.3 is a photograph of a very simple explosive device and trigger system. Packed with nails and screws, such a device becomes an extremely deadly weapon that can shower a large area with shrapnel.

Exhibit 11.3 Simple Package Bomb and Triggering System

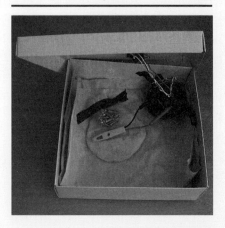

Equipment

A piece of equipment that you should consider purchasing for the mailroom is a specially constructed container designed to contain the effects of a small explosive device, such as a letter or package containing a bomb. Several companies manufacture these devices, including the Rav-Bariah Company, which we mentioned earlier as a good source for high-security doors. Rav-Bariah makes a device called a "Protectainer," shown in Exhibit 11.4, which is designed to absorb lateral blast energy and all lateral explosive fragmentation. The force of the blast will be directed upward, preventing the lateral dispersal of lethal shrapnel.

Exhibit 11.4   The Protectainer
by Rav-Bariah

Photo courtesy of Rav-Bariah.

Depending on your level of risk and the volume of mail you receive, you may wish to consider purchasing metal detectors, X-ray equipment, and other similar devices. Many locations X-ray every piece of mail. This is always a good practice. However, the cost of a large X-ray machine capable of dealing with large volumes of mail may be prohibitive. Many companies, therefore, scan mail with metal detectors, which is a less expensive alternative. This practice is based on the premise that a bomb cannot be made without metallic components. While this is generally true, the X-ray option certainly is among the better options to safeguard the office. Similarly, the new bomb detection equipment is an ideal way to prevent an attack that uses the mail as a delivery system.

One of the services offered by Global Security Group, LLC, our company, is a comprehensive assessment and overhaul of corporate mailrooms. This overhaul includes the creation of a company-specific mail-handling procedure and integrates the best and most cost-effective technological detection systems.

CHAPTER 12

Physical Site Security

IT IS AN AXIOM IN THE SECURITY INDUSTRY that physical security must be the primary focus while attempting to protect a business facility or home from attack or theft. Remember that even the most sophisticated alarm systems are designed to provide warning of the security breach, not to stop the breach itself. Video cameras allow for the remote monitoring of a location and, if an alert security officer is monitoring them, may provide advance warning of an intrusion attempt. Video also can provide a record for later use as evidence by law enforcement authorities. Similarly, infrared detection systems and electronic sensors do nothing to actually prevent an intrusion. These systems are designed to alert, not prevent.

This chapter is designed for corporate managers and executives as well as employees tasked with making general recommendations regarding necessary security upgrades. It provides a detailed look at how to enhance the physical security of your office or other facility. This process may be costly. Upgrading the security of a poorly prepared facility can easily cost several million dollars. While this may seem like a large and unnecessary expense, it must be viewed in the context of protecting the more valuable assets of the corporation. An appropriate capital investment now may ultimately save the corporation many more millions that may be lost in the event of a severe terrorist incident or criminal act. Many historical precedents support this position. For example, the rash of airplane hijackings in the 1970s led to the implementation of the sky marshal program. The goal was to have armed sky marshals on board American-based carriers to prevent armed hijacking. Unfortunately, people have short memories. After a number of turbulent years, the number of hijackings around the world was reduced, largely as a result of improved airport security measures. The government decided that the sky marshal program was an unnecessary expense. Prior to September 11, the sky marshal program had been all but eliminated. American-based air carriers were left unprotected, and members of Osama Bin Laden's Al Qaeda network pounced on that weakness. Loss of commerce, insurance payouts, and the government bailout of the airline industry as well as the total effect on the world economy have yet to be completely assessed. Recent estimates made by the city of New York place the economic loss at over $83 billion. By comparison, the several million dollars saved by eliminating the use of armed sky marshals is an insignificant sum.

Another example of how relatively minor capital expenditures for security concerns can prevent tragedies from occurring may be seen in the Oklahoma City bombing. On April 19, 1995, Timothy McVeigh parked a Ryder truck filled with a bomb made from ammonium nitrate next to the Alfred P. Murrah Federal Building. Virtually every American remembers the horrific sight of the front of the building after the explosion. One hundred seventy-three Americans lost their lives, including nineteen children. Until the attack on September 11, the Oklahoma City bombing had been the worst case of terrorism on U.S. soil. Just how difficult was it for McVeigh to acquire the means necessary to carry out this savage act? Unfortunately, the answer is that it was not very hard at all. The explosive he used, a bomb made from fertilizer, is easy to make; today, the instructions are available on dozens of Internet websites. Building this type of explosive is a simple task for the least sophisticated among us. All the necessary bomb components are readily available on the retail market. This method is still an easy way to create an explosive capable of destroying a building and has been used by Islamic militants before as well as domestic terror groups. All that McVeigh needed to do was to assemble the components and select a target that was both suitable for his needs and vulnerable to this type of attack.

The attack on the Alfred P. Murrah building was successful because McVeigh was able to park his explosive-laden truck in close proximity to the front of the building. Nothing in the design of the building or the surrounding area prevented the truck from being placed in a position where the explosives it carried would be most effective. In addition, statistics clearly show that bombings are the preferred methods of attack by international terror groups. Exhibit 12.1 compares the different methods that have been used in terrorist acts between the years 1995–2000. The number of bombing incidents greatly exceeds all other methods combined. Terrorists prefer bombings for the obvious reason that, absent an attack with weapons of mass destruction, no other method has the potential of causing the kind of catastrophic damage that these groups are seeking to inflict.

Exhibit 12.1   Terrorist Methods of Attack, 1995–2000

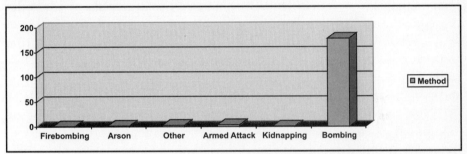

Source: U.S. Department of State, "Patterns of Global Terrorism 2001," Washington, DC: Office for Counterterrorism, May 21, 2001.

The tragedy of almost every bombing attack, excepting the 9/11 strikes which used commercial aircraft both as a bomb as well as the delivery system, could easily have been prevented by the placement of simple physical barriers placed around the outside of the building or targeted facility. Today, if you walk through the Washington D.C. area, you'll notice many changes relative to the security measures that are in place outside the other important federal buildings. Parking on the street near one of these buildings is only permitted when the front of the building is sufficiently far away from street parking. For example, parking is permitted along Constitution Avenue adjacent to the Washington Monument. This is true despite the fact that the Monument has long been thought to be a prime target for terror groups like Al Qaeda seeking to make a political statement. This is because the street is several hundred yards away from the monument. A conventional explosive hidden in a truck would not be sufficient to damage the structure at that distance. However, in cases where the front of the building is only a few short yards from the street, parking is not permitted. In situations like that, access is now effectively blocked off by the placement of bollards, cement wedges, and heavy cement planters.

These devices are designed to prevent a vehicle from being able to get too close to the building's exterior. These measures are relatively inexpensive but effectively prevent an attack such as occurred in Oklahoma City. If the bomb cannot be placed in close proximity to the structure, the blast will not be directed and much of the force will dissipate, resulting in damage that will be relatively light. In some cases, however, the actual physical location of a structure relative to a public thoroughfare will make the facility vulnerable notwithstanding the installation of barriers. There are literally thousands of sensitive facilities situated right along main traffic arteries that are open to heavy trucks and other commercial traffic. Under these conditions it is absolutely impossible to prevent an attack by a car or truck bomber. Even if bollards are placed along the roadway in order to prevent such an attacker from jumping the curb and detonating close to the building, an attack is still likely to be successful if the distance from the street to the facade of the building is a mere 15 to 20 feet.

Prior to running out and ordering millions of dollars of protective equipment, professionals should evaluate the overall security of your facility and a detailed report of the results should be prepared. Our firm, Global Security Group, LLC, is one of several capable and experienced enough to provide the type of detailed and comprehensive evaluation necessary for this process. The first step in the process is to have a complete risk assessment done for your particular circumstance. There are many factors that need to be considered, such as the nature of your business, the location of the facility, and its desirability as a political target, as well as any history of terrorist or criminal activity directed toward the company. Environmental factors are considered. The historical and present level of terrorist organizational activity as a whole is also of critical importance. Exhibit 12.2 is an example of a typical risk assessment format.

The actual physical security evaluation must be made only after the level of risk has been determined. Current security measures are then carefully analyzed and evaluated in relation to the perceived threat level. Exhibit 12.3 shows what a comprehensive evaluation should include.

Each category shown in Exhibit 12.3 will be analyzed and evaluated. A detailed report will be generated and specific recommendations for change will be made. The more competent firms will note deficiencies and will prioritize the corrective actions that must be taken. It is then up to the client to follow through and correct the noted deficiencies. The task of most consulting firms will end upon the delivery of the final written evaluation. Some firms, like our own, offer an additional service. They will

Exhibit 12.2   Risk Assessment Form

Company _____   Phone number _____

Location _____   Project number _____

Prepared by _____   Date _____

1. Brief Description of Company's Operations:

_____

_____

_____

_____

2. Threat Assessment

The likelihood that threats will occur based on the company's record and the industry's experience. (1 low–5 high)

Outside Threats

Criminal Acts (expensive materials, tools or products)	1	2	3	4	5
Competitor (competitive advantage)	1	2	3	4	5
Terrorist (political, animal rights, environmental, etc.)	1	2	3	4	5
Natural Disaster (flood, hurricane, fire)	1	2	3	4	5

Inside Threats

Employees, Temporary Employee
  (e.g., disgruntled employees)   1   2   3   4   5
Vendors, Contractors (expensive materials,
  tools, products, etc.)   1   2   3   4   5

                      Total   _____

                    General Threat Assessment
                        (total divided by 6)   _____

Comments:

_____

_____

_____

_____

(continues)

Exhibit 12.2 Risk Assessment Form *(Continued)*

---

3. **Loss Assessment** (1 low–5 high)

The value of loss that may occur as a result of actions against the company:

Loss Injury to Personnel	1	2	3	4	5
Damage to Facility	1	2	3	4	5
Loss of Products, Materials, Tools	1	2	3	4	5

Total _____

General Threat Assessment
(Total divided by 3) _____

Comments:

_____

_____

_____

_____

4. **Effectiveness of Security Measures Already in Place** (1 low–5 high)

Effectiveness:

Electronic Detection (alarm, camera, communication)	1	2	3	4	5
Access control (doors, gates, locks, barrier)	1	2	3	4	5
Procedures (emergency response, mail acceptance, visitor screen, information)	1	2	3	4	5

Total _____

General Effectiveness
(total divided by 3) _____

Comments:

_____

_____

_____

_____

_____

5. Recommended Preventative/Protective Measures to Reduce the Risk to an Acceptable Level:

_____

_____

_____

_____

_____

_____

_____

_____

Signed _____

Date of Assessment _____

Exhibit 12.3   Site Security Evaluation

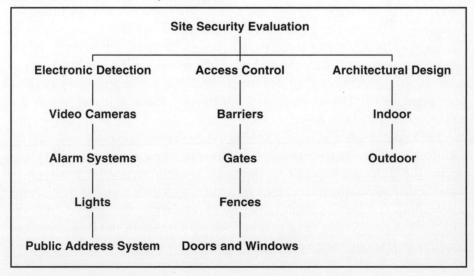

oversee the implementation of needed changes, often utilizing firms with whom they have professional contacts. In cases where many costly corrections must be made, the security consulting company should be clear on which upgrades should be addressed immediately. The better firms will show the client how the funds already budgeted for security may be used to greatest advantage. Often the allotted budget will be sufficient to provide for the security needs of the company. In such cases, the consultants will merely show the client where funds are being wasted and how they may be reallocated to accomplish the goal of greater security.

The security consultant should also be able to teach the client corporation how to make the best use of the security equipment they already have. For example, many companies already have extensive video surveillance and alarm systems. Quite often, however, these cameras are not used to their best advantage. Both authors have seen poorly used resources in the private and public sector. Many times, cameras are poorly aimed and out of focus. Often the security officer is sitting before a bank of video screens, half of which are nonoperational. More often than not, a simple repair is all that would be needed to bring most, if not all, of the cameras online. We will discuss alarm and video systems in greater detail in the following chapter.

In general, physical security refers to tangible impediments to attack or unauthorized entry. Fences, gates, barricades, bollards, and doors are just a few examples. An effective security system must integrate all different types of components, perhaps the most critical of which are the barriers that physically prevent the worst-case scenario: a truck bomb attempting to breach the perimeter at high speed. When we discuss barriers, we specifically mean bollards, barriers, and hydraulic wedges. While fences are also of critical importance, they serve a different function: to prevent and detect unauthorized intrusions. The better fences today combine some of the latest advances in perimeter alarm systems within the physical design of the fence.

Let's spend a bit of time focusing on perimeter security and understanding exactly what is necessary to prevent a truck bomb attack. Once again, the determination as to the need to defend against this type of attack must be made subsequent to a thorough risk analysis and threat assessment. If it is clear that the nature of the facility in question requires this level of protection, then it is necessary to focus on the installation of barriers sufficient to defeat the type of impact generated by a heavy-weight vehicle moving at highway speed. Barriers must be certified and independently tested to ensure that you have real, not merely cosmetic, security. How do you know which level of protection you require and whether the barriers you are considering have the ability to meet the anticipated threat?

Calculating the level of impact is a matter of simple mathematics and physics. Kinetic energy is a product of the mass (weight in kilograms) of an object and the square of the velocity (measured in meters/second) at which it travels divided by 2. Thus the speed at which the attacking vehicle is traveling has a greater effect upon the level of impact than does its mass. A Honda Civic hitting a barrier at 100 miles per hour has greater kinetic energy than a cement mixer hitting it at ten miles an hour. To make this calculation easier, we will use kilograms for mass and meters per second for velocity. For example, the kinetic energy produced by a cement mixer weighing 7,500 kilograms moving at 10 meters per second can be calculated as follows:

Kinetic energy = Mass (weight in kilograms) × Velocity (meters per second) squared divided by 2

7,500 kilograms × 10 meters per second squared (100) divided by 2 = 375,000 joules

In the case of a 1,000-kilogram Honda moving at 50 meters per second, the kinetic energy is calculated as follows:

1,000 kilograms × 50 meters per second, squared (2,500) divided by 2 = 1,250,000 joules

As you can see, the kinetic energy produced by the lighter and faster object produces greater kinetic energy. However, this calculation does not tell the whole story. Remember that the kinetic energy will be converted into heat, sound, and permanent deformation of the vehicle. In the case of the Honda, it is quite likely that the car would virtually disintegrate upon impact. A far more massive vehicle like the cement mixer will not. There are several other variables that enter into this discussion, but suffice it to say that controlling the speed at which a vehicle can approach an entry point is critical to preventing a successful attack. For that reason, most fortified entrance points are designed to require the driver to make a relatively sharp turn before reaching the barrier, thus preventing the attacking vehicle from attaining the same speed as it could if the truck or car had a long straight run. The next factor to consider is controlling the access of large trucks. Obviously, terrorists will prefer to use a truck when possible as they can pack it with greater amounts of explosives. Also, the more massive the vehicle, the lower the likelihood that it will be destroyed upon impact with a barrier. Realistically, the worst possible type of attack in the real world is more likely to be a very massive vehicle, 15,000–25,000 pounds attempting to drive through a barricade at fifty miles an hour. However, there also numerous instances where the bombers actually chose to use a car, rather than a truck, as their delivery device. Your perimeter system must be able to handle either possibility.

The industry leader in the design, manufacture, and installation of such security barricades is the Delta Scientific Corporation, a U.S.-based firm with offices in California, Virginia, and England. Their extensive line of barricades, gates, bollards and wedges are in use protecting sensitive government facilities, embassies, military bases, and private corporations throughout the world. The bollard itself may be fashioned from steel or cement and should be placed in such a manner as to prevent a car or truck bomb from being driven close to the structure. A sturdy barrier, improperly placed, will do little good. The question of how much distance is desirable is a difficult one to answer. A powerful explosive can do damage from even a considerable distance. However, the further away the bomb is placed, the less the resulting damage will be. Use as much distance as the circumstances allow.

The bollards themselves must be capable of stopping even a determined attacker attempting to drive through the barricade on a suicide mission. In addition, the bollard or barricade must maintain much of its effectiveness even if it is not in the fully deployed position in the case of movable barriers. This means the ability to stop a truck moving at highway speed, even if the bollard is only halfway deployed. This will not prevent an explosion, obviously, but it certainly will reduce the potential damage to life and property from the explosion by preventing the detonation from occurring in close proximity to the protected facility. The systems offered by Delta Scientific will do that and more (see Exhibit 12.4); they represent the state of the art in protective products. Contact information for Delta is listed in Appendix B. Their systems can be operated mechanically as well as manually in case of a disruption in the power supply or a pump malfunction. Strictly hand-operated systems are also available; these are suitable for use with portable systems set up in areas without a nearby power source. The normal speed of operation in mechanically operated systems is generally between 5 and 7 seconds. One very useful option Delta offers is a circuit that will allow the barricade to be deployed in six-tenths of a second in emergencies. The system can even be tied into sensors that will cause the system to be automatically deployed upon detection of a vehicle approaching at high speed. The system offered by Delta uses sensors embedded in the roadway remote from the guard booth. It can be set to trigger an alarm or deploy the barricades automatically without the need for human intervention. Exhibits 12.4, 12.5, and 12.6 are examples of several of Delta's excellent designs as well as tests of their effectiveness.

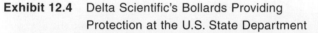

Exhibit 12.4   Delta Scientific's Bollards Providing Protection at the U.S. State Department

Photo courtesy of Delta Scientific.

Exhibits 12.5 and 12.6 show the DSC 720 bollard system, manufactured by Delta Scientific, during a crash test. Two of the three hydraulically operated bollards remained fully functional after this test despite the 1.2 million foot-pound impact. This is Delta's highest-rated system and is actually rated to stop even larger, heavier vehicles striking at high speed. It will stop a 15,000-pound truck even if it strikes the bollards at a speed of 50 mph.

Enhancement of physical security through the installation of such a system also has a deterrent value that should not be underestimated. The use of sturdy and effective barricades will likely encourage a potential attacker to find a "softer" and less well-protected target. However, there are always those not in favor of installing such systems. A common criticism while discussing the placement of bollards and barricades is the fact that no one wants to feel as though their place of employment is an armed camp. Bollards and barricades, critics say, have a less than aesthetically appealing look. Two responses come to mind. With current world conditions the way they are, there is an ever-increasing chance that you and your business will become someone's target. There is a tradeoff that must be made. Décor probably will suffer as a result of this need for security, but it is worth it if you avoid attack by improving security. Also, companies that manufacture these products are mindful that there is a need to

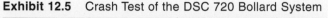

Exhibit 12.5   Crash Test of the DSC 720 Bollard System

Photo courtesy of Delta Scientific.

Exhibit 12.6   Truck as It Impacts the DSC 720 System
by Delta Scientific

Photo courtesy of Delta Scientific.

provide effective protection that is still somewhat pleasing to the eye. Delta Scientific, while primarily concerned with providing the state of the art in physical security products, also has a team of architects whose job is to tailor the designs of security systems to meet the decorative and architectural needs of their clients.

If bollards are not suitable to your company's specific needs, a good compromise option may be the placement of heavy cement planters. This option can be seen at many government installations all over the United States.

Many government agencies and business facilities opt for permanently placed heavy cement planters, which are both cost effective and aesthetically pleasing. A heavy cement planter placed properly will accomplish much the same thing as a bollard, wedge, or other physical impediment and can actually serve to enhance the beauty of the building. Planters cemented into the ground or sidewalk are preferable to those that are free-standing. For companies that are not concerned with aesthetics and favor a heavily fortified site, combinations of various methods may be used. Planters, however, cannot be lowered and raised to allow the passage of authorized traffic.

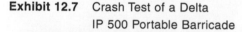

Exhibit 12.7   Crash Test of a Delta IP 500 Portable Barricade

Photo courtesy of Delta Scientific.

Most of the time there also must be provisions made to allow vehicles to access the building. Underground parking garages are common and deliveries must be made. Therefore, a secure guard gate must be used. Keep in mind that if you have a secure system of bollards or barricades, the gate will then become the weakest link that an attacker will attempt to exploit. The gate must therefore have the same ability to prevent a determined attack while allowing relatively smooth access for employees, visitors, and guests. Do not utilize a gate designed for parking control in a place that requires an effective impediment to a determined entry. The guard gate needs to be sturdy and ideally backed up by a heavy steel wedge that is hydraulically operated. The gates and wedges can be quickly opened or retracted to allow access but will be every bit as effective as the fixed bollards (see Exhibit 12.7).

The IP 500 portable barricade from Delta Scientific may be rapidly deployed; set up time is under two hours. It will secure a roadway up to 15 feet wide and is certified to defeat a 15,000-pound vehicle at 30 miles per hour. This system may be operated either manually or hydraulically and it is filled with cement once it is in place. It is also movable and may be deployed to other threat areas as necessary. For added security, gates should ideally be backed up by a hydraulically operated steel wedge (see Exhibit 12.8).

Exhibit 12.8   Hydraulic Wedge by Delta Scientific

Photo courtesy of Delta Scientific.

These systems have been used by extremely sensitive governmental facilities for decades and will, quite literally, stop a Mack truck. They have been rigorously tested and proven to be effective. This type of barricade will meet the demands of one of the worst-case scenarios: a bomb-laden truck, like a cement mixer, attempting to crash the perimeter at high speed. There is no way that an attack like that will be successful as long as the wedges are up and operational.

Another area of importance is the issue of access control. Simply speaking, this refers to making sure that only the right people are admitted into the facility. Prior to 9/11, there was very little effort made to properly screen individuals entering corporate buildings. Even in major corporations, anyone can walk right past the security desk and into the elevators without being challenged. After the 9/11 attacks, many businesses made the effort to limit access into their buildings. Unfortunately, as the events of 9/11 recede into memory, many companies have lapsed into their earlier practices and no longer follow appropriate access limiting procedures.

Controlling unauthorized access to corporate facilities needs to be strictly enforced for many reasons apart from concerns about terrorism. For example, criminal behavior is a far more common occurrence than a terrorist attack. Property theft, robbery, sexual assault, corporate espionage, and other crimes of violence are far more prevalent and may be virtually eliminated with the appropriate attention paid to limiting access. In addition, crimes of violence perpetrated by disgruntled employees are becoming quite common and may also be prevented if the security staff is doing its job.

The issue of access limitation is one of identification confirmation combined with the ability to physically prevent unauthorized individuals from getting it. Identification is generally an easy task. Corporate personnel may simply be issued identification cards or badges that must be displayed to the security staff upon entry. Secure electronic entry is also becoming easier to accomplish through the application of technology. Equipment is available that can recognize faces, hand size, voice, preset codes, and even the patterns in a person's retina. Confirmation is also an easy task. Guests and visitors to the building should be pre-screened through security. An employee expecting the visitor need only make notification to the security desk and provide the identity and anticipated arrival time of the individual. Many companies require that a simple visitor form be filled out and provided to security prior to the arrival of any guests. Exhibit 12.9 is an example of such a notification form.

This simple form will allow expected visitors to be admitted quickly and professionally, without unnecessary delay. Measures like this will also be noted by anyone with criminal intentions who is conducting a pre-operational surveillance. Do not underestimate the deterrence value of protocols such as these.

Exhibit 12.9   Visitor Information Form

Date _____

Host Information

Name   _____

Department   _____

Phone number   _____

Guest Information

Name of person invited   _____

Workplace of guest   _____

Phone number   _____

Address   _____

Has the guest been to the office previously: ☐ Yes   ☐ No

Level of Familiarity with the Guest

☐ Know the guest personally: _____

☐ Don't know the guest but familiar with his/her background: _____

☐ Don't know the guest at all: _____

Visit Information

Visiting date _____

Visiting time _____

Do you expect the guest to bring anything
special to the meeting (laptop, big bag, etc.):   ☐ Yes   ☐ No

If yes, describe: _____

Purpose of the meeting: _____

Other relevant information: _____

_____

_____

_____

CHAPTER 13

Technological Security

WHILE CHAPTER 12 DEALT WITH PHYSICAL SECURITY, specifically the use of physical impediments to limit access or vulnerability to a certain type of attack and protocols to limit access, this chapter explores the types of technological security devices currently available that will allow an individual or firm to dramatically enhance the capabilities of any security plan. Today there are devices of such sophistication available to the civilian market as to almost guarantee that it will be impossible to gain access to a protected facility without being detected and ultimately intercepted. We mentioned a few of these measures in Chapter 6 during our discussion of safety precautions in the home. Here we go into these systems in greater detail in regard to upgrading the level of security at an office, factory, or other corporate facility.

PERIMETER SECURITY SYSTEMS

Defensive measures always should be evaluated from the outer perimeter inward. The creation of an effective perimeter security system needs to be your first priority. One of the most practical of these technical security measures is a type of barrier known as a smart fence. These fences, such as those created by the Israeli firm Magal Security Systems, Ltd., not only provide a physical barrier but also incorporate a sophisticated web of sensing equipment that creates an alert if the fence is about to be breached in any way. An alert will be generated if anyone attempts to cut the fence, climb over it, or dig under it. Vibration sensors will even pick up the presence of individuals approaching the barrier on foot. Infrared technology and video monitors can instantly track in on the intruders and precisely pinpoint the area that is being scouted. Fences of this type are state of the art. They are also very expensive and require the client to dedicate trained personnel to maintain the system. Smart fences provide the most effective outer security perimeter for your sites short of an operational minefield. Magal is perhaps the premier manufacturer of this type of technology. The company designs, builds, and installs fences that can detect any type of intrusion, including attempts to approach, cut through, climb over, and even tunnel under the barrier. The Magal Security Systems' DTR-2000 Taut Wire Intrusion Detection System (TWIDS) (see Exhibit 13.1) has a long and proven history of reliability under some of the most challenging of circumstances. The design uses an electro-mechanical sensor that, when activated, sends a signal to a computerized control center, which then analyzes the signal and alerts the facility to the type and location of the attempted breach. The system is designed to virtually eliminate false alarms due to the fact that a force of less than about 15 kilograms (33 pounds)

Exhibit 13.1   Examples of Magal Security Systems: DTR-2000 Taut
Wire Intrusion Detection (left) and Inno-Fence (right)

Photos courtesy of Magal Security Systems, Ltd.

will not activate the sensor. Therefore, small animals or birds will not cause an alarm. The system is suitable for use under any climatic condition and is completely free of weather-related limitations.

Magal is also mindful, as is Delta Scientific, that security fences must be offered in configurations that are more visually appealing and do not make a corporate facility resemble a federal prison. Magal's Inno-Fence (see Exhibit 13.1) provides perimeter intrusion protection in a package suitable where aesthetics is an issue. The fence provides the necessary security while not making the secured area look like an armed camp.

INTRUSION DETECTION AND MONITORING SYSTEMS

Another extremely effective and sophisticated system from Magal is the DTS-1000. This system represents the state of the art in advanced digital video intrusion detection and allows for tracking on a personal computer (PC) platform. The system combines a sophisticated intrusion detection system with real-time imaging from closed-circuit television cameras. Up to four separate cameras are connected to a processor card, which resides in a slot in the PC. Each PC is capable of handling up to eight processor cards, and each card controls four cameras. This allows one PC to handle the interface of 32 surveillance cameras. The cameras are arranged so as to provide for complete and overlapping coverage of the entire site. Upon sensing an intrusion, the system will automatically track the intruder and instantly provide real-time tracking with a colored trace of the intruder's movements. Not only is each video frame stored on the hard drive for evidentiary or investigative purposes, but each new intruder gets a different color trace. In the event of multiple intrusions within the fields of view of more than one camera, the system automatically provides operator annunciation and priority display. This system is designed for outdoor use and is suitable for use in virtually all weather conditions. Exhibit 13.2 shows an example of the ability of the DTS-1000 to detect an intrusion and initiate a track and trace.

Another excellent Magal system is the MagNet, which is designed to allow one VGA monitor and one operator to control and integrate numerous security devices in a very large facility or in several locations. It is also a real-time control and display system suitable for use when complex graphics are required for integration with the live video signal such as: time, date, camera names, alarm icons, and tracking lines (see Exhibit 13.3).

Exhibit 13.2   Magal DTS-1000

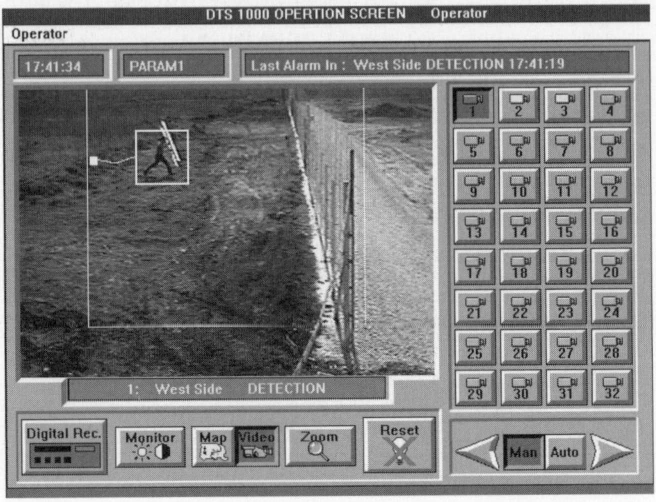

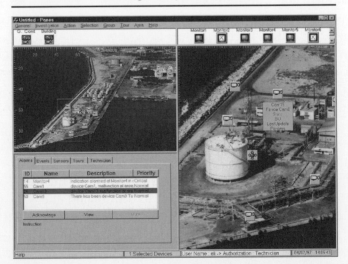

Photo courtesy of Magal Security Systems, Ltd.

These fences and monitoring systems represent the cutting edge in security technology and can be expensive. If the cost of such systems is prohibitive, less expensive alternates may still meet all of your security needs.

Exhibit 13.3   The MagNet System by Magal

Photo courtesy of Magal Security Systems, Ltd.

In addition, you often have the option of upgrading your current systems. In fact, you may not need all the features offered in the top-of-the-line models. For example, the layout of the location in question may such that it would be absolutely impossible to tunnel underneath the fence. Perhaps you only require a system that detects attempts at cutting through or climbing over the fence. At the low end of the tech scale is the standard cyclone fence topped with barbed or razor wire. These fences, of course, can be easily defeated but may be appropriate for your needs, given a careful evaluation of the nature and extent of the risk your site will face. If you currently have such perimeter fences, they can be inexpensively modified to provide more than just a physical deterrent. Magal is only one of several companies that can adapt detection technology onto conventional fences, providing increased security with a smaller capital expenditure. For example, the Yael-15 is a Taut Wire Intrusion Detection System that is designed for integration with any type of wire barrier. It combines the deterrent properties of an actual physical barrier (fence) with a highly advanced intrusion detection system. This is accomplished by having a sensor linked to all the fence wires through a stainless steel collector wire. A displacement of any of the wires during an intrusion attempt causes a change in the tension of the collector wire that the sensor translates into an analog signal proportional to the displacement. This allows for discrimination in the system, as displacement caused by a bird landing on the fence, for example, will not trigger an alarm. The system also has what is known as a self-balancing feature, which allows it to remain functional even after it is severely damaged.

LICENSE PLATE RECOGNITION TECHNOLOGY

Another new and very useful technology is the recognition technology produced by U.S. companies such as Perceptics and Israeli firms such as Zamir Recognition Systems Ltd. This type of technology can recognize and "read" numerical and alphabetic patterns on license plates, even while the vehicle bearing the plates is moving at highway speeds. The Zamir system operates in a way that makes it suitable for security-related applications. An approaching vehicle activates a trigger, which causes the system to take an image of the entire vehicle. The image is then sent to a data processing unit that identifies the license plate and separates and instantaneously recognizes each digit. The information is then stored along with the now-recognized license plate as well as the date and time the image was obtained. The information is available to be used to achieve a wide variety of goals. If the system is being used for access control in a corporate parking lot, the authorized vehicle is recognized and the security gate is opened automatically without the need for the driver to stop and enter an access code. The date and time of entry are also recorded and stored. Exhibit 13.4 (left) is a picture of a Zamir recognition device.

The system was originally used as a revenue-enhancing device for facilities with long-term parking, such as airports. In fact, the Zamir system was originally implemented at Israel's Ben Gurion Airport for just that

Exhibit 13.4   Examples of Zamir Systems: Zamir Recognition System (left) and Zamir System at Security Checkpoint in Ariel, Israel (right)

Photos courtesy of Zamir Recognition Systems, Ltd.

purpose. However, the system's applicability to enhancing security has recently caught the interest of governments and private corporations around the world. The potential uses of this system are impressive. If a road encircles your facility, you can place these systems so as to ensure that only authorized vehicles have access to the perimeter. The system also can be used to create an alert for a specific vehicle's license plate. If, for example, an employee is terminated, his or her access permission can be revoked immediately, denying the person access to all controlled areas. The system can be programmed to provide a specific alert to the security staff if the employee's license plate is identified on or near the perimeter. This system is seeing increased usage as a means of enhancing security in high-threat areas, such as Israel. The city of Ariel, Israel, utilizes the Zamir license plate recognition system to enhance security at the city's guarded entrance (see Exhibit 13.4).

In early 2002, we had the opportunity to meet with a senior executive from Zamir prior to the Israel Security Event, an event in which Israeli security firms showcase their products for the American law enforcement community. We got a firsthand explanation of the system and gained a real appreciation for the many applications this technology is suited for. In our opinion, the potential applications of this technology have yet to be fully appreciated. For example, every day alerts are put out to law enforcement agencies all over the world. Quite frequently, these alerts identify a particular vehicle and license plate that is being sought. It would be a simple matter to enter the data into the Zamir systems wherever they might be located. The systems would be able to alert law enforcement authorities that the sought-after vehicle was at a particular location at a particular time. What if the Federal Bureau of Investigation (FBI) receives information that a truck laden with explosives, or worse, bearing a particular plate was heading to New York City? Recognition systems in place at the city's bridges and tunnels would be an effective line of defense against this type of attack.

Other types of recognition systems are available, and new ones are being developed. Handprints, voiceprints, facial features, as well as retinal patterns all provide a reliable means of limiting access to only those people who require it. It is a very simple matter to use the same system for all employees and merely provide additional security authorization to different individuals. For example, every employee would be able to access the parking lot, but only those with special clearance could access the executive washroom or any other place you needed to limit.

Many types of screening systems available can be used to prevent weapons and dangerous objects from being brought into your facility. In reverse, screening systems also can be used to prevent employee pilferage. We spoke previously about x-ray machines in the mailroom. They are critical pieces of equipment if you are really serious about mailroom security. Other machines make it possible to detect explosives in a package. Still others can sterilize mail thought contaminated with a biological hazard or other toxic material. Metal detectors can help prevent individuals carrying weapons made from ferrous metal from getting inside your facility. Whatever your particular security concern, there is almost certainly a company that makes a machine to help you address it.

The authors' company, Global Security Group, LLC, also offers technological solutions to meet security needs. One company that we recommend to clients who need a state-of-the-art video surveillance system is Third Watch Digital, which provides a PC-based multichannel video surveillance system that uses advanced digital video compression technology. Up to 16 cameras can be connected and viewed live on a single system local monitor screen or through a TCP/IP network. Video can be recorded based on specified schedules or motion detection. Monitoring and even video playback can be carried out remotely from home, satellite offices, hotels, Internet cafes, wireless laptops, wireless PDAs, web-enabled mobile phones, or a central monitoring facility. Further information on the Third Watch system can be found at *www.thirdwatchdigital.com*.

New technology is currently being developed that will track and monitor individuals in much the same manner as mobile assets are now tracked. Global Security Group, LLC, has partnered with Orbcomm, one of the world's premier satellite communications companies, to develop and market small devices that will track and monitor people anywhere in the world. Orbcomm owns and operates a satellite communications network that consists of 30 satellites in Low Earth Orbit (LEO) and 12 terrestrial gateways that are deployed around the world. This system provides seamless worldwide coverage and is currently being used to track mobile assets such as truck trailers, rail cars, construction equipment, automobiles, and locomotives. It is also widely used to monitor fixed assets such as oil and gas pipelines.

The Orbcomm systems data transmission system delivers data messages to and from anywhere in the world; it is used by companies such as General Electric, Caterpillar, Hitachi, Komatsu, Volvo, Garmin, and British Petroleum. The authors' firm, Global Security, LLC, is currently developing new ways to apply the Orbcomm system to a variety of security-related applications. Personal tracking devices, roughly the same size as a PDA, can be tracked anywhere in the world and are also capable of two-way data messaging. Smaller units, the size of a wristwatch, are currently being developed. Additional information about this technology and other Orbcomm system applications is available at *www.globalsecuritygroup.com*.

CHAPTER 14

Emergency Response Planning

VIRTUALLY EVERY GOVERNMENT AGENCY, facility, and installation maintains an Emergency Response Plan. Command centers are activated during a crisis, and the agencies have anticipated emergency situations as well as the appropriate responses to initiate. Many corporations have adopted this practice and have emergency plans in place. The majority of businesses, however, have not. This chapter discusses the need for such plans and recommends specific courses of action that should be taken during a variety of emergency situations.

Why do you need an Emergency Response Plan? In a crisis, such as a bombing, bomb threat, fire, release of hazardous materials, armed attack, or natural disaster, stress, fear, and panic can lead to state of confusion. A confused workforce will rely on management to provide the appropriate direction. Managers, however, will be under the same stress as their employees. The state of panic will limit or prevent the ability of management, security officers, or other designated persons from making the right decisions during a crisis. A well-organized plan provides people with the ability to make the right decisions under pressure during an emergency. The plans must be well thought out and well organized. During an emergency, the prearranged plan need only be executed. The need for thinking under pressure has been eliminated. The right decisions can then be made, saving lives, protecting property, and eliminating disruption to the organization such as loss of productivity, increased financial expenses, and decline in employee morale.

DEVELOP AN EMERGENCY PLAN

How can an appropriate plan be created? The first step is to conduct a
risk assessment of the facility, weighing such factors as location, political
instability, level of terrorist activity, nature of the business, size, number of
employees, and degree of facility control. Once an accurate assessment has
been prepared by an experienced professional, the plan may be created.
The accurate assessment is crucial because the emergency plan must clearly
define which action should be undertaken in response to a specific attack
or threat. Besides our own company, Global Security Group, LLC, several
other very good companies provide this type of service. For American
businesses abroad, subject to availability of personnel, the diplomatic security service will provide additional guidance during the assessment phase.

Once the emergency situations have been defined, work on the plan
may begin. For each potential emergency, criteria for initiating an emergency protocol must be established. These criteria obviously include
actual emergencies as well as the threat of a potential emergency. Credible information—such as phone threats; intelligence information; suspicious mail; package, item, car, or other object near the facility—may
trigger the emergency plan. The emergency plan also must be prepared
with the assistance of experienced security personnel. Again, several very
good consulting firms provide this service. The security consultant will
enlist the cooperation and input from the necessary corporate departments and individuals.

A point that needs mentioning is that the emergency plan must be
prepared in such a way that it is easy for all employees to understand.
After the attacks on September 11, CNN broadcaster Jack Cafferty discussed on air the Emergency Response Plan that was prepared for the network by a security consulting company. Cafferty held up the handsomely
bound emergency response book and lamented that he couldn't understand what needed to be done in the event of an emergency. Furthermore,
no one at CNN made any attempt to explain the security measures to
CNN personnel. Nor had any drills been scheduled to practice the measures specified in the report. It is critical that the emergency plan be very
clear and understandable by every employee. Remember that cognitive
ability—that is, the ability to think—is severely impacted during a crisis.
Recall our discussion in Chapter 2 regarding these effects, such as tachypsychia, cognitive dissonance, and auditory exclusion. Clarity in the plan
will go a long way toward limiting general confusion when these effects

strike. Even more important is the scheduling of frequent drills so that every employee understands what to do during an emergency and how to do it. We discuss the importance of drill later on.

Also bear in mind that once the plan is created, it must continually be updated. It is a virtual certainty that emergency plans more than several months old will need to be reviewed and updated. For example, the emergency plan will direct certain employees to do specific things during an emergency. Employees may be designated as team leaders, searchers, and first aid providers or placed in other positions critical to the plan's success. Obviously the plan needs to be updated each time an employee is hired or leaves the company, unless that employee did not have a vital role in the plan. If the individual was a team leader, a revision is mandatory. In addition, the plan must be updated to reflect any changes in the facility's physical structure. For example, the closing of an exit, stairwell, or elevator is cause for a plan revision. Similarly, the addition of exits also must be reflected in the plan. The plan should be updated on at least a quarterly basis even if there are no changes to the facility or its personnel. However, when any change does occur, a determination must be made of whether it will impact the emergency response plan. No matter why an employee leaves, the personnel department must be required to check the plan and determine whether that person had an important role in the plan's execution. This also must occur whenever an employee goes on leave or is transferred to a different department. The personnel office must provide that information to security and must then work with security to coordinate the replacement of the missing individual in the plan. A similar requirement must exist with regard to the physical plant management department. Both the engineering and maintenance departments must be required to check the emergency plan and consult with the security department before they begin any construction or maintenance. A determination will then be made as to whether the planned activity will interfere with the execution of the emergency response plan. If it will, the plan must be adjusted to take the activity into account.

The key to developing a successful plan lies in cooperation between the various departments within the company. Each department must be included in every phase of the plan's development. Exhibit 14.1 details the departmental responsibilities by area.

As you can see, each department is involved in the planning and provides input unique to its specific function within the company. Management must coordinate input from the various departments to reach the

Exhibit 14.1   Departmental Responsibilities in Response Plan Development

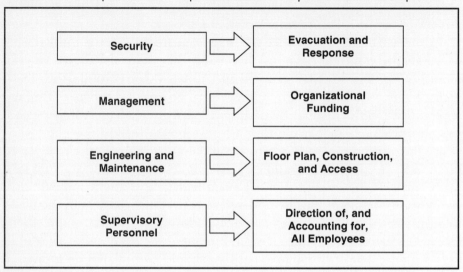

goal of having a workable emergency plan. Without such coordination, the plan will be unworkable and ineffective.

THE COMMAND CENTER

It also is necessary to have an emergency management command center within the company facility. It should be equipped with secure communications equipment, tape recorders, the company Emergency Response Plan, and a log to record all actions taken during the emergency. Ideally, the command center should have a backup generator as well as a supply of food and water. Command center personnel should have access to the complete list of employees and to employee emergency information forms. The command center must have a large printed list of the emergency contact numbers for officials in the local embassy or consulate as well as for officials of the host country's government. These contacts should be prominently displayed on poster-size charts (see Exhibit 14.2).

The command center phone should allow for direct access without going through a switchboard or a receptionist. It should be a distinct number that is familiar to every employee. The main number should never ring busy. It should spill over into other overflow lines to handle increased call volume during an emergency.

Exhibit 14.2   Emergency Contact Numbers

Embassy Contact Points:

Embassy (24-hour emergency #) _____

Marine Guard House   _____

Ambassador   _____

Deputy Chief of Mission   _____

Regional Security Officer   _____

Local Government:

Police Main Number   _____

Chief of Police   _____

Local Police Contact   _____

Head of State   _____

Mayor or Regional Governor   _____

State Department (DC)

Operations Center (24 hours)   _____

U.S. Foreign Disaster Assistance _____

Corporate Headquarters

Domestic Home Office   _____

Director Corporate Security   _____

There also must be a system for communicating with the home office, embassy or consulate, and employees that is not dependent on the local telephone system. If the host country's telephone system is operable, it should be used, with secure scrambling systems or while maintaining security-conscious telephone discipline. Some companies maintain their own satellite communications technology. In high-threat countries without reliable telephone systems, this capability is absolutely critical and is well worth whatever capital expenditure it requires. In addition, most embassies maintain an independent radio system used to communicate with embassy personnel. There are generally two systems, encrypted and unencrypted, or clear. The clear channels can be used to connect companies to the embassy radio net. In limited cases the embassy or consulate will permit certain companies to link with the embassy's local and non-secure VHF or UHF radio system. This will allow direct communication with the embassy in the event that local telephone communications is disrupted, either intentionally or as the result of a system-wide failure. The regional security officer in the host country can provide you with information on this subject and tell you whether it will be possible to do. The company should, at a minimum, maintain its own radio network to communicate with employees. Motorola can design a system to suit your company's individual needs. They can, for a few thousand dollars, set up a simple repeater system that can be used to alert employees in cases of emergency. They can provide radios to allow the use of the local VHF, UHF, or tracking system as well. Motorola can be contacted directly and a representative can discuss all available options with you. Remember, nonsecure systems may be easily monitored. Always assume that someone is listening to your transmissions and use strict radio discipline. For communication outside the local area but still within the confines of the local region, a national high-frequency system is necessary. Generally such a system requires the use of repeaters that rebroadcast the signal over greater distances. Shortwave radio will allow for the communication with the home office in the United States. Larger companies may own and operate their own satellite communications system and have it encrypted if it is likely that they will need to transmit sensitive information. Such systems can allow for communication even if local land lines are cut deliberately or as a result of a natural disaster. Similarly, commercial satellite technology is also available and provides effective worldwide communications. The Diplomatic Security Service uses this type of phone system to communicate with its personnel anywhere and under any circumstances.

The communications system also must provide for the broadcast of emergency information that is reasonably certain to reach all expatriate employees of the company. If you are American, you are familiar with the periodic testing of the emergency broadcast system. Years ago it was tested over radio and television, but in recent years it has become associated only with the commercial radio airwaves. If you are listening to the radio, you may hear a long, high-pitched tone followed by an announcer stating "This was a test of the emergency broadcast system." The announcer then goes on to explain that if this were a real emergency, the tone would be followed by official information describing the nature of the emergency and directing the public as to the action they must take. All major companies overseas should maintain a system that can operate along these lines.

Obviously the system is a more critical concern in some countries than in others. In most Western European nations, while there is always a level of risk to Americans living abroad, the threat that there will be large-scale terrorist operations, insurrections, or other dramatic types of political upheaval is relatively low. However, this system is critically important if you are located in some of the more volatile areas of the world. In Indonesia, for example, there is always the threat of violence against Westerners and their interests. In October 2001 the dependents and nonessential corporate employees of Nike Inc. were evacuated amid reports of escalating anti-American violence. In the Philippines, Pakistan, Malaysia, and many other countries, the need for quick communications cannot be overestimated.

EVACUATION OF PERSONNEL

In most instances, the nature of an emergency will not necessitate the evacuation of corporate personnel from the country. However, quite often it will be necessary to convey specific warnings to personnel about dangers in a particular area. For example, if there is a major, anti-Western demonstration near the main shopping area in a particular city, it will be necessary to warn personnel of this development and direct them to stay clear of the area. In some instances, a situation in a host country will deteriorate to the point that evacuation becomes necessary. The best thing to do under such circumstances is to mirror the policy of the embassy or consulate. Every year the State Department initiates evacuations, either partial or full, for many diplomatic missions throughout the world. Obviously when this action becomes necessary, the State Department also recommends the evacuation of nongovernmental U.S. citizens. If the State Department decides that dependents of embassy personnel are at risk, they will be evacuated first. It may well be prudent to follow the dictates of the State Department in this regard. Dependents will generally be evacuated before the situation deteriorates to the point of total collapse. It will therefore still be possible to leave the country on commercial airlines or via charter aircraft. The time to evacuate dependents is before even the trip to the airport will be fraught with danger. Essential personnel will likely stay on in the embassy as the crisis worsens. A large part of their function will be to look after the welfare of American citizens who have not left. If this is the type of situation you find yourself in, you must stay

in constant contact with the embassy. If closing the embassy is being considered, it is time for you to leave as well. The embassy staff will assist you
during an evacuation if you cannot leave safely on your own.

It is extremely irresponsible to ignore the reality that no matter where
overseas you are located, there may come a time when evacuation is necessary. It is critical, therefore, especially in high-threat areas of the world,
to have a complete evacuation plan in place. This plan must be coordinated with the local embassy. The regional security officer should be consulted during all phases of plan formulation. The plan must provide for
a complete or partial evacuation of employees and their families in the
event of civil unrest, terrorism, natural disaster, or medical emergency. An
appropriate country or location of refuge must be determined in advance,
and arrangements must be prearranged with facilities and agencies of the
country chosen to handle the arrival of all or some of your personnel.

Evacuation plans are solely the responsibility of the individual company. The embassy has neither the resources nor the mandate to provide
for the evacuation of private-sector employees. It does, however, have the
responsibility to apprise local U.S. citizens of any potential dangers to
their safety or property and will coordinate and assist in the development
of any evacuation plans. During times of crisis, embassy personnel will do
everything possible to assist all U.S. citizens in safely leaving the country
if it becomes necessary. Preplanning in conjunction with the embassy or
consulate is essential to make this happen without loss of life or injury.

Perhaps the most important role of the local embassy is the monitoring of the security situation within the country. Remember, embassy staff
have access to high-level governmental contacts and intelligence that private companies do not. Even large corporations having contacts at the
highest levels of the local government may not perceive the warning signs
of an impending crisis. The government often controls the media, and
content may reflect the government line and not necessarily the truth.
Close contact with the embassy is necessary to closely monitor a deterio-
rating situation and begin the implementation of steps necessary to effect
an evacuation if it becomes necessary

The State Department recommends that each company designate a
senior-level manager, assisted by appropriate individuals, to be responsible for the planning of any evacuation as well as to monitor the political
and security situation in the host country. The designated manager and
his or her support team should meet at least twice a year to review the
plan and the local situation. Regular meetings are particularly important,

as personnel changes may need to be reflected in the planning details. Any significant change in the stability of the situation locally or in the region in general should provoke the evacuation committee to meet on a more frequent basis. Prior to each meeting, a test of the employee notification system should be conducted. The results should be discussed during the meeting, and shortcomings should be identified and corrected. Again, in high-risk areas, the testing must be done on a more frequent basis.

The plan should identify a secure assembly area where employees can gather in the event an evacuation is ordered. The assembly area must be carefully selected for its defensibility as well as its proximity to the airport or point of embarkation. Particular attention should be given to the nature of the roadway between the assembly area and the point of departure. More than one possible route is preferred. The State Department strongly recommends that evacuees gather at a secure staging area rather than the point of embarkation to minimize the exposure of the evacuees. The plan must allow for the possibility that one or more of the planned routes will be impassible for one reason or another. Transportation of evacuees to the airport, for example, is done in appropriately sized groups that can be protected en route and will not overwhelm the ability of the carriers to transport them. The last thing you want is for your employees to be forced to wait for hours or even days to get on a flight.

The plan also must identify secondary assembly areas in the event that a disturbance or natural disaster renders the primary staging area unsafe. Similarly, secondary points of departure should be identified in the event the airport or other primary choice is closed. If your company is in constant contact with the embassy and is monitoring the situation closely, it should be possible to evacuate the staff smoothly via commercial carriers before the condition reaches a critical level. In the event commercial carriers are filled or not available, arrangements for a charter flight can be made in conjunction with other local companies also ordering an evacuation. Contacts with charter airlines should be made long before the actual emergency arises. If the situation results in a complete breakdown of all services and governmental functions, the State Department advises staying put in a secure area and not attempting to move around the country in an attempt to get out. Moving around exposes personnel to far greater danger than does sitting tight and waiting for the conditions to stabilize, the State Department has found. Once an evacuation is deemed necessary, no company personnel should unilaterally attempt to leave the country or travel internally. The assembly area should be amply stocked with non-perishable food items, fresh water, and medicine. Anyone taking prescription medication should have enough on hand to weather the crisis.

The State Department has identified three phases of an evacuation and a fourth that necessitates staying in place. Each stage has a specific set of procedures attendant to it. The phases are:

Phase I, Alert Stage: A warning to companies and individuals of host country instability.

Phase II, Limited Action: Increased preparation for evacuation includes those preparations made under conditions of increased tension or instability that could lead to partial or complete evacuation of expatriate employees and their dependents.

Phase III, Evacuation Phase: Final preparation and/or evacuation includes those preparations made under conditions in which the decision to evacuate is imminent or has already been made. Withdrawal and cessation of business is imminent or under way.

Standing Fast: Could be implemented in the event that evacuation is not considered prudent. Under this concept, employees and their dependents would remain in their quarters (or other designated location) for an extended period of time until tensions abate.

In Phase I, a situation begins to develop in the host country or region that engenders some concern from the embassy. Typically, the embassy will issue a warning or simply advise the expatriate community of the nature of the incident causing some concern. This notice should be considered akin to a hurricane warning or perhaps a report from the U.S. Geological Survey detailing some minor seismic activity that may foreshadow an earthquake. It is at this stage, the earliest twitch, that preplanning should be done. The evacuation committee should meet and discuss the recent events. The evacuation plan should be reviewed and assessed. Every what-if should be pondered, and the employee notification system should be tested.

The State Department recommends that evacuation priorities be established. It suggests:

- First priority—dependents
- Second priority—individuals other than key expatriate employees
- Third priority—key expatriate employees

This is basically the same system that is used by the government. If you will pardon the sexism, it is the modern equivalent of "women and children first." Dependents are, quite naturally, the first concern. The government then makes the distinction between "essential" and "nonessential" personnel. In the private sector, this is defined as the difference between ordinary employees and key personnel. In a gradually developing situation, an evacuation will be ordered for government employees along these lines. Dependent family members are considered most vulnerable and evacuation is generally attempted before any real danger develops. If conditions worsen and operations are gradually curtailed, nonessential employees are sent home next. Essential personnel remain until the last possible moment, generally assisting nongovernmental citizens who disregarded earlier warnings and stayed in country too long. Evacuation plans should be organized along those lines for corporate employees. Throughout Phase I, evacuation plans should be constantly updated and all personnel must be made aware of the process if evacuation is necessary. In the office, planning should include the protection of assets and proprietary information in case evacuation becomes necessary. Backups of corporate records and computer files should be made and sent to a secure site or to the home office. Teams should be assigned to identify what documents or equipment might need to be destroyed or what computer information would need to be removed from computer hard drives. Assume that in an unstable situation, foreign assets will be deliberately searched, looted, and possibly destroyed.

As conditions continue to worsen, Phase II is reached. Evacuation may be a real possibility or may be imminent. Additional planning is made and all assets are placed in a standby status. Management must continue to monitor the situation and know the whereabouts of all employees and their family members at all times. Management should be in constant contact with the embassy, the home office, and with other local companies with which cooperative evacuation protocols have been established.

Phase III is reached when the senior corporate manager, who has been in constant contact with the embassy and home office, determines that the situation has become dangerous, volatile, or otherwise unstable and nonessential employees and all dependent family members be evacuated. Assets should have already been put in place to support the evacuation in Phase II. During this stage, the senior manager must decide whether to assemble all personnel to a secure staging area or allow everyone to remain in their homes pending the actual call to evacuate. The staging area should be assessed again for its defensibility, and routes to the airport or other departure points should be scouted and assessed for safe passage.

Under certain conditions, staying put and "hunkering down" may be determined to be a safer choice than evacuating. Employees and their family members would be instructed to remain in their homes or report to alternate secure assembly points. Families should have prepared stocks of food, water, and medicine in case this becomes a necessity. The decision as to where to "hunker down" will be made by management in conjunction with the RSO.

Before we address some of the specifics that must be included in an emergency plan, we must emphasize that merely having a plan is not enough. For the plan to be effective, it must be thoroughly and regularly drilled. At first the drills must be frequent. Once personnel become familiar with the plan, unscheduled drills should be conducted on a quarterly basis at the very least. Ideally the plan should be drilled each time critical personnel are changed. More frequent drilling is indicated in high-risk locations or if the nature of the business is inherently dangerous or a high-profile target.

In military operations and tactical law enforcement, there is a concept known as a postoperational brief back. This is nothing more than a critical review, conducted by the participants, of the operation. The purpose of this review is to provide the necessary feedback required to make subsequent operations even more successful. Similarly, postdrill reviews must be held after any run-through of the emergency plan. Representatives of each of the departments must attend these reviews for the reviews to be effective in eliminating plan weaknesses.

In addition, for the plan to be effective, it must be coordinated with the appropriate departments or agencies with the local government. Representatives from the local police and fire departments as well as any of the emergency management agencies should be consulted. Unless there is some security reason to prevent it, these governmental contacts should be consulted in the planning stage and also should be invited to sit in on operational meetings. If the agency representatives are willing, they should become involved in drilling the plan once it is in place as well as in any "tabletop" exercises designed to prepare management to implement the plan in an emergency and evaluate performance during a mock crisis.

EVACUATION OF PREMISES

One of the most common elements of any Emergency Response Plan deals with the full or partial evacuation of the facility. This type of evacuation refers to a location-specific evacuation and not a general "flee-the-country" evacuation discussed above. Often a timely evacuation literally means the difference between life and death for the employees, visitors, and guests present in facility during a catastrophe. Nearly 3,000 people were killed in the World Trade Center attack. Apart from the several hundred who died instantly as the planes crashed into the towers, the rest died because they were unable to get out. Literally thousands of lives were saved by the heroic firefighters and police officers who helped evacuate the occupants of the buildings at the cost of their own lives. Interviews with many of the survivors revealed that most had no idea what to do in the moments after the impacts. Many people who had escaped gathered in the immediate area at the base of the Twin Towers. Prior to the second impact, many were told it was safe to return to their offices in the second tower, which had not yet been struck. Still others stayed in their offices and were not evacuated. They were unsure what to do and had no idea of what was yet to come. Few businesses had Emergency Response Plans; instead, they relied on building management to conduct drills and advise the tenants if evacuation was necessary. Few had considered just how long it would take to walk down 100 flights of stairs in stairwells filled with panic-stricken people. No provisions had been made for special-needs people, such as people in wheelchairs. How many additional lives were lost by this failure to prepare for disaster?

Still, there were some exceptions. A former soldier and Vietnam combat veteran named Rick Rescorla was the vice president of security for Morgan Stanley Dean Witter. His office was on the forty-fourth floor of the South Tower. Rescorla was serious about the need for training and preparation and conducted evacuation drills at least twice a year. He had been present during the first World Trade Center bombing in 1993 and personally ensured that every one of his firm's employees was safely evacuated. On September 11, Rescorla was at work when the first plane struck the North Tower. In an error of monumental proportions, the Port Authority officials at the trade center did not order an evacuation but rather told the tenants of the untouched South Tower to remain in the building. Rescorla, grasping the significance of what had happened, ignored their directive and personally initiated and led the evacuation of Morgan Stanley's 2,700 employees occupying floors 44 through 74 of the South Tower. He acted so quickly and decisively that most Morgan Stanley employees had been safely evacuated by the time the second plane hit the South Tower. All but six of Morgan Stanley's workers survived. Rescorla was one of the lost six. The last time he was seen, he was walking back into the stairwell in the South Tower to make sure everyone had gotten out safely.

The critical element in an emergency is decisive action. The cliché "to ponder is to perish" is never truer than under these circumstances. Fortunately for the employees of Morgan Stanley Dean Witter, they were led by a man who knew how to act and lead. In an adjacent eight-story building, over 800 employees of the U.S. Customs Service worked on the World Trade Center site. Every one of those individuals made it out safely. A publication later issued by the Office of Compliance, the enforcement arm of the Occupational Health and Safety Act of 1970, noted that the fact that both Morgan Stanley and the Office of Customs had spent a great deal of time and effort restructuring their evacuation plans after the 1993 bombing attack allowed almost all their employees to escape.[1] Each of these entities had a well-thought-out plan and practiced it. In the final analysis, the key element was that they also had managers who were decisive leaders who chose to act and execute the plan. This was not true for many others, who sat in their offices waiting for someone to tell them what to do. There is no way of knowing how many people owe their lives to Rick Rescorla. Whether he saved all 2,700 employees or just one is irrelevant. He took the right action.

It is up to each one of you to decide right now to act as he did, should you face a similar situation. Do not wait for someone to get up and lead. Get up, grab your things, and tell everyone to do the same. Most people are followers. It only takes one person to galvanize an entire office into action.

How is the decision to evacuate properly made? The decision to conduct a partial or full evacuation is based on the type of the building, the nature of the emergency, and the number of people present at the time. For purposes of the Emergency Response Plan, there must be a clear and unambiguous set of criteria for initiating an evacuation protocol. If a certain event occurs, then an evacuation is initiated. This must be done without hesitation, second-guessing, or discussion. Get your people out to a place of safety. Your emergency plan must cover all contingencies; plan for evacuation via several alternate routes; and designate assembly areas where employees, visitors, and guests may be accounted for. Depending on the nature of the facility, an internal assembly area may be utilized in lieu of an evacuation if it is deemed a safer alternative. This internal assembly area should be the strongest room in the most secure area in the facility that is as far from the effects of bomb blasts as possible and free from the risk of secondary explosion.

The actual evacuation may be preceded by an upgraded security condition, which will be in place once the Emergency Response Plan is activated. In most instances there is ample time to communicate with employees and prepare them prior to the order to evacuate. For example, say anti-American demonstrators are conducting a protest outside your facility. All of your employees are aware of the demonstrators' presence because you have kept everyone informed, as is called for in the Emergency Response Plan. At some point the demonstration turns violent. This information is also immediately conveyed to the workforce. At that time no evacuation has been called for. However, everyone knows what's going on, and all team leaders have been given specific instructions pursuant to the Emergency Response Plan of what to do if the situation deteriorates even further. If the demonstration reaches the point where the safety of the employees is being threatened, then a partial or full evacuation may be ordered. If exiting the building would be too dangerous, personnel may be directed to the internal assembly area.

Several situations will cause the emergency protocol to be initiated. Car bomb attack, bomb threats, suspicious objects, physical attack, violent demonstrations, natural disasters, and fire are all incidents significant enough to trigger the emergency plan. Each of the situations will call for a different response. For example, if a fire alarm is sounded or if smoke is detected, a general evacuation will be ordered. The plan must also establish specific procedures that must be followed prior to evacuation relative to securing vital documents containing classified information. In case of fire, the immediate goal is the rapid removal of company personnel from the building. Unless specific exit points are blocked, the nearest exits should be used, excluding the elevators. Other types of emergencies may call for other specific measures or different routes of evacuation. Let's suppose that a suspicious vehicle has been parked near the main exit. At approximately the same moment, a bomb threat is phoned into the company, and the caller states the bomb will explode in 10 minutes. Obviously, any route of evacuation that includes the exit adjacent to the suspicious vehicle must not be used. In this case, an alternate escape route must be employed. Therefore, the emergency plan must clearly define which routes will be indicated during which type of emergency and be able to clearly direct employees toward the route they need to take.

Now we need to discuss how exit routes should be identified to avoid confusion in a crisis. Virtually everyone has been in a building where the emergency exit signs are located high up close to the ceiling or are labeled in a very confusing manner. We can all relate to trying to leave an unfamiliar building and spending several frustrating minutes trying to figure out exactly where the exits are. Remember, this type of confusion only gets worse during a crisis. We recommend a very simple approach, one that has been successfully used in Israeli government buildings for many years: Paint colored lines indicating direction on the walls close to eye level, in such a way so as not to unduly affect the decor building decor. For example, say that in a particular section of the building the colors red and blue are used. The red line will lead personnel toward primary evacuation point A. The blue line will direct personnel to alternate evacuation point B. This system is simple and, more important, easy to follow during an emergency. It also allows personnel to move in the right direction in a rapid manner. All management needs to do is to direct all employees, visitors, and guests to exit the building using primary route A or alternate route B, which may be done by following the red or blue lines on the walls. This system has been proven to work well under even the most extreme conditions.

We've spoken a great deal about the importance of communication and timely notification to company personnel. How should such notification be made? Several effective methods can be used. A fire alarm is one very common choice. However, this type of alarm conveys only one message: Exit immediately. Alerts of this nature can convey no additional information. However, combining the fire alarm with the simple lighting system utilizing the same colors used to designate the primary and alternate escape routes may convey more information. For example, if we are using red and blue to mark the evacuation routes, we also use red and blue lights in conjunction with the fire alarm to alert personnel of the need to exit the building and which fire route to use. Telephones also may be used as a means of notification. The number or length of rings may convey simple messages. An example of this would be to designate two short rings on each phone to mean a demonstration is going on outside the building. A long ring may be used to indicate the fact that the demonstration has become violent and employees should stand by for further instructions.

Similarly, information may be conveyed over the public address system, via direct verbal communication by supervisory personnel, or via use of alternate alarms. The critical point is to make sure that the messages that must be conveyed to the workforce are clear, unambiguous, and easy to understand.

Another lesson learned in countries familiar with terrorism and that was made clear during the evacuations of the Twin Towers in New York is that simple preparatory measures make a tremendous difference in allowing individuals forced to evacuate during an emergency to do so successfully and safely. Hundreds of women trying to get out of the World Trade Center learned how difficult it is to negotiate stairs quickly while wearing high-heeled shoes. If you are accustomed to wearing such shoes to your place of employment, it is prudent to leave a pair of sneakers or similar type of footwear at your workstation. If there is a call to evacuate, it is a simple matter of changing shoes. This can make all the difference in the world. Other items of importance also should be considered. Flashlights are a necessity and should be kept available in the office. Other very useful devices are packaged emergency respirators that will provide protection against many types of toxic fumes, smoke, and biohazards. Many are also available with self-contained oxygen supplies to allow an escape in situations where there is no breathable air. These escape hoods are manufactured by such firms as Duram (see Appendix B on this book's website).

Every Emergency Response Plan also must establish procedures to deal with visitors and others not familiar with the plan. The way to accomplish this is to direct the person who is being visited to be responsible for the visitors. If that person is designated to perform a particular function during an emergency, it is his or her responsibility to find someone else to provide direction to the visitors. The plan also must provide for special-needs individuals. There are many ways to do this, but they must be preplanned before the emergency. For example, an individual confined to a wheelchair may be quickly evacuated using a chair-type stretcher. This equipment must be both available and accessible, and specific personnel must be trained to use it. Understand that during an emergency, there is no time to think about the plan, only to do it. The success is completely dependent on the level of training given to your employees.

Once the building has been evacuated, specific procedures established to account for company personnel as well as visitors at designated assembly areas. There also must be an established procedure for preventing employees from coming to work in the event an evacuation protocol is initiated before normal working hours. The presence of newcomers will only lead to confusion and hamper any attempts at rescue. In addition, the plan must facilitate a return to normal conditions once the event is over.

A properly prepared Emergency Response Plan requires both expertise and the input from all relevant departments. An effective plan can be designed only by an experienced and well-trained person. Companies should hire a well-trained security officer to supervise the security needs of the company or hire a reputable security consultant to coordinate the task. It may also be advisable to utilize the services of a consulting firm to periodically update the emergency plan, conduct surprise drills to gauge its effectiveness, and provide specialized security training for your staff. Exhibit 14.3 is a sample of an Emergency Response Plan form to provide you with a guide for creating one for your own company. Remember, we do not recommend that you create such a plan without the assistance of trained security professionals. The office of compliance has published the following recommendations.[2]

1. **Be thorough and comprehensive in planning for emergencies.** Try to cover all contingencies, not just the quickest way out of the building.

2. **Train all new people when they come on board about the contents of the plan.** Interns, like other short-term employees, should be familiar with emergency evacuation information.

3. **Implement a system to back up and store data in a remote location that can be retrieved later.** Newspaper articles reported that some workers in the World Trade Center complex lost their lives when they returned to their offices to collect information.

4. **Keep the plan current.** As staff members leave the organization, be sure to assign new employees to fill their roles in the emergency plan.

5. **Do practice drills.** Often problems are discovered when the drills are practiced.

6. **Plan for the unexpected.** During an actual emergency, there may not be telephone service or emergency lighting, and certain doors or passageways may be blocked or inaccessible.

7. **Follow the plan once it has been activated.** Once the plan is activated for whatever reason, complete the evacuation. Unless directed otherwise by law enforcement at the scene, follow the plan. Morgan

Stanley and U.S. Customs experienced no or very few fatalities because they followed the plan and left their buildings quickly.

8. **Once the fire alarm is sounded, do not wait for an announcement over the public address system.** The fire alarm is your signal to evacuate the building. There may not be an announcement.

9. **Know the facts, make no assumptions.** Do you know how to open an emergency exit that has a delayed opening device? Can the fire alarms be heard inside the rest rooms? How will people needing assistance get out of the building?

10. **Ask questions.** Know what your role and responsibilities are in an emergency evacuation. Your life can depend on it.

Exhibit 14.3   Emergency Response Guide

Why Do We Need to Create a Plan?

- In a crisis such as a bombing or bomb threat, stress, fear, and panic can lead to a state of confusion. This can result in the loss of organizational control and the lives of employees.
- A well-organized plan and the ability to make the right decision in a crisis can limit interruptions to the organization. Potential interruptions include: daily activity, lost production time, additional financial expenses, and the reduction of employee morale.

Preplanning in the form of a structured, detailed, and well-practiced system of evacuation can limit these emotional reactions and organizational interruption and increase the level of safety for all personnel involved.

General Information

Name of Organization: _____

Location: _____

Size of facility: ☐ Small   ☐ Medium   ☐ Large

Control of facility: ☐ Company-controlled   ☐ Management company
                        ☐ Multiple corporations

Number of employees: _____

Risk factor: ☐ Low   ☐ Medium   ☐ High

(continues)

Exhibit 14.3   Emergency Response Guide *(Continued)*

Basic Plan Requirements

1. Representatives from each group should be included in all aspects of planning:

   ☐ Management   ☐ Security   ☐ Plant Engineer   ☐ Maintenance

2. Instructions must be prepared in a format that is easy for employees to understand.

3. The plan must be continually updated and reflect changes in personnel and the physical structure of the facility.

4. A regularly scheduled drill of the evacuation plan must be mandated.

5. A schedule review of the plan must be established after each practice.

Critical Elements in Plan Development

1. Define departmental roles and responsibilities.

Department	**Responsibility**
Security	Evacuation and response
Management	Organizational and funding
Engineering and maintenance	Floor plan, construction, access
Supervisors (site responsibility)	Direct personnel and account for all employees

   ### *Departmental Representatives*

   Security: _____

   Management: _____

   Engineering and maintenance: _____

   Supervisory personnel: _____

   _____

   _____

2. Define emergency situations and establish criteria for initiating an emergency for each.

   Situation based on:

   • Credible information: phone threat, intelligence.

   • Suspicious item, mail, or other object in or near facility.

Type of Emergency	**Criteria for Initiating an Emergency**
Car bomb	_____
Bomb threat	_____
Suspicious object	_____
Violent demonstration	_____
Physical attack	_____
Fire	_____

3. Identify the assembly area. This must be strongest place in the facility and should be as far as possible from the bomb blast effect and free from risk of secondary explosion.

   _____

4. Define evacuation routes and assembly areas for each situation.

   Situation A: _____
   Route _____
   Assembly area _____
   Situation B: _____
   Route _____
   Assembly area _____
   Situation C: _____
   Route _____
   Assembly area _____
   Situation D: _____
   Route _____
   Assembly area _____
   Situation E: _____
   Route _____
   Assembly area _____
   Situation F: _____
   Route _____
   Assembly area _____

(continues)

Exhibit 14.3   Emergency Response Guide *(Continued)*

5. The decision to conduct a partial or full evacuation is based on the type of building, type of event, number of employees.

   Full evacuation:

   Situation: _____

   Partial evacuation:

   Situation: _____

6. Establish a method of evacuation notification that insures all employees receive the instruction.

   ☐ Fire alarm   ☐ Public address   ☐ Microphone

   ☐ Telephone   ☐ Alarm

7. Establish a procedure for visitors or others who are not familiar with the evacuation plan.

8. Establish a procedure for accounting for people in the assembly area and during the evacuation.

9. Establish a procedure to account for and evacuate visitors at the assembly area.

10. Establish a procedure to prevent people from coming to work when an evacuation protocol is initiated before normal work hours.

11. Establish a procedure to go back to normal once the event ends.

Nature of Emergency	Criteria for Initiation	Method of Notification	Partial/Full Evacuation	Routes	Assembly Areas
Car Bomb	Suspicious car or vehicle next to facility	Public address	Full		
Phone Threat	Phone call to one of the employees	Alarm Microphone	Partial/Full		
Suspicious Object	Object discovered by an employee	Alarm Microphone	Partial/Full		
Violent Demonstration	Demonstration outside with the potential for violence	Alarm Microphone	None		
Fire	Fire, Smoke	Fire Alarm	Full		

In addition to having an Emergency Response Plan to deal with general emergencies that affect the entire company, it is also necessary to have an employee-specific emergency plan. Management must maintain information on each employee that includes emergency contact numbers, the names of family members and where they can be contacted during the work day, relevant medical history, and special instructions in case of emergency. Having this information readily available will not only enhance the personal safety of the employee but also will make it easier to support the family of an employee who is injured, killed, or experiencing a medical emergency. Management should strongly consider having a family support unit within the human resources division to coordinate any help that the family might require. Both the employee's immediate supervisor and the human resources department should maintain copies of the employee emergency information form in an off-site facility. This will ensure that the information is available even if the entire facility is destroyed. See Exhibit 14.4 for an example of such a form.

This form is a sample that is recommended for every single employee in the company. During a crisis, such as a terrorist attack, fire, or natural disaster, there will be a need to have as much information as is possible to aid in treating the injured or identifying the dead. In either case, the families of employees who have become casualties will need assistance, both spiritual and material. A simple employee information form will make that task easier during a time where speed is of the essence. This form also can include fingerprints and DNA samples. It is a morbid subject even to discuss, but considering that the identification of victims from the attacks on the World Trade Center continued for more than a year after the fact, it is an option that should at least be considered. Fingerprints are easy to obtain, and a small envelope with a tuft of hair is all that is needed for DNA sampling. It is unfortunate that this has become part of the discussion in the field of emergency planning and management, but the fact is it has.

A variety of other emergency situations may arise that will require coordination rather than evacuation. Management may need to handle a kidnapping or hostage situation in a satellite facility. A natural disaster may affect the region and impact on the company personnel. There may be civil disturbances such as protests, riots, or attempts to overthrow the local government by coup d'état. It is the function of the managers staffing the emergency command center to assess the situation and verify and validate the threat to company personnel or property. They must carefully

Exhibit 14.4   Employee Emergency Information Form

Name _____ Date of Birth _____

Address _____

Department _____ Ext. _____

Telephone (home) _____ Cell _____

Marital status: ☐ Single   ☐ Married   ☐ Separated   ☐ Divorced
                  ☐ Children

Spouse _____ Daytime contact number _____

Spouse's Address _____

Physician _____ Phone _____

Address _____

Minor Children	**Age**	**School Address**	**School Phone #**
1.			
2.			
3.			

Adult Children	**Address**	**Contact**
1.		
2.		

Special Health Conditions or Allergies: _____

_____

Blood type _____ Living will: ☐ Yes   ☐ No   ☐ (If yes attach)

Religion _____ Clergyman _____ Phone _____

Special Instructions:

_____

_____

_____

_____

_____

assess the situation and explore possible outcomes. This assessment typically should include a best-case, worst-case, and middle-case outcome projection. It is also critically important to immediately enlist the assistance of the regional security officer. If the officer cannot be physically present, advise him or her or other appropriate official at the U.S. Embassy or Consulate of the actions being taken and get their assistance and input. Remember, they will have access to contacts that you may not have. Involving the embassy often will allow you to reach the appropriate contact person within the host government faster than you would be able to by yourself. You also will be able to clearly define which duties are best performed within the corporate command structure and which should more properly be left to the expertise of the embassy security staff. The command center must also stay in close contact with the home office and security staff to inform them of the situation and of the actions being taken. The home office in the U.S. should activate its own crisis and command center to allow for the acquisition of whatever assets or other assistance the beleaguered office is facing. Home office assistance will be needed when decisions are being made to protect the assets in country. It is desirable to be able to protect an asset under attack while not compromising the security of additional corporate assets elsewhere. Often the larger corporate picture must be considered, and the home office and top-level executives will need to determine the company options in responding to the emergency.

In kidnap or hostage situations, the command center will be utilized to coordinate rescue efforts with the local government or with U.S. government personnel. Part of your emergency plan will include the response to a kidnapping. The plan should include a team prepared to implement a negotiated agreement. This may require the payment of ransom and/or the promise of concessions.

The center will also be activated on receipt of a threat made against corporate employees, dependents, or property. On receipt of a threat by terrorists or other criminals, there must be an immediate effort made to ascertain its severity. This should be carried out by the Embassy Security Staff. They will, for example, be familiar with local terror organizations and activity and will be able to assess immediately whether the information received is consistent with available intelligence data. They will also have contacts with the local law enforcement community and be able to evaluate the information with the assistance of their local counterparts. While all of this is going on, local management must keep the home office abreast of the developing situation. A formal report process to facilitate this transfer of information back home should be established in much the same way as the various governmental agencies are required to notify their headquarters' command center of details about an emergency or developing crisis. Local federal law enforcement offices are required, for example, to notify the command center in Washington, D.C., about shooting incidents involving their agents. Typically, most agencies are required to make a phone-in notification to the watch commander and provide the who, what, where, when, why, and how of the situation. This information is then logged in the command center duty log. Within 24 hours, a formal teletype must be sent that provides greater details about the incident as well as an account of all actions taken to that point. A similar protocol should be established for your company as well.

NOTES

1. "Ten Safety Recommendations for Every Office," *Office of Compliance Bulletin,* Vol. 1, No. 1 (November 2001).
2. Ibid.

CHAPTER 15

Bomb Threats
and Bombings

IMAGINE YOURSELF SITTING IN YOUR OFFICE and the phone starts to ring. You answer and hear the voice of a man saying "I hate your country (or your company, race, religion) and within a few minutes a bomb in your facility is going to explode." What can you do to prevent injury, loss of life and what, if anything, can you do to minimize the damage? Although many bombings occur with no warning, on occasion an individual who has placed an explosive device in a particular location will call or otherwise contact the targeted facility to warn that a bomb will go off within a certain amount of time.

Although it hardly makes sense to speak of bombers as having a sense of humanity, a warning allows the occupants of a building to evacuate, thereby reducing the number of human casualties. The resultant damage will be to property, not people. Unfortunately, the reality of the period in history in which we live has shown that damage to property alone will not satisfy many of today's terrorists. No distinction is made between combatants and noncombatants or among men, women, or children. Still, a bomb threat protocol must be included in any Emergency Response Plan. If a bomb threat is received, it is crucial that as much information be obtained from the caller as is possible, given the fact that time is of the essence. Initially the goal is to find out, if the caller is willing to provide the information, when the device will explode, where it has been placed, and what will cause it to explode. Obviously, the amount of time to effect an evacuation is of paramount importance. The bomb's location is equally as important because it will determine which evacuation route will be selected. And of course the question of what will cause the bomb to explode is important because it might provide information that will prevent the device from detonating. Exhibit 15.1 is a sample bomb threat checklist. We reviewed similar checklists published by the Bureau of Alcohol Tobacco and Firearms, the Federal Bureau of Investigation (FBI), and various other federal state and local police agencies. In the exhibit we've included the elements from each that we think are most important. Before we discuss some of the other questions on the checklist, we should make it very clear that the first and foremost priority after receiving a bomb threat is to quickly gather information that will help save lives. The checklist contains a number of questions to ask the caller. As we have mentioned, the person receiving the call should ask the safety-related questions first and act on them. If the caller states that a bomb will explode in several hours, there probably will be time to ask all the questions listed on the checklist. Some questions may be answered and some may not. The first five questions (they should be color coded in red when you use this checklist in printed form) are the safety-related questions, which must be asked first. Questions 6 through 10 are investigative in nature. These are designed to obtain additional information that will be needed later by investigators. The checklisted items are also geared to assist in a subsequent investigation of the attack or threat. These questions do not need to be answered during the phone call. However, they will be very useful to assist the person receiving the call in remembering as much detail as possible. The instructions at the bottom of the form say to call 911 and report the threat, but of course police emergency numbers vary from country to country. Every employee should know the local equivalent of "911" or how to contact the police as quickly as possible.

The other suggestion is to keep the caller talking as long as possible. That suggestion, of course, gets tossed right out the window if the caller tells you the bomb will explode in several minutes. Otherwise, try to get as much information from the caller as you can. When you evacuate, take the form with you and try to fill it out while the information is still fresh in your mind.

Remember, the overriding concern when receiving a bomb threat is safety. You must not waste precious time attempting to engage the caller and obtain additional information if by doing so you put your life or anyone else's life at risk.

Exhibit 15.1   Sample Bomb Threat Checklist

Exact date and time of call: _____

Received by: _____

Number receiving call: _____

Exact words of caller: _____

Questions to ask caller:

1. When will the bomb explode? _____

2. Where is the bomb? _____

3. What does it look like? _____

4. What will cause it to explode? _____

5. What kind of bomb is it? _____

6. Did you place the bomb? _____

7. Why did you place the bomb? _____

8. What is your name? _____

9. Where are you calling from? _____

10. What is your address? _____

Background noise:

Factory   ☐

Street   ☐

Airplanes   ☐

Office sounds   ☐

Voices   ☐

Trains   ☐

Party   ☐

Quiet   ☐

Music   ☐

Animals   ☐

Familiarity with threatened facility:

Much   ☐

Some   ☐

None   ☐

Did the caller sound familiar?

Yes   ☐

No   ☐

If yes, whom did he sound like?

_____

_____

(continues)

Exhibit 15.1   Sample Bomb Threat Checklist *(Continued)*

Voice		**Speech**		**Accent**	
Loud	☐	Fast	☐	Local	☐
High pitched	☐	Distinct	☐	Foreign	☐
Raspy	☐	Stutter	☐		
Intoxicated	☐	Slurred	☐	**Language**	
Soft	☐	Distorted	☐	Educated	☐
Deep	☐	Nasal	☐	Fair	☐
Pleasant	☐	Lisp	☐	Poor	☐
Other	☐	Other	☐	Abusive	☐
				Foul	☐
Manner		**Sex**			
Calm	☐	Male	☐		
Rational	☐	Female	☐		
Coherent	☐	Approx. age: _____			
Deliberate	☐	Caller ID: _____			
Righteous	☐	Ethnicity _____			
Angry	☐	Remarks _____			
Irrational	☐	_____			
Amused	☐	_____			

CALL 911 (or its local equivalent) **IMMEDIATELY.**
Keep caller talking as long as possible.

One additional safety point that must be discussed is what to do in the seconds immediately after a bomb blast. For example, you are seated at your desk and hear a loud explosion outside the building. Your natural reaction is to jump up, rush to window, and look to see what has happened. In all likelihood you will reach the window a second or two before the pressure wave from the explosion blows it out and sends shards of glass through you and anyone else standing in an unprotected area. According to the U.S. State Department, this is exactly what caused the death toll to be so high from the Al Qaeda bombing attack on the U.S. embassy in Nairobi. The physics are quite simple. The speed of sound is faster than the pressure wave generated by the blast. If you hear an explosion, you must overcome your initial reaction to run to the window and look outside and instead drop to the floor, under a desk if possible. Do not attempt to stand up and run until after the effects of the blast reach you and blow out the windows.

Another word of caution is warranted. The Israelis learned the painful lesson that often terrorists plant two or more explosive devices in the same general area. The first device detonates. After the initial shock, police, rescue workers, and additional civilians rush to the scene and try to help the victims. The bombers watch from a safe distance until they are satisfied with the number of people at the scene, then they remotely detonate the second device. This is a no-win situation. Very few people can suppress their humanity and allow fear to prevent them from helping the wounded. If possible, try to allow trained professionals to secure the area before you rush in. This type of dual explosive attack is also being used to kill civilians who survive an initial attack and then run to seek cover in the closest protected area. It is a favorite tactic of groups like Hamas, which routinely try to kill additional civilians in Israel in this way. The bombers plant the first explosive device in an area calculated to kill the greatest number of people. They place a second device in an adjacent area to which the survivors would be likely to run to to seek shelter. The terrorist murderers watch from a safe distance until enough men, women, and children have reached the area of presumed safety and then detonate the bomb with a simple cell phone call to a phone attached to the device. Make sure that you factor this information in to any part of your Emergency Response Plan (see Chapter 14) that deals with evacuations and bombings.

There have been more than 75 suicide bombings in Israel over the last two years. Each of these attacks has been extensively analyzed to allow the Israeli police and intelligence agencies to come up with a profile of suicide bombers, which can be used to detect such bombers before they can strike. An Israeli journalist named Etgar Lefkovits[1] wrote an interesting piece on this very subject for the *Jerusalem Post*. He reported that the first 40,000 copies of the bomber profile brochure were released to the general public after months of debate about whether the information would benefit the public or just allow terrorists to review their methods of infiltration and disguise and come up with new ways to deliver their deadly explosives. After six months of debate, the police and Israeli government decided it would be more advantageous to disseminate the information to the Israeli public. The police decided that the terrorists had already been changing their tactics to try to stay ahead of the police response, so releasing the information would not hinder police action. Palestinian terrorists were already using many innovative methods to allow their bombers to infiltrate Israel and reach their targets without detection. They routinely changed their appearance to try to blend in by dyeing their hair blond, using gel in their hair as many teens do to create "wild" hairstyles, wearing look-alike or stolen Israeli Defense Force (IDF) uniforms, and donning kippot (skull caps). Some signs that the brochure advises Israelis to pay attention to are:

- Someone wearing heavy clothing not appropriate for the climate
- A young man or woman who seems to be attempting to fit in with the surroundings even though he or she clearly does not
- Something obviously sticking out of someone's clothes
- Someone who is nervously scratching or rubbing an article of clothing
- Someone perspiring heavily while walking slowly and looking around
- Someone seen muttering, hesitant, or nervous, or attempting to avoid security officials or police

The brochure urges people who see anyone with these characteristics to immediately call the police emergency number and, if possible, to keep the person in sight from a safe distance. The guide also offers tips on identifying a potential car bomb; people should be aware of vehicles with unclear or distorted license plates, plates that don't match in the back and front, a car that looks weighted down in the rear, or a car that is parked in a suspicious manner.

NOTE

1. Etgar Lefkovits, *The Jerusalem Post*, August 28, 2002.

CHAPTER 16

Hotel Safety
and Security

THUS FAR, THIS BOOK HAS DISCUSSED how to maximize security in areas over which you have daily control. We have discussed how to secure your residence, your vehicle, and your place of employment. However, often you will be traveling either on business or for pleasure. Traveling presents a variety of additional security concerns. The next several chapters provide you with the necessary information to maximize your personal security while en route to your intended destination and while staying in local hotels.

Making security enhancements at your home or workplace is easy because you have both control over the location and the time to make the necessary improvements. Obviously, as a guest at a hotel you have neither of these advantages. Therefore, the best thing you can do to enhance your physical security while traveling is to select a hotel that meets your security needs. The single best way to find a good and secure place to stay is to contact the embassy or consulate. Ask where diplomats and other government officials stay when they are in country. The regional security officer (RSO) is a good source for information. You can be sure that the RSO has a list of several thoroughly vetted hotels that are used to house VIPs when they come to the officer's area of responsibility. Another easy suggestion to follow is simply to stay at the better hotels belonging to a reputable chain. Major hotel chains generally are managed by Americans or Europeans and have security standards that are comparable to the security standards in the United States. These hotels recognize the tremendous negative impact that will occur should something unfortunate happen to one of their guests. They have a security division with officers on duty around the clock. While this certainly does not take the place of using common sense and adhering to your basic security guidelines, it does make a difference. There is always a deterrent value in having a guard force present regardless of its level of skill. No security is foolproof, but some security is better than none at all. The bottom line is that you shouldn't try to save a few dollars by staying in cheap hotels that are short on service as well as security. Although everyone wants to save money, avoiding a more secure place to stay to save a few bucks is not worth it.

KNOW THE AREA

Prior to checking in, there are several things you should research. First, check the overall location of the hotel and make sure it is in an area that is safe and easily accessible. Again, if you aren't sure, call the embassy and ask about the hotel and the area. By the way, this is also a good way to find out a great deal of information about a lot more than security issues. The staff at the embassy will know the hotels with the best restaurants and overall service as well as where to get the best value for your money. Call and ask anyone you talk with where they would tell their own family or friends to stay. They will be glad to help. A quick check with the embassy also can alert you to specific problems in whatever area you are intending to stay in. For example, perhaps there has been a rash of car thefts or assaults in the part of town you are going to, and that information is too current to have made it onto the State Department website.

Make sure there is a secure parking area adjacent to the hotel. It is better if the parking garage is physically on the premises and there is no need to walk back to the hotel from the garage if you happen to return late at night. The lot should be well lit, guarded, and have access limited to hotel staff and guests. Valet parking is also a plus.

When you check in, try not to use your name or, at the very least, inform the desk not to release any information about you to anyone. That way you will make it harder for people to find out if you are staying at the hotel or to identify your room number. Also, ask the front desk not to deliver any packages to your room. Use the services of the hotel bellman to transport your luggage to your room. Anything of extreme value or sensitivity should remain in your possession. Let the bellman open the door to your room, and have him turn on the lights for you as well.

ROOM SELECTION

After you have chosen a reputable hotel to stay in, the location of your room is the next thing you can do to improve your level of security. Most security experts recommend getting a room that is at least one story above ground level but no higher than seven stories up. The reason to avoid the first floor should be obvious to everyone by now. It is always easier for someone to break into a room at ground level. While it is possible for someone to climb to higher floors and break in, it is far less likely to occur. The restriction not to stay above the seventh floor is because the seventh floor is the last that is within reach of most firefighting evacuation buckets and ladders.

While this is true, in many parts of the world you will be lucky if there is a professional fire department, let alone firefighting equipment. The better option is always try to stay on the second floor and no higher than the third floor. If your hotel room is engulfed in flames, you have the survivable option of jumping out the window. If you need to jump from the second floor, it is likely that you will receive only minor injuries, depending on your physical condition and age. From the third floor, your odds of being injured go up but are still within acceptable limits, especially if your only other alternative is to die of smoke inhalation or burns. You can make crude but effective ropes from sheets that can allow you to descend out a window to a safer level, once again depending on your physical ability. Higher than the third floor and the fall will likely prove fatal if you are forced to jump. We discuss some additional fire safety measures below.

IDENTIFY EMERGENCY ESCAPE ROUTES

Note the location of the emergency exits and all stairwells. Make sure you know which direction you must take to get to an exit from your room. Make it a practice to physically count the number of doors between your room and the exit. First locate the nearest emergency exit. Then locate an alternate exit. Beginning from your room, count the number of doors between your room and the nearest exit. For example, if the closest stairwell is down the hallway to the left, count the number of intervening doors. Perhaps the stairwell is down the hall to the left and is on the opposite side of the hallway. In that case you simply count the number of doors until you must cross the hallway to find the exit. Do the same thing for exits that can be reached by making several turns down other hallways.

Count in this manner: I exit the room and there are eight doors until I reach the end of the corridor. I must then make a right, pass four more doors, and cross the hallway to reach the exit. Doing this will allow you to find your way to an exit even if the power is out and you are attempting to get out in darkness or heavy smoke. If you can't see, you can still feel your way down the hall and get to safety by counting the doors you pass. Do the same thing for an alternate exit point, if one exists, so you always have a backup plan in case the primary escape route is impossible to reach. If you exit your room and can't reach the primary exit, you just take the secondary exit route. Also, it is a good idea to prepare yourself to be able to retrace your steps back to your room. If, when you reach the primary exit, you find that route is impassable, you will need to retrace your steps and make for the secondary exit. Never use the elevator in a fire or other emergency.

YOUR HOTEL ROOM IS NOT YOUR HOME

One thing that must be understood is that your room is never truly secure. It is not your home, and you cannot control the number of people having access to your room. Your room will be cleaned, generally on a daily basis. In many fine hotels housekeeping pays a second visit to your room to turn down the bed. Therefore, every chambermaid in the hotel has a key that will open your door. Similarly, hotel managers, maintenance workers, and security officers also have keys to your room. Not only do these people have access to your room; they also are expected to be there for a variety of reasons.

Keep in mind that in many countries, the police and local intelligence services will have nearly unfettered access not only to your room but to the phone system as well. In hotels in Russia, the People's Republic of China, and Cuba, many of the rooms are wired with both listening devices and video monitors. Hotel managers know which guests are to be given which rooms.

In many countries, the employees at local hotels make a weekly salary that, although it may be higher than the average for local factory workers, is less than you may spend weekly on cigarettes. Do you think these people would be susceptible to bribery? For example, if you are a businessman engaged in sensitive negotiations with a local company, it is quite conceivable that the local corporate interest would be able to have a chambermaid check your room for documents you may have left out. It would be a simple matter for the company to pay a maid a few dollars to place your room trash in a separate bag and deliver it later. Could a local competitor obtain anything that might be useful in that manner? The answer is yes, unless you never leave anything of importance unsecured in your room. Assume that your room is under electronic surveillance, that it will be searched, or both. If you keep that thought in mind, you will never discuss anything of importance in your room or leave sensitive documents there.

Avoid rooms with connecting doors. It is common among law enforcement agencies to hold undercover meetings in hotel rooms with a connecting door. The backup team monitors the meeting from the next room and is prepared to move into the meeting room to assist the agent if there is trouble or if an arrest must be made. Criminals, terrorists, and local intelligence officers can do the same thing. It is very easy to disable the lock from your side of the room. While you can check it and it will seem secure, actually it can be opened easily from the adjoining room.

There are a few other tips that we all know and understand, but they bear repeating anyway. We all know that we shouldn't invite strangers into our room. We know it but ignore the rule as soon as we've had a few drinks and an attractive member of the opposite sex indicates a willingness to accompany us back to our room. This prohibition is certainly even truer if the person in question is a prostitute. Don't do it. This means not under any circumstances. It is a breach of basic safety rules. Should you let such a person into your room, you are completely vulnerable to a whole host of dangers. Sexually transmitted diseases are rampant in many parts of the world. In Bangkok, Thailand, it is estimated that fully half of the working girls are HIV positive. In South Africa the rates are even higher.

Consider as well that prostitutes commonly go back to the room of an individual they think is affluent. Once there, it is a simple matter for them to slip any one of many drugs into your drink that will render you unconscious while they ransack the place. Even if no drugs are used, just consider how vulnerable you are once you have fallen asleep. In addition, beyond the danger of disease or theft, there is also the very real chance that you are being compromised for blackmail purposes. A few photos of a married executive with a prostitute can convince anyone to cooperate with local intelligence operatives or to divulge sensitive corporate information.

Along that same line of reasoning, do not invite anyone up to your room unless you are well acquainted with the person. Avoid meeting business contacts in your room as well. Make it a point to treat your hotel room like your bedroom at home. It is your living space and the place where you sleep.

ROOM SECURITY

Be sure you always secure your door with the dead bolt as well as the door chain. By the way, consider this more of a privacy measure than anything else. We can personally attest to the relative ease with which a door chain can be defeated. The chain is especially useful if you are sleeping or in the shower and the chambermaid enters because you forget to put out the "Do Not Disturb" sign. It also may be a deterrent to some types of crime. While a door chain provides very little protection to a determined individual, it will hinder a thief attempting to gain quiet entry to your room at night. You can buy small electronic devices to use as a room alarm. The devices consist of a buzzer that is activated when two metallic prongs are separated. The prongs are flat and thin, and they slide easily in between the closed door and the door frame. If the door is opened, the prongs separate and the buzzer sounds. It is also a good idea to keep the "Privacy Please" sign on your door at all times as an additional deterrent.

Another thing that can help you determine if someone has entered your room while you were out is to place a small piece of paper between the door and the frame. Ilan, in his former capacity as a diplomat, used hotels very often and found this simple method to be very effective to see whether someone had entered his room while he was gone. He placed a small piece of paper between the door and the frame every time he left the room. Upon his return, he looked for the piece of paper before he entered the room. If the paper was not where he put it, there was a good chance that someone entered the room. If the paper was present but in a different location then it is likely that someone skilled entered your room. Once your room has been cleaned, simply put up the "Do Not Disturb" sign. Leaving the television or radio on while you are out is another way to help keep out anyone who doesn't belong there.

FIRE

In the event of a fire, there are several things that you should do. Remember, the time to plan for this contingency is the moment you ask for a room on the second floor. By now you have already counted the number of doors between your room and the nearest stairwell, as described above. You also have noted the position of the fire alarms and extinguishers, if any. If you have elected to stay in a reputable hotel, there probably will be an active sprinkler system as well as smoke detectors. These systems can alert you to the presence of a fire or smoke before the actual alarm is even sounded. It is good practice to carry your own smoke detectors that also can detect the presence of carbon monoxide in the area. You always can check whether the detector installed in your room is working by pressing the test button. However, there is no way for you to check whether the unit is as sensitive to the presence of smoke as devices manufactured in the United States. In any event, it is unlikely that the hotel-installed smoke detector will protect against carbon monoxide poisoning. Therefore, it is a good idea to use your own and gain peace of mind. Take extra batteries with you, and store the detector in your checked luggage with the batteries out of the unit.

In the event of a fire, never open the door unless you have physically felt it and the knob to see whether they are hot. If the door and knob are hot, you can assume that there is fire in the hallway outside of your door. Opening the door will cause the flames to rush into your room as a new source of oxygen becomes available. The air that will be drawn in is most likely toxic and is certain to be superheated. Inhaling in such an atmosphere will bring the high temperature air into your lungs and will burn them. If the door and knob are hot, turn the water on in the bathtub and wet all the sheets and towels you can. Fill the tub with water. You are in immediate danger from smoke inhalation, which can suffocate you even if the flames never get near you. Place the wet towels on the floor below the door to prevent smoke from coming in. Seal any other cracks as well. Try the phone. If the call goes through, tell the desk that you are trapped in your room and give your name and room number. Obviously, if you are on the second floor, this is the appropriate time to open the window and jump or climb to safety. If you are on a higher floor, you should wait as long as possible to see if rescue equipment is being brought to the scene. Open your window and place a white sheet or towel outside. This is a universally recognized distress sign and will alert rescue personnel to your presence. Do not break the window unless there is no other way of opening it. You may need to close the window if smoke begins to come into your room from outside. Unfortunately, most hotel windows do not open, and you will need to break the glass.

Keep wet sheets and towels at hand. If the room becomes smoke filled, place the wet towels over your mouth and nose and breathe through them. This will filter out a great deal of the particulate matter. Stay low, because smoke rises and will be thinnest the closer to the ground that you are. Several emergency escape hoods are available (see Chapter 10 for a discussion of such devices). They are self-contained rubber and plastic respirators built into emergency hoods. Some products are effective only against smoke and a limited number of toxic gases. Others are better and actually provide protection even against carbon monoxide. Others still have their own self-contained supply of oxygen, typically enough for five to twenty minutes. These are effective but are also bulkier and more expensive and may be difficult to travel with. Some of the models made by Duram and Supergum fit into very small packages and still provide protection against a variety of poisonous fume that will be released during a fire. Do not fail to appreciate the danger of fumes that are released when plastics and other manmade materials are burned. Most people who are killed during a fire die as a result of smoke inhalation, poisonous fumes, or having their lungs burned by inhaling superheated air.

If the fire is burning intensely outside your door, it is only a matter of time before the door will be consumed. If you are trapped in your room, you have little choice other than to try to keep the door as wet as possible. Take the ice bucket, drinking glasses, or the wastepaper basket and continuously douse the door with water from the bathtub. This will buy you a little time. It is hoped that that is all you will need. The filled tub may become your last place of refuge if help has not arrived. If all else fails, get into the tub and immerse as much of your body as possible, covering your head and face with wet towels. Do this only as an absolute last resort because you are now going to be engulfed in flames with little chance of rescue. You are also in danger from the likely event that the fire is burning below you and that the structure has been weakened to the point that the floor might give way. Still, this may provide you with time to survive while the fire is being brought under control by the sprinklers and fire department. Even so, before either of us would opt for this choice, we would first make absolutely sure that there was no way to get out around the fire, perhaps via an adjoining room or by escaping out the window onto a ledge.

CHAPTER 17

Hijacked

THE SUBJECT OF HIJACKING is perhaps the most difficult on which to provide instruction. The traditional school of thought, advocated by experts who had studied the hijackings perpetrated in the 1970s and 1980s, always focused on compliance with the hijackers and cautioned against taking any action against them. The State Department published a set of guidelines that listed the most effective ways to survive a hijacking by keeping a low profile. The guidelines stressed that the most important thing to do was to remain below the hijackers' radar by being docile and unobtrusive. The material posted by the State Department and other related government departments provides instruction on how to avoid being noticed or singled out and how to stay away from the area that will be the focus of attention by terrorist hijackers. This material suggests that you begin planning to avoid such focus even as you purchase your seat on the airplane. You should ask for a window seat rather than an aisle seat. If the plane is hijacked, you will then be close to the window and farther away from the attention of the bad guys. Keep as much distance between you and them and avoid catching their eyes. Obey the terrorists and don't do anything to get them upset. The most dangerous moments of a hijacking are the initial takeover and during any attempt at rescue. The terrorists are likely to be nervous as well, the guidelines say, especially during the initial assault. Of course they will be nervous; after all, they are only human. In fact, the guidelines say that later on you may be able to use this common thread of humanity that you both share. They suggest trying to develop a rapport with the captors and gradually make some small requests for items to enhance your personal comfort. If you have family pictures with you, it will be to your advantage. Everyone has family. It may be the way to bridge the gap that exists between you and the hijackers. (This advice is sounder when applied to a long-term hostage ordeal.) You will be humanized to them, and they will be less likely to harm you.

The guidelines remind you that you also must maintain your dignity while being held hostage by the hijackers. This seems to be quite a tall order under the circumstances. On the whole, these guidelines are very similar to the suggestions given by most experts about how to behave during a kidnapping or hostage situation. Because in some cases a hijacking can degenerate into a prolonged hostage situation, there are common elements to both scenarios. However, there are also marked differences and, therefore, reasons to approach each scenario differently.

CHANGE OF TERRORIST GOALS WARRANTS CHANGE IN STRATEGY

Recent events have caused airline security experts all over the world to rethink the traditional school of thought on how to behave during a hijacking. Prior to the events of September 11, 2001, airline security experts almost uniformly recommended the docile and nonconfrontational approach during a hijacking crisis. The reason was obvious. Traditionally, hijackers had taken planes to use them as bargaining chips. They tried to gain control of the plane and then divert it to somewhere from which they could get other terrorists aboard to assist them. Then they would begin to threaten to kill the hostages one by one unless and until their demands were met. The premise was that the lives of the hostages had value; therefore, the hostages wouldn't harm or kill anyone without provocation because doing so would be contrary to their goals. The advice was always to "Obey the hijackers," "Keep a low profile," and "Avoid eye contact with the hijackers." As we noted above, lesson plans went into great detail about where to sit to stay below the terrorists' radar. Passengers were encouraged to fly wide-bodied aircraft because hijackers thought the large number of passengers and multiple aisles made them too difficult to manage. All of these theories (except the fact that wide-bodied planes are still not preferred by hijackers) went out the window on September 11. All of a sudden the goal was to turn passenger planes into missiles. This eventuality was not factored into the equation while attempting to formulate effective guidelines for passengers who found themselves in the middle of a hijacking. Silently obeying the commands of fanatics whose actions would certainly result in your death was no longer the best advice. Suddenly the experts were recommending passenger rebellions and pilots armed with pistols.

The bottom line is that no one really knows what to do. It is easy for anyone to Monday morning quarterback every terrorist incident. Unfortunately, the majority of us can't read minds. If you knew that all your assailants wanted was to take you on a nice plane ride to Cuba, the advice of "Listen to the nice terrorists and do what they say" would seem to make sense. Now, however, you don't know if they intend to fly the plane into the airspace of a country friendly to them or into something they wish to destroy. In fact, in Bin Laden's taped discussion of the attacks, it is clear that most of the hijackers themselves did not know what the true nature of the mission was. Apparently only a few of the terrorists knew that the mission was actually a large-scale suicide bombing. Once it becomes clear that the planes are to be flown into buildings, passengers have no choice other than to act. To do nothing is certainly to perish. As Ambassador Francis X. Taylor told the Congressional Committee on International Relations:

> One result of the terrorists' stark "us" vs. "them" attitude is their willingness to kill large numbers of innocent people in suicide attacks without claiming responsibility or stating a measurable demand. In the past, when terrorists hijacked aircraft or took over a building, they did so in pursuit of specific and quantifiable political goals, such as forcing governments to release previously captured colleagues or the media to publish manifestos. The September 11 attacks were a continuation of the trend to inflict maximum casualties, without regard to loss of life or likelihood of achieving specific demands. The planners used a ghastly scenario of the kind that could be imagined only by people so full of hatred that they are beyond the civilized pale.[1]

This tactic represents a quantum shift in the mind-set of those terrorists who continue to use airliners in furtherance of their goals. This change also has caused airline security experts to rethink the standard approach to a hijacking that suggests docility. Almost every American is aware of the now-famous last recorded words of Todd Beamer, a passenger on United Airlines Flight 93. The passengers on board knew they were the fourth plane hijacked that day, and they knew the fate of the other three planes. Beamer and several other passengers decided not to go as sheep to the slaughter. Instead, they fought the terrorists and prevented them from crashing the plane into the White House or another major government target. Ordinary citizens, untrained and unarmed, fought with five armed terrorists and won. Tragically, they were only able to save the lives of their fellow Americans on the ground at the cost of their own. Beamer's words, "Let's roll," have entered the American lexicon and will always be remembered. The passengers aboard the first three planes—two of which hit the World Trade Center and one that hit the Pentagon—apparently followed the advice given by our federal government. They sat quietly and tried not to be noticed as the terrorists flew the planes into their targeted objectives. The passengers on Flight 93 out of Newark decided not to take that advice and refused to "go gentle into that good night." While they lost their lives, their valiant behavior saved the lives of countless others who would have been killed had the fourth plane been allowed to proceed against its intended target.

RECOMMENDATIONS

Is there currently a consensus on what to do in the unlikely event that you are aboard a hijacked airline? Probably not. The truth of the matter is that there are knowledgeable security experts on both sides of the issue. Our approach is to cover both methods that are being recommended by experts in this field. If you are ever the unfortunate victim of this type of attack, you will need to make that decision for yourself. If the terrorists seem to be using passengers as bargaining chips, then you opt for the traditional advice: Maintain a low profile and try not to be noticed. However, if it even appears as if something more imminently dangerous is happening, then you must begin to switch your mind-set to fight back with every bit of strength and ferocity you have and destroy those who would otherwise destroy you. The philosophy that we have espoused in this book is somewhat different from that in most other security publications. You need to be able to understand how to play both cards. At the onset of the hijacking, it is probably sound advice to try to keep a low profile and avoid having the attention of the terrorists focus on you. However, this is a means to an end, not an end in and of itself. There may come a time when you personally need to act. The situation is, quite literally, one of life or death. If you don't have to physical ability to fight, then perhaps you can support others who can. You may need to be a leader and to rally others. This approach means that every single person must make a conscious decision not to sit and do nothing while vicious and depraved sociopaths take away your life and your future.

Do not make any moves right away. It is possible that there is an armed air marshal on board who may be planning to take action, and you need to stay out of the way if shooting starts. Armed security agents typically wait to assess the nature of the opposition before they act. They will be readying themselves to attack the hijackers as they try to ascertain how many bad guys they will be facing. They will prepare themselves to go for their weapon even as they wait for the terrorists to become distracted and turn their attention away. When the agents move, it will be quickly and decisively. Remember, if you are on board an aircraft during this type of emergency and a security agent takes action, do not get out of your seat and try to help once the shooting starts. The agent does not know who you are and will likely view you as another target who must be engaged. Hijackers may have an accomplice or "sleeper" sitting among the passengers. Keep down and cover your head. If you are traveling with children, get on top of them. If the time comes and you need to fight, you must fight with a level of ferocity foreign to most civilized people. You will now be in a fight for your life and the lives of your family. You need to get angry and to utterly annihilate the inhuman monsters who would take your future from you. They care not at all if your spouse loses you or if your children grow up without dad or mom around. This is not being melodramatic. Todd Beamer knew this when he led an unarmed and untrained group of passengers into hand-to-hand combat with the terrorists. Could they have been successful in retaking the plane? It seems that they were close to doing just that. The point is that they did not accept their fate quietly. It is certain that their actions saved lives on the ground. The passengers of Flight 93 denied the terrorists their goal. Perhaps they saved the White House or Capitol building from destruction. Who knows what effect that could have had on our government's ability to respond? They did better than anyone could have hoped they would. Would that they had been able to kill the terrorists and survive themselves.

CONFRONTING THE THREAT

The recommendations put out by the State Department have not been changed as of this writing. The advice is still for passengers to do nothing and not fight back. Travelers are advised not to get involved if they observe a disturbance or attack. We reject this as a generally accepted theory. While in some instances such behavior may be appropriate, today the people likely to confront you on a plane don't need you alive to bargain with. In fact, your presence is actually incidental to them. To sit by and do nothing only makes it easier for them to end your life.

If you must fight, these rules must be burned into your mind:

- Maintain the will to live.
- Do not give up.
- Fight despite your fear or injuries.
- Initiate immediate violent, effective action to terminate threats to your life, your safety, or that of others.

We are aware that this seems to be an almost impossible task, but be assured that fighting for one's life is well within everyone's ability. The attackers have a plan. Dealing with determined resistance is not something they are counting on. Their plan is to attack violently, perhaps brutally murdering passengers before your eyes to cow everyone into obedience. Having to fight dozens of enraged passengers is not in their realm of expectation. It may very well be your only way to survive. There are many instances to observe just how ordinary citizens rose up to meet a threat to their lives and the lives of their fellows. On December 7, 1993, a gunman opened fire on passengers aboard a Long Island Rail Road Train near the Merillon Avenue station in Nassau County, New York. Three heroic passengers physically attacked the gunman, Colin Ferguson, while he was reloading his 9 mm pistol and ended the rampage, which left 6 dead and 17 wounded. On December 22, 2001, an airline passenger named Richard Reid, a 28-year-old British citizen of British and Jamaican ancestry, attempted to blow up a plane with explosives hidden in his shoe. Passengers and flight attendants overpowered Reid, who has since been linked to radical Muslim terrorist organizations, when they observed him trying to touch a lit match to his sneakers during the Paris-to-Miami flight. Federal Bureau of Investigation (FBI) agents later testified at Reid's bail hearing that the explosive in his shoe was of sufficient quantity and destructive power to have blown a hole in the plane's fuselage. Incidents like these as well as dozens of others are leading aviation security experts to encourage passengers to take action during a hijacking or other crisis.

As a general rule, the most dangerous times of a hijacking occur during the initial takeover and during any assault on the aircraft to end the event. Obviously, this was not true of the hijackings of September 11.

Still, there are enough data relative to the more "traditional" hijacking scenarios to support this statement. The initial assault may well be an extremely violent experience as the hijackers take control of the plane. Passengers and crew may be randomly shot or beaten, and the attackers may be screaming out orders for everyone to follow. At this time they are seeking to terrify those on board into following their orders. Yet this is not always the case. There have been incidents where the hijackers have managed to take control of the plane by quietly gaining access to the cockpit.

RESCUE ATTEMPTS

Attempts to retake the aircraft also present extreme dangers to the passengers and crew of the aircraft. Ordinarily, hijackings are treated in much the same way as hostage situations; trained hostage negotiators attempt to end the situation peacefully by establishing a dialogue with the hijackers. The assault option is held as a last resort to implement if negotiations fail or if the hijackers begin killing the passengers. If an assault is attempted, it will, if the entry team is well trained, be fast and violent. The doors may be breached by explosive charges, and flash bangs (stun grenades) will likely be used both as a diversionary tactic and to disorient the hijackers. If the assault team is wearing night-vision equipment to give them a tactical advantage over the hijackers, the lights may be cut, plunging the plane into total darkness. Your only option is to get yourself and those with you as low as possible. Do not stand up for any reason. The assault team will be yelling for you to get down. Anyone standing, especially if the person gets up quickly, will in all likelihood get shot. Once the plane is secured, everyone will be ordered off. Standard procedure is to have the passengers exit with their hands up. This is done because the police or military team conducting the rescue has no way of knowing if you are a passenger or a hijacker. There have been several documented cases of hijackers attempting to escape by exiting quietly along with the passengers. Until the rescuers are sure of your identity, expect to be considered a possible suspect. Most Americans recall the sight of terrified children running out from Columbine High School with their hands up after the horrific mass-shooting incident.

Once you have been properly identified, you will in all likelihood receive considerable assistance from the State Department officials monitoring the situation. Your health and safety will be their first concern, as will letting you contact your loved ones as soon as possible. You also can expect to be extensively debriefed by law enforcement and intelligence personnel, especially if you have not been freed as a result of a crisis-ending assault but have been released through negotiated efforts while others are still being held. Your duty will be to assist officials and provide as much detailed information as you possibly can. It may well be that something you remember or noticed while you were held will facilitate the release of others.

If the hijacking leads to a drawn-out situation where passengers are being held for a long period of time, try to remain as calm and clear-headed as possible. Everything is being done to facilitate your release. The U.S. government's policy is firm: It will negotiate but not make concessions. It is the responsibility of the host government to deal with the situation. This may or may not be good news. If you are in Britain, Germany, or Israel, you will be in good shape. The governments there are responsible, and they possess the ability to mount a rescue operation if necessary. If you are being held in Lebanon or Uruguay, however, you may be in trouble.

Avoid resistance and sudden or threatening movements. Do not struggle or try to escape unless you are certain of being successful. You should weigh many factors carefully before making such a decision. You must take into account your personal ability and physical condition. Have you had any training in unarmed combat or escape techniques?

If you are being held, prepare yourself for the possibility of a long ordeal. Now is the time to follow the State Department's suggestions and remain inconspicuous. If addressed, speak normally. Do not be argumentative or belligerent, and comply with all orders and instructions. If the hijackers' interrogate you, cooperate and answer their questions as briefly as you can. We go into further detail on this subject in Chapter 18.

NOTE

1. Testimony to the Committee on International Relations, House of Representatives, by Ambassador Francis X. Taylor, Coordinator for Counterterrorism, U.S. Department of State, September 25, 2002.

CHAPTER 18

Hostage Survival

A GREAT DEAL HAS BEEN WRITTEN on the subject of how to survive being held as a hostage. Former victims, some of whom were held by their captors for many years, have penned scores of books. As you read this book, many people, including American citizens, are being held against their will in countries all over the world by individuals seeking money for ransom or by those using human beings as bargaining chips to try to further their political agenda.

The first thing to accept regarding this subject is that while your odds of being kidnapped are very low, anyone can be taken hostage. If you are a high-profile individual, you can safely assume that your odds are somewhat higher than others. However, sometimes you can just be in the wrong place at the wrong time and wind up a victim of this terrible crime. In many countries kidnapping has become an industry. Foreign business personnel are likely to be snatched as the kidnappers realize that a corporation will pay a hefty ransom for their release.

COOPERATE OR RESIST?

Here again, this is a subject where traditional techniques of hostage survival are being rethought as a result of the change in the abductors' goals. Hijackings used to turn quickly into hostage-taking events, often for long periods of time. Kidnappings often were perpetrated for the same reason: Gain a valuable hostage and trade him or her for something of value to the hostage taker. This was thought to be a constant motive, and therefore the victim of a kidnapping was taught to remain passive and not resist the kidnappers. The problem with the automatic application of the passive approach is that your kidnapper may have no intention of using you to trade. Often individuals are kidnapped for interrogation, torture, and execution. The kidnapping of *Wall Street Journal* reporter Daniel Pearl is a recent example. From the very beginning of that incident, it was clear that his kidnappers had no intention of releasing him. Kidnappers' demands must have some level of reasonableness.

For example, a group that kidnapped an American tourist is not likely to say that the victim will be safely returned once the United States has deactivated every one of its military bases overseas. On its face the demand itself shows that the intention of the terrorist is not to bargain. Daniel Pearl was taken not to bargain but to terrorize. His abductors took him to savagely strike back in a way that only pathetic and vicious sociopathic criminals know how to do: by inflicting pain on someone helpless to prevent it. Did murdering Pearl further anyone's cause? Of course not. Nothing tangible could have been gained from such a senseless act.

Terrorists aren't the only ones who kidnap people just to kill them for their own personal pleasure. In 1986, Drug Enforcement Administration (DEA) Special Agent Enrique "Kiki" Camarena was kidnapped in Guadalajara, Mexico, by police officers working for drug traffickers. He was tortured to extract information about law enforcement knowledge of the traffickers' operation. Then Camarena was tortured to death for the amusement of his abductors. The traffickers even had a doctor present to keep Camarena alive for as long as possible to prolong his agony.

The point in discussing these stories is to emphasize that no one blanket approach is correct. In hindsight, it would have been better for Pearl and Camarena to resist their kidnappers to the point of death, since that would have spared their families and themselves further agony and pain. The problem is that there is no way of knowing whether you are being taken for trade or to simply be murdered at the convenience of the abductors. Ultimately, the decision can only be yours. As in the situation discussed with hijackings, you must decide whether to cooperate or resist. This is an old conundrum that has plagued women discussing the best response to an attempted rape: submit or resist. If you are being kidnapped, will the situation get better or worse? There is no way of knowing. Each of us must decide for ourselves how we intend to react if we are placed in that situation.

As a general rule, most authorities and experts on the dynamics of hostage situations still recommend cooperation. This is even truer if you are taken hostage in a known location and not kidnapped and taken someplace convenient for the kidnappers. For example, if you are taken hostage by bank robbers after a botched robbery, it is likely that law enforcement has been alerted to the situation and will dispatch appropriately trained negotiators and assault personnel to end the crisis. In that case, unless an opportunity presents itself for you either to escape or to overcome the bad guys, you should wait and allow the professionals to handle the job. According to security experts, even if you are being abducted, you still have a better chance of survival if you cooperate and comply with the demands of the kidnappers.

WHAT TO EXPECT

If you have chosen to be compliant, you must expect to be handled roughly, even brutally. Physical violence is likely even if you follow the abductors' demands. There are those who seek to explain this wanton use of violence by blaming the captors' frightened mental state. In reality, there is no need to search for any rationale other than the fact that the people capable of perpetrating this type of crime are vicious criminals for whom violence is a way of life. Physical abuse of a helpless captive, much the same as the abuse perpetrated by a rapist on his victim, is one way for abductors to feel important and powerful. Expect to be blindfolded. There are several reasons for this. First, blindfolded people are more helpless as a natural result of the disorientation they feel being deprived of their sight. Second, the blindfold prevents victims from learning where they are being taken. This will reduce the chance that they will try to escape, even if the chance arises, because of the uncertainty of not knowing where they are. It will also prevent victims from disclosing where they are being held in the unlikely event they are able to pass a message or communicate with the outside world.

Many other indignities will be perpetrated on victims of a kidnapping. While it is difficult to prepare to endure them, at least knowing about them beforehand may allow you to anticipate what is going to happen next. The kidnappers will almost certainly continue to try to keep you disoriented. Disorientation, by the way, is a favorite technique of hostage takers and kidnappers, especially if they believe you may have information useful to them. Common tricks are to vary your sleeping times, serve you meals you would associate with certain times of day at the wrong times, and keep you in total darkness to prevent you from being aware of whether it is daylight outside. It will be important for you to try to maintain a sense of the passage of time. If you can hear the sounds of the street, it is a safe assumption that activity is higher during the daylight hours and lower at night. Also, since it is usually cooler at night, you can determine the time of day from paying attention to the temperature. Observe the condition of your guards or others with whom you come in contact. They are people, too, and are affected by the human biorhythmic cycle. If it is three o'clock in the morning, it is very likely that the guards will look lethargic and sleepy. Try to count the passage of days and record the date. Scratching a simple tick mark someplace to mark the passage of every day is an easy way to do this.

You may continue to be physically abused throughout the ordeal. You may be beaten to obtain information or merely to amuse the criminals holding you. Women, and to a lesser extent men, may be sexually abused. Remember, you must do everything you can to stay alive. If you are assaulted in this manner, you will probably be forced to endure it. There is no shame in this. Do what you must to survive the ordeal.

KEEP PHYSICALLY AND MENTALLY ACTIVE

Try to exercise whenever possible. Keeping your body as physically fit under the circumstances is vital to your survival. A healthy, fit individual is likely to be more resistant to disease. Exercise is also one of the best ways to relieve stress, which will be one of your most difficult challenges during captivity. Eat whatever you are given, whenever it is offered to you. Your appetite will certainly not be what it should be, but food is a basic necessity and you need to survive. You have no way of knowing whether food will be withheld as a punishment or whether the kidnappers have sufficient resources to "waste" on their victims.

It is also extremely important to exercise your mind. If you have never seen the movie *Midnight Express*, rent it to see a depiction of how the mind of a captive can deteriorate over the course of the captivity. Any mental exercise you can come up with will keep your wits intact. Try to remember the soliloquies of Hamlet, Macbeth, or any of your favorite Shakespearean characters. Try to recall the names of your classmates from the first grade. Mentally relive your favorite vacation. You can see the point here. Think actively and vigorously. If you are given writing materials, you can compose the great American novel.

Pray. Pray often and earnestly and rely on the Creator of the Universe to sustain you. Prayer is an extremely powerful thing, even more so in captivity. While communication with other prisoners is also important if possible, it is always possible to talk with God. If you are of Jewish or Christian heritage, recall the Psalms as best you can. Admiral Jeremiah Denton, a pilot held captive by the North Vietnamese during the war in Vietnam for over seven and a half years, has written of the way that prayer sustained him as he endured one hellish day after the next. Denton was confined to a coffin-size cell and tortured. In fact, while being filmed as a prisoner of the North Vietnamese in 1966 just 10 months after his capture, Denton used Morse code to blink the word "torture" to the outside world. His devout faith as a Roman Catholic sustained him during his incarceration. As a fascinating aside, Denton has spoken at length of how he kept his mind active. He stated that his clarity of thought became such that he was able to calculate the formula for centrifugal force in his head, something he couldn't do with pencil and paper at the U.S. Naval Academy.

Mentally take notes of as much detail as you can concerning the location where you are being held and the people holding you. Not only will this help keep your mind active, it also will provide assistance to those trying to locate and identify the bad guys after you are ransomed or rescued.

Try to notice the weak points in your abductors' security. Escape is a difficult prospect even for well-trained individuals, and we will discuss it in a moment. For now, consider escape foremost as a mental exercise. Plan your escape, even if it is not an option for you.

The general consensus regarding escape is that attempts are not recommended. Many factors lead to this recommendation. You probably don't know where you are being held. If you managed to escape, you have no idea whether you are in the middle of a hostile neighborhood or terrorist enclave. Or perhaps, like the dozens of people kidnapped and held in the jungles of the Philippines or Colombia, you may be many miles away from any help. Could you find your way out of a jungle with no equipment, food, or water?

If you do try to escape and are recaptured, you probably will be severely punished for the attempt. Certainly, any rapport you have managed to build with your captors will be gone. You may be beaten, starved, or otherwise abused. The rule to follow is not to do anything that may antagonize the kidnappers, including escape, unless some extraordinary opportunity occurs. Even then you must accurately assess your own personal abilities. Can you fight if necessary? What is your physical condition and your level of fitness and strength? Can you run long distances swiftly under difficult conditions? Would you know how to orient yourself without a compass? Only you will be able to assess your own abilities and your chances for success.

CHAPTER 19

Commercial Espionage

Espionage, commonly known as spying, dates back to pre-history. Ever since the first primitive clans competed against one another for survival and primacy in the ancient world, the value of collected intelligence has been recognized as having supreme importance. Before Moses led the Israelites into the land of Canaan over 3,000 years ago, he sent out 12 spies to scout the land and the opposition. More than 2,000 years ago, the Chinese warrior Sun Tzu penned *The Art of War*. In it, he discusses every aspect of preparedness for a successful military campaign: when to fight and when to withdraw, how to choose terrain to your advantage, how to lead, and how to feint. The work, still relevant after more than two millennia, values one thing above all else: intelligence, or information gathered from spies. In Chapter XIII, "The Use of Spies," Sun Tzu says:

> *Thus, what enables the wise sovereign and the good general to strike and conquer, and achieve things beyond the reach of ordinary men, is foreknowledge. Now this foreknowledge cannot be elicited from spirits; it cannot be obtained inductively from experience, nor by any deductive calculation. Knowledge of the enemy's dispositions can only be obtained from other men.*

Spies, he notes in paragraph 14, have a value beyond all others and warrant special treatment:

> *Hence it is that which none in the whole army are more intimate relations to be maintained than with spies. None should be more liberally rewarded. In no other business should greater secrecy be preserved.*

231

Sun Tzu advises his readers to:

> *Be subtle! Be subtle! And use your spies for every kind of business.*

Sun Tzu's final words in this masterwork underscore the value of intelligence acquired through the use of spies:

> *Hence it is only the enlightened ruler and the wise general who will use the highest intelligence of the army for purposes of spying and thereby they achieve great results. Spies are a most important element in water, because on them depends an army's ability to move.*[1]

These words have not been lost on corporate managers who have recognized their applicability to the business battlefield.

Virtually every government in the world has an intelligence-gathering apparatus. Knowledge of the intentions and capabilities of your enemies or competitors provides an advantage that can be obtained through no other means. Information must be gathered, analyzed, and used in a strategic manner. Intelligence may be obtained through technological methods, such as satellite monitoring and the intercepts of radio and telephone communications. It may be the result of deductive reasoning after analysis of the actions of the subject in question. Or intelligence can be obtained from the oldest and most basic method: the use of spies. Spies can make visual observations, overhear conversations, or gain the confidence of specifically targeted individuals having information of value to the nation supporting the intelligence operation. A spy may be a trusted member of a targeted government, agency, group, or corporation and may be passing valuable information helpful to the opposing side. This type of spy, or "mole," is most dangerous as, by necessity, he or she is privy to highly classified and compartmentalized information. The information that moles can provide is the most valuable and provides the greatest advantage to the group gathering the information.

Governments seeking security or the advancement of their own national interests are not the only ones to recognize the value of spying. Corporate espionage or economic spying has long been a vital tool for industries competing for dominance in a competitive world market. Often the interests of a government and a particular industry coincide. The reasons are obvious; if a country can dominate a market, the strategic situation of that country will also be enhanced. A strong market position and a healthy and productive economy are always in the national interest of a country. For that reason, national intelligence-gathering organizations often provide acquired intelligence of an economic nature to domestic industries that might benefit from such knowledge. This poses an extremely difficult problem to solve. As former Federal Bureau of Investigation (FBI) director Louis Freeh noted during a speech to the Executive's Club in Chicago, "At least 20 nations are actively engaged in economic espionage."[2]

AREAS OF VULNERABILITY

Most corporations are not equipped to counter espionage attempts directed by a country. If the highest levels of government agencies, such as the Central Intelligence Agency (CIA) and the FBI, can be penetrated, then so can a corporation. Local employees are often susceptible to pressure from the intelligence services of their country. They can be threatened, bribed, or even approached to cooperate willingly based on their feelings of patriotism. American employees may be co-opted through the use of financial inducement, feelings of resentment, or even ideological reasons. Remember, information doesn't have to come from the president of a company to be valuable. The president's secretary, driver, or office cleaner may be in a position to provide access to exactly the same information.

What type of information is of value to an economic competitor? If you are in business, you know how to answer that question better than we can. Think of the type of information you wish you had from your most direct competitor. In merger discussions or hostile takeovers, what type of knowledge about the target firm would help you take advantage of a company's weakness or prepare you to protect your own company's interests? Or perhaps your direct competitor would benefit by stealing your research or developmental ideas. What about your cost structure, bids, customer lists, and marketing strategies, or personal information about your top-level executives? As former FBI director Freeh noted in the speech quoted earlier:

> This kind of information can be intercepted from fax and satellite communications. It can be monitored from cellular and microwave telephone links. It can be retrieved from inadequately protected computer systems.

Information of this type is also vulnerable if it isn't disposed of properly: burned or shredded. You would be amazed at how frequently vital clues are obtained during a criminal investigation by going through a suspect's trash. An executive's wastebasket can be equally rewarding. Information is easily obtained if documents with any sensitivity or proprietary information are not secured at the end of the day. How difficult do you suppose it would be for your competitor to hire an operative as part of your cleaning staff? Cleaners have access to every location in the facility and are there when everyone else has gone home. They can copy or take important documents, rifle through unlocked office drawers and filing cabinets, and examine the garbage. Trained professionals can easily install a room monitor or "bug" in a matter of seconds.

The first stage in creating an informational security system for your company is to have each individual department conduct a security audit. Each department head must first understand the type of information that should properly be labeled as sensitive and subject to security regulations. As a general rule, any information, process, procedure, practice, or performance unique to your company that gives you a competitive advantage falls into this class. With respect to operations abroad, the definition is a bit broader. If certain types of information, skills, or techniques are not commonly employed outside the American business community but clearly make American industries more competitive in a given field, then they should be included in this category. The information in question may be quite commonplace in the American industrial sector but not abroad. Any innovation, no matter how mundane, may provide an edge to your company and should be guarded. Each unit manager carefully must consider the individual operation with these parameters in mind and compile a detailed list of anything unique that makes the company more competitive against corporate rivals. Once these areas have been identified, an informational security specialist should be engaged to compile a plan detailing the steps required to correct the noted deficiencies. Ideally this evaluation should be part of an overall security and risk assessment report. The recommendations of an overall site security plan will address many of the concerns regarding the protection of information.

How can your company protect itself against such attempts at corporate espionage? A series of measures can and should be taken to secure your company against such economic intelligence gathering (or just plain stealing). Basic security protocols must be established dealing with such issues as:

- Classification of documents and computer disks
- Handling/storage/disposal procedures for each classification
- Clean desk policy
- Access limitation
- Electronic surveillance countermeasures
- Use of secure communication systems for conversations that are considered sensitive
- Computer security and hacking

CLASSIFICATION

Classification is an issue common to anyone who has ever worked for the government or the military. In fact, virtually everyone has an idea about what it means, for example, to mark a document "Top Secret." Basically, the classification system is a method of determining the number and identity of persons authorized to read certain documents. The system also provides instruction as to how to use and handle a particular item classified in a particular way. For example, an unclassified document has no security limitation placed on it at all. Anyone may see it, read it, or use it in any manner. There is no handling restriction placed on it. It may be discarded as ordinary trash and does not need any protection at all. Each step up the classification ladder requires the application of more stringent rules regarding how the document must be stored, who can see it, and how it must be destroyed. The first step to take is to establish a method to classify and mark all materials generated during the course of business. Management needs to determine exactly what criteria should be used to determine classification level. Actually, this is quite easy to do. Information that you don't want unauthorized individuals to see will get classified. If only a few individuals need to know something, then you classify the document with the higher "Need to Know" standard. Information that might be ruinous to your business if a competitor obtained it can be classified as having the highest level of restriction. Classification must be identified by marking the document, usually with color codes. An example would be to stamp a document as "ROUTINE" with black ink and "SECRET" or "RESTRICTED" with red ink. Colors also may be used to separate physical data storage items, such as floppy disks. For example, sensitive information goes on a red floppy disk, and routine items go on disks of another color. Red disks will, of course, be subject to specific handling requirements that will be discussed below.

HANDLING/STORAGE/DISPOSAL PROCEDURES
FOR EACH CLASSIFICATION

We have already briefly touched on this subject. Each classification level requires its own specific handling instructions. Obviously, items given a higher classification require greater care and handling. Special care must be given to the manner in which a classified document is destroyed. The most sensitive items must be completely destroyed beyond any attempt at restoration. Remember, trash is often a great source of intelligence. Many criminals are in jail today because of incriminating items they discarded in the trash. Similarly, proprietary information may be compromised if it is simply tossed out with the garbage. Any document that could hurt your business or give a competitor or firm contemplating a takeover an advantage needs to be destroyed. The only acceptable methods to use are shredding and burning. In each case, measures must be taken to ensure that destruction is complete. If a shredder is used, it needs to be a multilayer cross-cut shredder that turns the document into an almost powdered state. This is the level used by the government in destroying highly classified documents, as it is virtually impossible to put what comes out of the shredder back into the original document or a portion thereof. Make sure your shredder meets this level of function. Inexpensive, single-row shredding machines create very narrow and very fine strips of paper. While it is difficult to reassemble such strips, it is possible. A veteran detective of our acquaintance was an expert in such document re-creation and was able to obtain much useful and incriminating evidence that the target of many investigations thought had been permanently destroyed. If burning is used, you must be certain that combustion is complete, that no scraps are left, and that none has been blown out the smokestack by the rising current of hot air in the furnace.

Storage is another issue in handling secure items. Common sense applies. If you don't want the information lost or stolen, store it in a designated area, under lock and key, limiting access to as small a number of persons as possible. Information that is proprietary but does not rise to a higher level of classification may be kept by individual employees as part of their work product or files as long as they lock the documents in their desks or filing cabinets. Higher-level documents should be placed in a heavy, fire-resistant filing safe with access limited to a few select people. Files that need to be taken out for use should be signed out by the responsible party.

There also must be strict regulations controlling which documents may be copied or may be taken out of the office. This includes physical documents as well as floppy disks and compact disks (CDs). Laptop computers containing sensitive data on their hard drives must be similarly regulated. Documents of the highest level of secrecy should be numbered and color-coded to avoid any misidentification. The storing of sensitive information on only red floppy disks, mentioned above, is one example of a coding system. Those disks must be treated as classified documents in the government and may not be removed from the office. Many employees take work home. Employers love this because they are getting extra productivity out of their workforce. However, this action opens up another avenue of attack for those seeking to acquire information. Just as an individual on a cleaning crew at work may be a planted or co-opted spy, so too can an operative be placed as a domestic employee. Sensitive information that must be taken home must be subject to the same types of safeguards as are used in the office. If you are like most people working at home, you will have work strewn out all over the kitchen table. When you get up to use the bathroom or take a walk, your household help has unhindered access to the material. Since there is no way to monitor employee behavior at home, there are really only two choices: either forbid the removal of sensitive information from the office for any reason whatsoever or allow it and educate employees regarding the risks of not securing information at home. David recalls a case where an informant was receiving suspicious phone calls from a man pretending to be from a utility company. This was a ploy intended to learn whether the informant was home in order to follow him. David and his supervisor tracked the calls to the home of an unlicensed private investigator who provided a convincing explanation of how the calls could have originated from his home office. He even agreed to provide access to the office to show that he had nothing to hide. He had forgotten that he had left a computer printout of the informant's criminal history and motor vehicle information in plain view on his desk. His failure to adhere to a home "clean desk policy" tripped him up. The following sections lay out the specifics of an office policy.

CLEAN DESK POLICY

Sensitive documents must not be left out on a desk that is open to plain view. Whenever the employee leaves his or her workstation, the desk must be clean of any sensitive materials. Generally, employees can simply lock sensitive work product in their desk. If they are working with extremely sensitive documents that they had to sign out for, then they must return the documents to the proper storage area and remove them later. The same is true for computer screens. Screens need to be turned off and everything password protected. If you have someone handling documents of the highest level of security, you should be cognizant that even reading such material near a window may compromise the data. It is not a difficult task to use telescopic equipment to look into an office. It is just as simple to take photographs of material in the office and have the pictures enhanced to retrieve useful data. It is done every day by intelligence agencies worldwide. Cleaning crews should be allowed to work only after sensitive or proprietary information has been secured.

These policies need to be enforced if you are serious about information security. Even during an evacuation, real or drill, there must be a minimum level of response calling for the securing of vital documents. It only takes a couple of seconds to throw everything into a desk drawer and lock it. Then you shut off the computer and out you go. Total time elapsed is less than 10 seconds. In the past, spies have activated fire alarms and even set fires to cause an evacuation and gain access to competitive information. Security is part of the drill. If, of course, the emergency is so severe— say an earthquake or bomb attack—that these seconds may make the difference between life and death, then the security protocol is abandoned in favor of saving lives. If time is not that critical, then the informational security protocols should be followed. Even during an ordinary workday, attention must be paid to securing your computer workstation and keeping classified documents out of the reach of unauthorized individuals.

ACCESS LIMITATION

The concept of access limitation refers to limiting physical access to specific locations and limiting those persons having access to particular information. The former concept is easy to conceptualize in theory but is often less so in practice. For example, the physical safety of corporate employees will require the establishment of security procedures to control access to the site and admit only those persons with legitimate business inside. These steps have the added benefit of preventing unauthorized persons from gaining entry to production facilities, research areas, and other areas where company-sensitive information might be found. Visitors must be escorted to ensure that no one can "accidentally" wander into a design center or research lab. The difficulty with access control often comes in regard to friends or close business associates of those working at the facility. Our open and easygoing nature as Americans leads us to be hospitable to those who visit us. Remember that even friends and relatives require escorts. If a rival company or foreign power really believed that a product, concept, or idea being developed in your company had substantial value or could undermine a competitor's market share or a nation's economy, it will attempt to target those individuals with access to that information. How difficult would it be for a rival corporation or government to have an intelligence operative befriend one of your employees? Seduction also has been a tool since time immemorial. Men and women have been romanced, seduced, and even married by operatives seeking only to gain access to information. While this may sound far-fetched, it happens with regularity.

The second component of access limitation relates to specific items. This concept is very simple and follows along the lines of the classification system itself. Basically, the need a person has to see a certain type of document determines the security classification given to that person. An employee with a need to see sensitive documents is given a clearance level of "Sensitive" or "Secret" or whatever you choose to call it. That person now has unrestricted access to documents identified with that level of secrecy. Documents of extraordinary sensitivity may be limited to a special level of clearance given to individuals on a case-by-case basis. This is comparable with the "Eyes Only" classification you may have read about in a Tom Clancy novel.

The issue of limitation must extend to the creation of a method to prevent the unauthorized removal of a sensitive document, even by an individual cleared to see it. Information of high levels of sensitivity must be controlled in such a manner as to prevent them from being copied and/or being removed from a secure area. These materials may be signed out and then limited to use in an area that is monitored or devoid of any copy equipment. Problems arise when a trusted employee manages to take a document and secrete it on his or her person, or use a miniature camera to photograph the document. Before you dismiss this idea as being overly paranoid, consider how valuable some internal company correspondence may be to the right person. This type of activity is happening every day, often with negative results to the company that has been victimized. If individuals are working with documents of the highest security classification, there should be precautions in place to prevent the intentional removal or copying of such documents. Physical searches may be the only way to ensure that documents of great sensitivity don't get taken outside of the secure environment.

ELECTRONIC SURVEILLANCE COUNTERMEASURES

As we mentioned before, there are many ways to use technology to remotely obtain information from your subject. Imagine this. You are the president of a corporation preparing a final bid on a government contract worth hundreds of millions of dollars. What would a copy of this document be worth to your closest competitor for the contract? Now look out your window and see if there are any office buildings nearby that have offices slightly higher than your own. Don't just look next door. Can you see any in a straight line of sight? If the answer is yes and if you do not have mirrored or heavily colored window glass, then someone can look into your office and see what you are reading, what's on your computer screen, or what you left out on your desk. There is a reason that the Pentagon has painted windows.

It is also a relatively simple matter to plant a transmitter, or "bug," in an area. Although such devices are small and have a finite range, they may be used to compromise your private conversations. Several years ago police observed an individual using an earpiece outside the State Department in Washington. He was stopped and identified as a Russian national, and it was quickly discovered that he was listening to a bug that had been placed in a State Department conference room. Since that room had been used for meetings by then Secretary of State Madeline Albright, it is likely that the bug provided extremely useful information to the Russians. However, since these devices must transmit information, trained experts in the field of counterespionage generally can detect them. Doing so entails the use of sophisticated monitoring equipment to "sweep" an area and attempt to detect the presence of unaccounted-for radiation from a particular area. The battle is always between the developers trying to make a transmitter that is harder to detect and the companies building more sensitive detection equipment.

USE OF SECURE COMMUNICATION SYSTEMS FOR SENSITIVE CONVERSATIONS

Many military manuals on communications by radio or telephone begin with the words "The enemy is listening." Telephones may be tapped. The same is true for lines used to fax documents. If someone has access to the phone line, it is a simple matter for him or her to gain access to every conversation or any bit of information that goes across it. Corporate telephone transmissions are highly vulnerable targets, especially overseas. In fact, because of the volume of information transmitted over the phone, such transmissions are often the primary targets for intelligence gathering. The reason why this is even more of a problem overseas is because, in many nations, the phone company is owned by the government, which has unfettered access to the system. In other countries the legal safeguards that we have in the United States and the Western world are nonexistent. You must assume that all telephone and facsimile transmissions from overseas are being monitored.

What, therefore, can you do to defeat this type of intelligence gathering? Several products on the market allow for completely secure communication between individuals. The government has long used these secure telephone unit, or "STU," phones to prevent the interception of sensitive conversations. These phones work by encrypting the signal as it goes through one phone and decrypting it on the other end. Any attempt to intercept the conversation will only result in the acquisition of incoherent electronic noise that cannot be decrypted. The same principle is used for the secure fax machines and computer e-mail. Many countries, however, prohibit the use of encrypting equipment within their borders. In such regions, the use of trusted couriers to hand-carry extremely sensitive materials is a more secure means of transferring data.

COMPUTER SECURITY AND HACKING

Everyone is aware of the dangers of loss of sensitive information by computer hackers able to surreptitiously gain access to your company's database. Hackers have been able to penetrate virtually every computer system on the planet. Even teenage hackers have been able to penetrate highly classified and supposedly secure systems, such as the system maintained by the Pentagon. Microsoft itself has been hacked on several occasions. Companies and government institutions, tired of this embarrassing phenomenon, have at times hired former hackers to create security systems for them.

The entire business and financial world is automated. The use of computer technology has rapidly become the backbone of how business is done. Computer systems have made the storage and flow of information move at incredible speeds. They also have opened up a new front in the war on terrorism. As we have seen, terror groups have without question shifted their targeting priorities to the economic infrastructure of the United States and other Western nations. Economic disruption, they believe, has a far greater impact on the policies of a nation than attacks on traditional military targets. Thus far, Al Qaeda and their ilk have used bombs, guns, and fully fueled jet aircraft to effect these attacks. It is only a matter of time before terrorists acquire the technical sophistication to achieve the same results through massive attacks on the computer systems that control our economy. Of even greater concern is the potential of a cyberattack made in conjunction with a conventional attack. For example, vital services such as electric power generation and communications systems could be disrupted electronically through a cyberterror strike. If this were done at the same time as a massive bombing attack or the dispersal of biological, nuclear, or chemical materials, the combined effects would be catastrophic. Governments all over the world have become greatly concerned over this looming battleground and have mandated that business institutions, particularly those involved in providing essential services, take immediate action to protect themselves against this new threat. The U.S. government has even begun conducting "war games" in conjunction with private industry to simulate a coordinated attack on the country's computer infrastructure and gauge the effectiveness of current counter-measures.

The basics of computer security are generally the same whether here or abroad, although there are some additional concerns that apply to the foreign environment, which we will discuss below. The first element always to deal with is physical security. As we have repeatedly stated, physically protecting a site or item is the primary concern. The best security system in the world, for example, will not do the company much good if a laptop with sensitive data is stolen. Care also must be taken to secure the individual computer stations to prevent unauthorized access by intruders. Proper site security, alarm systems, and access control systems will help in this regard.

Information stored in the company database must be backed up with the copies stored off site. We saw the importance of this procedure in the aftermath of the September 11 attacks. Some companies without off-site backup faced a nearly insurmountable task of re-creating data that was permanently lost when the towers fell.

A strict protocol must be put in place mandating that computers be shut off when employees step away from their desks. Password protection is not much use if the authorized user logs in and then leaves the station unattended. Modems in particular must be disconnected or turned off when not in use. This will prevent a skilled party from being able to communicate with your computer and being able to hack into the system.

As we discussed in the chapter on corporate espionage, proper disposal methods of discarded trash containing sensitive information must be implemented. A floppy disk or CD containing sensitive data must be thoroughly destroyed. If your printer uses film ribbons, the ribbons must be destroyed, as they can yield information in much the same way as old-style typewriter ribbons could be read and some of the words written on a particular ribbon re-created.

Individual access to PC stations must be protected by passwords unique to each individual, which must be changed on a regular basis. In systems used by the federal government, passwords are randomly generated and assigned. Individual users do not create their own passwords. This is done to prevent an intruder from guessing a user's password. Despite all warnings to the contrary, most computer users still create passwords that are based on birthdays of children, spouses, or themselves or addresses or other numerical or alphabetical combinations that would be easy to guess. Hackers are experts in guessing passwords. They know all the tricks. First they will try the user's birth date, then that of the spouse or children. Then the same numbers in reverse. Then combinations like the user's birth date combined with the spouse's birth month and child's birth date. Randomly generated passwords prevent this kind of guesswork from being successful.

One approach that is used by many governmental agencies is the actual removal of computer hard drives. All work is stored on a disk that is secured at the end of the day. This denies sensitive information to anyone who manages to gain access to the computer.

Remember, while many computer systems are secure, the transmission lines into them are not. This is especially true overseas, as we discussed above. Because virtually all corporate information is found in the corporate database and because the volume of information transmitted via computer e-mail is increasing at an exponential rate, the targeting of computer systems is the fastest-growing choice of intelligence-gathering organizations. Installation by experienced professionals is your only means to secure your system against such intrusion.

NOTES

1. Sun Tzu, *The Art of War,* translated from the Chinese by Lionel Giles, 1910.
2. Address by former FBI director Louis Freeh to the Executive's Club, Chicago, IL, February 17, 1994.

CHAPTER 20

Violence in the Workplace

I T IS IMPORTANT TO REMEMBER that any comprehensive security program must be sufficiently broad to include all conceivable risks to health and safety and not merely dwell on the dangers presented by terrorism. As we have already pointed out several times, you are more likely to become a victim of common crime than you are of being the victim of a terror attack. This also holds true for a threat that is becoming more and more common every day: the potential of violence in the workplace from disturbed or disgruntled employees. Such employees are dangerous because typically they have unrestricted access to the facility, unless they have already been terminated. Often employees do not go through security screening, which generally targets unfamiliar visitors to the building. However, despite the fact that access control measures are not designed to stop these types of individuals, violent workers are often the easiest to identify and deal with.

In almost every instance of workplace violence, there have been warning signs that should have been picked up on and acted on but were not. In literally dozens of instances, not only were obvious warning signs of impending violence ignored or not recognized, but actual and direct threats were ignored as well. It would seem obvious to anyone, regardless of their level of security training, that an individual who has just been fired and who states that he is going home to get a gun and then will come back and kill everyone needs to be given the appropriate level of attention.

However, often management does nothing, even in these extreme cases. Management does not call the police, and often the security department is not even notified that this individual has made threats and must not to be admitted into the building. Tragically, many times these individuals are as good as their word and do return, with deadly results. The circumstances are all the more heartbreaking because they could easily have been averted.

The initial step to take to prevent workplace violence is basic training that teaches the employees of your company to recognize the warning signs that a particular employee may be planning acts of violence. Very often a person may seem disgruntled or angry about certain situations in the company. Perhaps the person has been passed over for promotion, either justifiably or unjustifiably, and is expressing anger over what he or she perceives as unfair treatment. Sometimes the violence may be triggered by relationships with coworkers. In many of the horrible school shootings in the United States during the last few years, there often has been a pattern of systematic bullying of the shooter before the violent act. The child, most likely already suffering from personality disorders, lives in dread that each new day of school will bring more harassment, more name calling, and more physical abuse. Finally the child begins having revenge fantasies where those bullying him are punished. Thoughts of revenge allow the victim of harassment to feel more in control of the situation. If the circumstances are not addressed, they can fester until ultimately the victim of the day-in, day-out bullying can take it no more. One day the person decides to turn fantasy into reality. While this explanation does not excuse the violent conduct, it shows how timely intervention could easily prevent tragedies from happening.

Management needs to implement explicit notification procedures to ensure supervisory awareness and action. These programs must include a complaint process that transcends the usual chain of command in instances where, for example, procedures call for employees to notify the first-level supervisor, when it may very well be this person who is causing the problem. There also must be a clearly defined procedure for employees to follow when they notice unusual behavior in a coworker. Management must be made aware as soon as possible to allow for the implementation of appropriate intervention techniques. Often the human resources department can employ the services of a mental health professional familiar with employee-related crises. An evaluation by such a trained person is a very good first step to take before a problem becomes more serious.

RESPONSES

Let's discuss some appropriate security-related responses to employee violence. Definitive measures should become standard protocol when a person is suspended or dismissed. For example, after a person is terminated, he or she must immediately be denied access to every area of the facility. Certainly there will be matters that the person will need to take care of. Desks need to be cleaned out, final paychecks cut, and other financial matters such as the disposition of any funds in a company pension fund or thrift savings program. The company should appoint a single individual to act as a liaison between the employee and management to handle these matters. Anything that needs to be resolved must be handled by this designated person. The employee should not be allowed to contact anyone in the office, barring personal friendships of course, to discuss matters related to separation from the company.

What is an appropriate response to make when an employee actually threatens violent behavior? First, security needs to be made aware of the circumstances of the incident and the nature of the threats. The ability of the guard force to handle the matter needs to be evaluated. In most cases the local authorities need to be alerted immediately and their input should be obtained. In many jurisdictions in the United States, laws make the utterance of threats of violence a crime, often a felony. In such a case, the ability of the police to make an arrest will depend on what the individual actually said and the availability of evidence to support a charge. We suspect that the same is true in many foreign nations. Consult the local police.

In the event that the employee is an American citizen, it is also a good idea to contact the embassy or consulate and ask the regional security officer (RSO) for advice. The RSO will also have a relationship with the local authorities and may be in a position to obtain their help faster than you can. In addition, the embassies will have liaison offices that may be able to provide appropriate support from a social services standpoint.

While all this is being done, security needs to prepare an individual-specific threat upgrade. If, for example, an employee has stormed off stating he is going home for a gun, then this threat must be taken seriously and prepared for. Again, an evaluation must be made. What type of security force do you have? Are its members armed? What do local laws say about the use of deadly physical force in these circumstances? Is there a sufficient access-limiting system in place to stop an armed intruder?

These points must be assessed, and local law enforcement must be contacted immediately and asked to respond. Once the local authorities arrive, they will take charge of the situation. Until then the security staff has the responsibility of protecting the employees present on premises.

Consideration also must be given to what measures are to be taken if an armed individual has either taken hostages or is randomly shooting company employees. Plans for hostage rescue situations must be made. Before we discuss such plans, it must be understood that the level of professionalism, training, and ability in any hostage rescue team must be quite high if you expect the team to be able to conduct such an operation. To our way of thinking, every company with the wherewithal to fund a highly proficient force should do so. This matter is even more critical in countries where the local police are not well trained or well equipped. The internal security force will be the only option available if a critical situation occurs in a country low on law enforcement assets. This is not so formidable a task as you may think. If the caliber of the security employees is high and if they have been given the appropriate training (reinforced by regular practice and drill), then such a force is not difficult to maintain on the premises. Your company will need to decide whether the safety of its employees is worth the expense of such a security staff.

SUPPORTING LOCAL AUTHORITIES

What is the function of the security staff in the event that local police are responding to an armed attack or hostage situation? Quite simply, it is to provide as much support and intelligence to the police as they can. To facilitate that role, it is recommended that every Emergency Response Plan include information that a police tactical unit would need if it had to respond to an emergency in your facility. The information should include diagrams of the facility and surrounding areas. This will allow a tactical team leader to evaluate the location before initiating any operation. The location of all windows, access points, and vents and crawl space areas must be included. If there are active security systems that can be used to monitor the subject, someone from security will need to be with the police and be responsible for providing whatever technical assistance required. Several very capable firms can prepare a complete emergency package of this nature. One Israeli firm, Tandu, specializes in preparing emergency crisis guides for schools. The company provides details of the entire facility, identifies appropriate points of entry if assault is necessary, and identifies appropriate areas for helicopter support or Medivac units. Tandu develops intelligence on students with a violent history and maps out the locations of the nearest hospitals and trauma centers in relation to the school address. This type of plan is suitable for incorporation in a corporate Emergency Response Plan and is strongly recommended. In a hostage situation or an armed attack, the time an assault team needs to prepare itself costs lives. If a team comes upon a situation where there is a professionally made operational plan waiting for it, the team will be able to act much more quickly and decisively.

CHAPTER 21

Criminal Activity

THE CHANCES THAT YOU WILL BECOME the victim of terrorism abroad are relatively low. Adherence to the basic rules of safety will bring those odds down even further. As mentioned, you have a far greater chance of becoming a crime victim, at home or abroad, than you have of winding up in the middle of a terror operation. The question that you should be asking yourself at this point is "If I am more likely to become a victim of common crime, then why is the chapter on crime prevention the next to last one in a book about security?" The answer is simply that all of the counter-terrorism techniques that we have discussed are effective against the criminal element as well. As a rule, the potential for harm is greater during a terrorist incident. Therefore, we elected to discuss terrorism as the subject of prime concern in this book. If you learn how to defeat a terrorist, you will learn crime prevention techniques as well. There are just a few additional important items that the issue of criminal activity requires us to address.

Criminal activity may be broken down into several types for purposes of our discussion. At home, we frequently hear about white-collar crime as distinguished from violent crime, and property crime as opposed to crimes directed at the person. Whatever the nature of the crime, we all run the risk of being affected by criminal activity. We must take precautions to prevent all types of criminal victimization; we need to secure both our property as well as our person.

The first step in taking specific precautions to prevent criminal conduct is to learn as much as possible about the specific criminal trends present in the country you are traveling to or residing in. Every country has its own particular criminal industry. Often you can obtain information about the local crime problem and also get statistics about the types of crime targeted against tourists or resident Westerners. Many countries are conscious about the impact that crimes against foreigners have to their local economy. These countries have government divisions that analyze the criminal threat to guests in their country and develop strategies to combat them. In Thailand, for example, there is a branch of the police identified as the Tourist Police. These officers are specially trained to handle crimes against foreign nationals and are taught how to interact with foreigners who may have been crime victims. Candidates for this unit must be well educated and speak at least one language other than Thai, usually English. The unit also publishes bulletins for the foreign national community describing common types of local criminal behavior and ways to avoid being a victim. And since Thailand is known as a great place to buy gold and gemstones, another benefit that the Tourist Police provide is the enforcement of antifraud laws to protect tourists from being cheated by unscrupulous jewelry merchants.

RESEARCH

The U.S. State Department website is a great resource to learn about the crime situation in the country you are traveling to. Each embassy and consulate also will be able to provide you with details about the numbers of Americans victimized by crime in a particular country.

One issue that deserves special attention is the way crimes are punished in different countries. Often the potential for serious punishment actually causes certain crimes to be carried out in a specific manner, rather than being a deterrent to crime. Here in the United States, we experience this phenomenon as well. For many years in New York state, for example, there was no charge for capital or first-degree murder. The most serious murder charge was murder in the second degree, punishable by 25 years to life in prison. That penalty was not reserved only for murder. Armed robbery was also punishable by 25 years to life in prison. Furthermore, New York law provided for concurrent rather than consecutive sentencing for crimes arising out of the same event. Think about that and you will soon see the folly in the approach. Both murder and armed robbery have the same punishment if someone is convicted. Therefore, if you commit armed robbery, you are already subject to the maximum allowable sentence. If you murder someone during the armed robbery, you get the same sentence and, since the sentences run concurrently, no additional penalty is meted out for a killing during the same robbery. What message does that send to criminals? Basically, it says they can kill somebody for "free" if they do it while robbing the person with a weapon. In fact, since they get the same penalty anyway, they might as well kill the victim to avoid leaving a live witness behind who can put them in jail forever. Thankfully, this is no longer the situation in New York. A death penalty statute, albeit a restrictive one, is on the books in New York today.

This same reality exists in foreign countries. During a Security Overseas Seminar, an excellent speaker from the State Department gave an informative presentation on sex crimes abroad. The instructor made a similar point regarding the crime of rape in the Philippines. In the Philippines, rapists are subject to the death penalty if caught and convicted. Following the same thought process as the armed robber who kills his victim to avoid leaving a witness, the Filipino rapist also often kills his victim. The speaker made this point not to criticize the Filipino justice system but in the context of a discussion about the appropriate response if a rapist is attacking you. There is always disagreement about whether a rape victim is more likely to survive an attack by passively complying or resisting strongly. But if you were attacked in the Philippines, and you knew that rapists there often murder their victims, wouldn't that information affect your decision as to whether to fight or comply?

USE COMMON SENSE

Generally the same rules apply while attempting to avoid becoming a victim overseas as within the United States. You know which neighborhoods and areas to avoid in your home city. Your task is to learn which areas in your country of residence also should be avoided. In the chapter detailing general recommendations, we stressed that maintaining a low profile was a security necessity. It is worth stating again. Don't be overly flashy and loud. Avoid wearing expensive clothing or jewelry when you are out enjoying the local nightlife. A handmade suit or gown, Rolex Presidential watch, and diamond necklace may be perfectly appropriate to wear if you are invited to an embassy dinner party hosted by the ambassador. However, while you are out for dinner in town, the overt appearance of wealth draws attention to you and makes you an attractive target for street criminals looking to make a fast few dollars. This is especially true if you are living in a country where a factory worker earns as little as $100 a month. An expensive watch may very well represent several years of savings to a local. It is just foolish to flaunt your wealth in that manner.

CHAPTER 22

Studying Abroad

$\mathbf{A}$T ANY GIVEN TIME, THERE ARE more than 100,000 Americans spending at least one semester studying abroad. In fact, according to a study by the Institute of International Education dated November 13, 2001, a record 143,590 American college students were receiving college credit for study abroad that year. This number only reflects college students. The survey did not count the thousands of dependent children of Americans working overseas and attending local grade, middle, and high schools. Moreover, the trend also shows that the number of U.S. students going to less traditional destinations is increasing. Over the last 15 years, the shift has been away from the formerly most popular areas, especially Europe, to the less developed regions of the world, such as South and Latin America, the Middle East, Africa, and Asia. The percentage of students going to European countries declined by 18 percent between 1985 and 2001. Europe remained the most popular destination, with 89,593 students during the year 2001, but Latin America had 14 percent of the total number of American students abroad, an increase of 7 percent since 1985. The Middle East, despite the unrest there, also experienced a 15 percent increase. Exhibit 22.1 shows this trend in more detail.

The security concerns attendant to this shift is readily obvious. Many of the nations experiencing the highest growth in student enrollment are also experiencing very high rates of terrorist activity. Less developed countries also pose a greater health risk to the student. The prevalence of disease and the lack of modern medical facilities is a serious concern. Civil unrest, always a danger to the foreign population, is always greater in

Exhibit 22.1   Americans Studying Abroad in 2001

Country	Number of American Students	Percentage Increase[a]
China	2,949	30%
Brazil	717	21%
Cuba	553	11%
Egypt	388	45%
Czech Republic	1,248	25%
Nepal	389	31%
India	811	15%
Kenya	695	24%
Vietnam	142	50%

In addition, almost all the top 12 host countries have also experienced an increase in U.S. enrollment:

United Kingdom	29,289	6%
Spain	13,974	14%
Italy	12,930	15%
France	11,924	14%
Mexico	7,374	0.1%
Australia	6,329	18%
Germany	4,744	5%
Israel	3,898	18%
Ireland	3,810	24%
Costa Rica	3,421	−1%
China	2,949	30%
Japan	2,679	8%
Austria	2,246	20%
Netherlands	1,545	5%
Greece	1,449	8%

[a]Since 1985.

developing countries as well. Clearly, there is a need for students and their parents to consider security while selecting the country in which to study. And, in any event, it is also necessary for American students to become familiar with basic security concepts before traveling.

CHANGE IN RECENT PATTERNS

Let's take a look at the local situations in countries experiencing the greatest increase in student enrollment. A good place to look is the State Department website, which provides travel alerts and other information relative to each country around the world. One note of caution, however: Statistics are not perfect. They are only as good as the reporting system providing the data, which are collated and analyzed before the charts, tables, and graphs come out. Several years ago, David was discussing the elements of a recently released Federal Bureau of Investigation (FBI) crime report with some of his colleagues. The report contained a section on assaults perpetrated against law enforcement officers for that particular year. The report stated that there had been three assaults against Drug Enforcement Administration (DEA) personnel during that same year. As the four people discussing the report personally knew of many more instances than that, it was safe to assume the statistics were incomplete to say the least.

The State Department Report of Patterns of Global Terrorism, which was released by the Office of the Coordinator for Counterterrorism on May 21, 2001, lists the countries of the world along with the number of reported incidents for the year 2000, the latest data available. Not having any personal data ourselves, we looked intently at the figures, initially accepting them at face value, until we got to the entry for Israel. According to this report, there were between six and eight terrorist incidents in the State of Israel that year. We both reacted in the same way: Did they mean last year or just last week? There is no possible way that this statistic is even close to being accurate. Once you find such a glaring error, you may safely assume that there are more lurking about somewhere. In addition, there is also the troubling habit of arguing what constitutes a terrorist act in the first place. Most of you probably have heard the ridiculous cliché that "one man's terrorist is another man's freedom fighter." Recall the shooting at the El Al counter on July 4, 2001. Initially, the FBI said that there was no link between that act and terrorism. An Egyptian male armed with a gun decides to shoot to death two people at the ticket counter for the national airline of Israel and they can't find any justification to classify this incident as a terrorist act?[1] Clearly, the reluctance to call this an act of terror is not based on anything other than political sensitivities. Our preference when making judgments of this type is more along the lines of Supreme Court Justice Potter Stewart's comment when he declined to specifically define obscenity in 1964, stating "I know it when I see it." Perhaps terrorism cannot be universally defined in a manner that satisfies the FBI or United Nations, but we all know it when we see it. Months later, however, the FBI finally came around and said it was investigating the case as a terrorist incident. The question is: Would that shooting have been included in a statistical report about the incidence of terror attacks within the United States or not? Perhaps not, and that certainly would call into question the validity of the statistical analysis.

LOCAL CRIMINAL HISTORY

Let's go through the analysis for some of the countries listed above to show how to research the country of destination for security concerns. These items of importance should, at a minimum, include local criminal activity, terror cell activity, anti-American sentiment and/or demonstrations, and the state of emergency medical care. In the year 2001, approximately 2,949 American students were studying in China. As you can see, this represents an increase of 30 percent from the previous year. If you are a student contemplating an educational experience in China, it is essential that you research the current situation before you finalize your decision. This is what the State Department website says about the level of criminal activity in China:

> Overall, China is a safe country, with a low but increasing crime rate. Pickpockets target tourists at sightseeing destinations, open-air markets and in stores, often with the complicity of low-paid security guards. Violence against foreigners occurs, but it is rare. The number of violent incidents against Americans is very low on a worldwide basis (there were nine reported violent attacks on American citizens between 1999 and 2001), but such incidents do occur. Robberies, sometimes at gunpoint, have occurred in western China, and there have been some reports of robberies and assaults along remote mountain highways near China's border with Nepal. Travelers are sometimes asked by locals to exchange money at a preferential rate. It is illegal to exchange dollars for RMB (the local currency) except at banks, hotels and official exchange offices. Due to the large volume of counterfeit currency in China, unofficial exchanges usually result in travelers losing their money and possibly left to face charges of breaking foreign exchange laws.[2]

This synopsis gives a quick overview of the criminal situation in China as it relates to foreigners. The information is concise and is certainly easy to act on. The alert warns against pickpockets, so it is reasonable to assume that more than a few Americans have been victims of this type of criminal activity. Safeguard your wallet by keeping it in your front pocket. The report also gives a specific warning about the remote sections of western China and the border with Nepal. Perhaps you had better cancel a trip to those areas. Use your common sense. Believe it or not, there are people who go to New York City and wish to sightsee in Harlem. While there are many interesting places to see and cultural events to experience in Harlem, visitors really need to be familiar with the area or go with someone who knows it, in order to avoid problems in the dangerous high-crime areas. The State Department report on China goes on to say:

> Throughout China, women outside hotels in tourist districts frequently use the prospect of companionship or sex to lure foreign men to isolated locations where accomplices are waiting for the purpose of robbery. Travelers should not allow themselves to be driven to bars or an individual's home unless they know the person making the offer. Hotel guests should refuse to open their room doors to anyone they do not know personally. Sexual assaults in China reported by American women usually involve acquaintances rather than strangers.[3]

To the male readers of this chapter, that paragraph really needs to sink in. There are many old tricks in the book, but this one is one of the oldest and is common the world over, certainly not just in China. A man alone, especially after having just enough to drink to switch off the common-sense center of the brain, is extremely vulnerable to this practice. In many countries it is possible to engage the services of a prostitute for about the same price as the breakfast special at IHOP. Beautiful women offering the promise of a sexual encounter for such little money can be an extremely tempting proposition. To quote the words of former first lady of the United States Nancy Reagan: "Just say no." Even if you do have a purely sexual encounter, you are taking your life in your hands regarding the possibility of being exposed to HIV. However, you also have a pretty good chance of being drugged and robbed or lured to a place where the woman's associates will rob you by force. Once again, if such a warning is included in the State Department travel advisory, you can be sure it has happened to Americans before.

The advisory on China also provides very important information regarding the availability of medical care consistent with Western standards:

> *Western style medical facilities with international staffs are available in Beijing, Shanghai, Guangzhou and a few other large cities. Many other hospitals in major Chinese cities have so-called VIP wards (gaogan bingfang). These feature reasonably up-to-date medical technology and physicians who are both knowledgeable and skilled. Most VIP wards also provide medical services to foreigners and have English-speaking doctors and nurses. Most hospitals in China will not accept medical insurance from the United States. Travelers will be asked to post a deposit prior to admission to cover the expected cost of treatment. Many hospitals in major cities may accept credit cards for payment. Even in the VIP/ Foreigner wards of major hospitals, however, American patients have frequently encountered difficulty due to cultural and regulatory differences. Physicians and hospitals have sometimes refused to supply American patients with complete copies of their Chinese hospital medical records, including laboratory test results, scans, and x-rays. All Americans traveling to China are strongly encouraged to buy foreign medical care and medical evacuation insurance prior to arrival.[4]*

The advisory continues:

> *Ambulances do not carry sophisticated medical equipment, and ambulance personnel generally have little or no medical training. Therefore, injured or seriously ill Americans may be required to take taxis or other immediately available vehicles to the nearest major hospital rather than waiting for ambulances to arrive. In rural areas, only rudimentary medical facilities are generally available. Medical personnel in rural areas are often poorly trained, have little medical equipment or availability to medications. Rural clinics are often reluctant to accept responsibility for treating foreigners, even in emergency situations. Foreign-operated medical providers catering to expatriates and visitors are available in China. SOS International, Ltd., operates modern medical and dental clinics and provides medical evacuation and medical escort services in several Chinese cities.*
>
> *Americans are advised not to travel to China without both health insurance and medical evacuation insurance (often included in so-called "travel" insurance and provided as part of a tour group package). U.S. medical insurance is not always valid outside the United States. Medicare/Medicaid programs do not provide coverage for medical services outside the United States. Even when insurance does cover services received in China, it will usually be necessary to pay first and then file for reimbursement with the insurance company upon returning to the United States. Supplemental insurance with specific overseas coverage,*

including provision for medical evacuation, is strongly recommended and can be purchased in the United States prior to travel. Please check with your own insurance company to confirm whether your policy applies overseas, and if it includes a provision for medical evacuation.

Recent medical evacuations by air ambulance from China to nearby areas have cost over US $30,000. Two private emergency medical assistance firms, SOS International, Ltd., and Medex Assistance Corporation, offer medical insurance policies designed for travelers. Both of these companies have staff in China who can assist in the event.[5]

Based on the foregoing, it would seem that the best advice is not to get sick or injured in China. However, the advisory tells you what you need to do, just in case. Have appropriate travel insurance that is accepted in the country you are traveling to. As we have mentioned before, International SOS is an excellent resource to contact to cover you in case you have an unexpected medical emergency. The cost of such protection is reasonable, especially given the fact that your life may depend on it. In any event, SOS International has many years of experience assisting Americans abroad and is your best choice in case an emergency medical evacuation becomes necessary.

LEARN AND RESPECT LOCAL LAWS AND CUSTOMS

Those who will travel abroad for school need to become familiar with the laws of the host country. For some reason, most Americans assume that what is legal or overlooked in the United States will likewise be dealt with the same way abroad. This may or may not be so. The responsibility, however, is yours to find out about the local laws before you violate them. Many people remember the story of the young American boy arrested in Singapore for defacing property with graffiti. The penalty in Singapore, an extraordinarily clean and well-kept country, is extremely harsh for this crime. If you vandalize public or private property in New York City you will, at worst, receive a summons or you may be compelled to participate in a public service program where you will scrub graffiti off walls. In Singapore, the penalty is caning. This is an extremely painful form of corporal punishment that will definitely dissuade someone from repeating the crime. For weeks, the U.S. State Department tried to have the boy's sentence changed or rescinded. Finally, the young man was given a reduced number of lashes with the cane. We are certain that it wasn't pleasant. Remember, when you are in a sovereign country, you are subject to their laws, not ours. Each year more than 2,500 American citizens are arrested in foreign countries. Many of them are students who get arrested for drugs, drinking, and disorderly conduct. Approximately half of those arrested are charged with narcotics violations. Some of these arrests are of persons involved in the large-scale smuggling of illegal and controlled substances. Most, however, are arrested for simple possession of small amount of drugs and are stunned to learn that an activity they assumed was a violation at worst was actually a serious felony. In addition, there are often dramatic differences in the laws of even countries with common borders. What is legal in the Netherlands, for example, may not be legal in Belgium or Germany. Although it seems as easy to go across Europe as it is to go from state to state in the United States, local laws may differ greatly. The German police do not want to hear "But it is legal in Amsterdam." Do not assume the police will be soft on you because you are a young American student either. Maybe they will, if a good-natured cop catches you. But if the officer in question has had a fight with his or her spouse that morning or is just fed up with getting called to disturbances caused by drunk and disorderly foreign students, you will be locked up. By the way, the same recommended guidelines in Chapter 3 apply to you as well. Think from your own personal experience about friends or others you may know who have gotten into trouble while drunk or stoned. In our experience, once your senses have been impaired, your judgment follows right along. How many Americans get drunk abroad and are robbed, raped, or worse because they left their common sense at the bottom of a bottle of beer? If you really need to cut loose, do not do it in public. If you are drunk or even just a bit impaired, do not drive. Stay home when the urge to behave in this manner takes hold of you. If you are out, the same precautions apply overseas as they do here. A designated driver, who is also likely to be the designated thinker as well, is a necessity. And before you engage in underage drinking, remember that in some countries the punishment will not be the police officer taking you home to mom and dad. It may very well be arrest and jail.

A bit of advice that we mentioned earlier in the chapter about pre-travel research bears repeating: Know as much as you can about the culture you are going to. You should, in particular, become familiar with the customs of the country to which you are traveling and pay particular attention to the country's values, etiquette, and dress code. Wearing a miniskirt in a society where most women are clad in burqas will definitely get you in trouble, either legal or physical.

Before you go, try to learn as much of the language as you can. This will not be an issue for the 8 percent of students who are abroad studying the language of the country. It will be for the other 92 percent. English is rapidly becoming an almost universal language. However, don't rely on the fact that locals in the country where you are traveling might speak English. Your ability to communicate in the local language actually may be the difference between life and death. If you have any special concerns or health considerations, write them on a piece of paper you keep in your wallet or purse. This applies especially to conditions requiring constant care or regularly administered medications, such as diabetes. Written instructions and some facility in the language will make requesting assistance easier should you require help of some sort. For less dire situations, you will be able to handle the basics of ordering a meal, negotiating cab fare, or getting travel directions.

The pretravel checklist, discussed in Chapter 3, is a good start for students preparing for their trip. However, students traveling abroad should take certain additional steps. Obviously, they require a valid passport and possibly a visa. It is a very prudent idea to make sure that the passport will not expire during the duration of the expected stay. An expired passport may, of course, be renewed at the embassy or consulate in the country in which you are staying. But why not avoid that extra headache and make sure the expiration date is a long way off before you leave? And while you are making sure that your passport is valid, have your parents apply for one as well. If you experience some difficulty abroad, such as a medical emergency, for example, they will need a valid passport to do what parents do best: Come to your rescue.

Make sure your vaccinations are appropriate and up to date. Information available from the State Department and the Centers for Disease Control will advise you on the potential health hazards where you are going and tell you what shots you need to take. As with anyone traveling overseas, make sure you have medical insurance that covers emergency care abroad. Check specifically whether the country of your destination accepts the type of international insurance that you are considering subscribing to. Make sure, as noted above, that the policy covers evacuations for medical reasons.

Once you arrive in country, learn the location of the nearest embassy or consulate and be sure you know how to find your way there on foot, by car, or by public transportation. Register with the embassy. Make sure someone there has all your pertinent information, including your address and phone number and the name of the school you are attending. If any of the contact information you provide to the embassy changes, call the embassy and make sure your profile is updated in its system.

NOTES

1. Terrorism is defined in the U.S. Code of Federal Regulations as: "the unlawful use of force and violence against persons or property to intimidate or coerce a government, the civilian population, or any segment thereof, in furtherance of political or social objectives" (28 C.F.R. Section 0.85).
2. U.S. Department of State, Bureau of Consular Affairs, *Consular Information Sheet for China*, April 11, 2002.
3. Ibid.
4. Ibid.
5. Ibid.

INDEX